# EMOTIONALLY RESILIENT
# TWEENS AND TEENS

# EMOTIONALLY RESILIENT TWEENS AND TEENS

EMPOWERING YOUR KIDS
*to* NAVIGATE BULLYING, TEASING,
*and* SOCIAL EXCLUSION

Kim John Payne, M.ED., *and*
Luis Fernando Llosa

SHAMBHALA

Shambhala Publications, Inc.
2129 13th Street
Boulder, Colorado 80302
www.shambhala.com

Cover art: Labib Retroman/Shutterstock
Cover design: Daniel Urban-Brown
Interior design: Claudine Mansour Design

9 8 7 6 5 4 3 2 1

First Edition
Printed in the United States of America

Shambhala Publications makes every effort to print on acid-free, recycled paper.
Shambhala Publications is distributed worldwide by Penguin Random House, Inc., and its subsidiaries.

Library of Congress Cataloging-in-Publication Data
Names: Payne, Kim John, author. | Llosa, Luis Fernando, author.
Title: Emotionally resilient tweens and teens: empowering your kids to navigate bullying, teasing, and social exclusion / Kim John Payne and Luis Fernando Llosa.
Description: Boulder, Colorado: Shambhala, [2022]
Identifiers: LCCN 2021062074 | ISBN 9781611805642 (trade paperback)
Subjects: LCSH: Resilience (Personality trait) in adolescence. | Bullying. | Rejection (Psychology) in adolescence.
Classification: LCC BF724.3.R47 P39 2022 | DDC 155.5/1824—dc23/eng/20220111
LC record available at https://lccn.loc.gov/2021062074

# CONTENTS

*Introduction*                                                    1

## PART ONE: ADVICE TO PARENTS

1. What to Do and What Not to Do                                  9
2. Belonging Is a Process, Not a Right                           24
3. Bullying without Borders: Cyberbullying                       31
4. "I Can Help. I Am Here for You."                              45

## PART TWO: YOUR TEN-STORY TOOLBOX

5. The New Kid: Anika's Story                                    63
6. But What If It's True? Daniel's Story                         81
7. How I Got My Confidence Back: Sara's Story                    98
8. A New Group, a New Me: Joey's Story                          118
9. It's Life That's Bullying Me: Sophie's Story                 137
10. The Shy Kid's Gift of Inner Strength: Destiny's Story       159
11. Stop Pushing Me Around: Michael's Story                     177
12. Rumors and Whispers: Elena's Story                          204
13. Truth Telling and Tattling: Emma's Story                    228
14. Standing Up and Speaking Out: Darpan's Story                249

*Acknowledgments*                                               281
*Notes*                                                         282
*Additional Resources*                                          284
*About the Authors*                                             286

# EMOTIONALLY RESILIENT
# TWEENS AND TEENS

# INTRODUCTION

Our greatest wish for our children is that they will be okay. When they are hurt or excluded by other kids, we feel our family foundation lurch. Teasing, social exclusion, and bullying strike at the core of our family identity, awakening our primal urge to protect them. That is why any solution needs to involve the whole family.

Here in *Emotionally Resilient Tweens and Teens*, you will find the tools you need to help your child. You will also learn how to avoid fighting your kid's battles for them. Because when you attempt to solve their problems for them, you unintentionally block their pathway to personal growth. Better, instead, to stand behind and beside them; and to avoid getting frustrated, overreacting, and angrily calling their school, which inevitably embarrasses them and causes them to stop telling you about what is really going on.

The first four chapters of *Emotionally Resilient Tweens and Teens* offer you specific, practical advice on how to handle your own reactions when you learn that your child, tween, or teen is excluded or bullied, whether in person or online. You will also learn how to support them through this difficult situation in a way that builds family connection and trust, and, most importantly, helps them develop "I can do this" self-confidence.

## WHAT DOES EMOTIONAL RESILIENCY REALLY MEAN?

When we were young, few of us ever experienced anything close to the frenzied pace of life, competing demands, and heightened expectations that our children face every day. Though we can certainly help reduce some of the pressures our children encounter, others are hardwired into modern living. That is why we hear terms such as *resiliency* so often these days. Our kids, we are told, need to develop the inner fortitude to *bounce back*, learn from what's happened, and move on without a significant loss of confidence.

The aim of *Emotionally Resilient Tweens and Teens* is to help you understand how to better support your child to make a behavioral course correction while their social challenges are still moderate.

But what exactly is emotional resilience? A good way to sharpen our understanding is to juxtapose its characteristics with trauma responses as laid out in the chart below:

| What is an EMOTIONALLY RESILIENT RESPONSE? | What is a TRAUMA-BASED RESPONSE? |
|---|---|
| Responding freshly to each situation. | Reacting habitually; repetition, looping patterns of response. |
| Returning to a restful state between events. | Maintaining low-grade vigilance between events, rising to high vigilance for all events. |
| Able to enjoy new things and people. | Maintaining low-grade vigilance between events, rising to high vigilance for all events. |

| | |
|---|---|
| Finding interest in emotionally neutral information and quiet situations. | Attending only to emotionally charged, highly relevant information. |
| Engaging socially and enjoying friendships, play, and humor. | Experiencing social isolation, fixed routines; avoiding play; unable to generate or respond to humor. |
| Accepting positive performance feedback. | Rejecting affirmation and consistently seeing success as failure, as an accident, or as evidence of not being good enough. |
| Able to bracket negative events. In time: it's only happening now. In space: it only affects this aspect of my life. | Magnifying negative events; In time: it's always going to be like this. In space: it affects my whole life and contaminates everything. |

*Sincere thanks to Dr. Dee Joy Coulter,*
*whose work was the basis for this chart.*

## SOOTHING TRAUMA AND BUILDING EMOTIONAL RESILIENCE THROUGH STORYTELLING

Stories are the language of childhood. Children learn from them and empathize with them. That's why stories have been so effective in helping to heal social wounds. Starting with chapter 5, you will find ten stories that help teach our children how to shape their reactions and minimize their vulnerability. Targeted kids need to understand that they can't *make bullies stop*, because attempting to do that just hands the bullies more control. But they can learn how to stand their ground and take back power by controlling their own responses. That way they can influence a difficult situation rather than passively accept what is happening.

In essence, *Emotionally Resilient Tweens and Teens* is a toolbox that leads to the development of empathy, promotes problem-solving, and provides hope during your child's socially crucial elementary- and middle-school years.

The subtle but clear messages in these stories will teach your kids how to navigate their own way out of challenging social situations. They will identify with the characters' struggles and realize, "Oh, it's not just me. Others like me have gone through this and found ways to deal with it. If they are okay, I can be too."

Parents who read *Emotionally Resilient Tweens and Teens* will better understand what their kids are up against and learn how to *coach them* through the social landmines of their developing world. After you have read these stories yourself, sit down with your elementary- or middle-school child and read together about the trials, tribulations, and eventual triumphs of their peers. Then you can team up to devise effective ways to handle the teasing, social exclusion, or bullying that they encounter.

Right when you and your child are at your most vulnerable, these uplifting stories will soothe your parental anxieties, help your child break free from a vicious cycle of blame and victimization, and provide you both with new direction and hope. Your child will feel validated and become empowered: "We figured this out and then I did it on my own!" Then the whole family will realize, "Whatever the future brings, we can work it out together."

We cannot rely on schools and state policies to solve social-exclusion problems. To begin with, the resources schools have to identify and combat teasing, exclusion, and bullying are limited. School counselors are overwhelmed, and schools are often slow to implement change. Furthermore, the anti-bullying programs they *do* employ can be ineffective because they tend to focus on the bullies and inadvertently disempower the targeted child.

*Emotionally Resilient Tweens and Teens* provides kids with first-hand examples of peers who've been through it all and learned how to take control of their own lives. Our ten teenaged narrators have each worked through a perplexing problem and resolved it by the end of the story. They are fellow students—teen mentors who have struggled with teasing, subtle social exclusion, or bullying and become masters of their own destinies rather than remain mired in victimhood—tormented for months, sometimes years.

## AS YOU EMBARK

I have spent over thirty years coaching children through difficult social situations, raised two children of my own on our New England farm, and tried and tested each of the strategies you will read about in these stories. My epiphany came when I asked older children and teens to tell their own stories of struggle, mistakes, and success to other children who were excluded or bullied. They listened with rapt attention and with unmistakable relief and hope.

And my coauthor, Luis Fernando Llosa, has spent twenty-five years coaching children's sports teams and raised five children of his own. He discovered that overly aggressive kids learned patience and self-control when teaching their expert moves to younger ones, and their adepts learned faster.

Luis Fernando and I met when he attended a lecture I gave on boys and overwhelm at the Rudolf Steiner School in New York City. Over the following decade, we met regularly in a quaint little valley village in Harlemville, New York, to discuss all manner of topics related to raising kids and shepherding them through play and youth sports. Those conversations sparked our collaboration on *Beyond Winning:*

*Smart Parenting in a Toxic Sports Environment*, a sports parenting book we coauthored with the former National Football League youth sports director Scott Lancaster.

In *Emotionally Resilient Tweens and Teens*, Luis Fernando and I present stories in the voices of mature, experienced young people who have freed themselves from teasing, exclusion, or bullying. Read them through until you find the one that most closely parallels the events taking place in your child's life. Feel free to combine strategies from different stories if that best fits your child's particular situation. Read the story slowly and deliberately. Pause when you get to a point that resonates with your child.

When you get to the end, ask them what stood out for them and whether they think doing what the kid in the story did might help their predicament. They might say that only some or even none of the strategies in the story would work for them. That's perfectly okay. The stories will, in any case, serve as a springboard. You have started a conversation with your child about how they can face their problems differently. In doing so, you have begun to build a new bridge between you and your child as you transform a time of vulnerability into one of promise and possibility.

*Part One*

---

# ADVICE
# TO
# PARENTS

# 1

## WHAT TO DO AND WHAT NOT TO DO

Every parent dreads the moment when their child says, "Mom! I'm being left out of everything. I don't have any friends." So many emotions and questions flood in.

First comes our instinct to protect:

> "Is someone picking on my child?"

> "Do I need to speak with someone at the school?"

> "Just exactly what is going on here?"

Then memories from our own childhood bubble up to the surface:

> "I know *all* about this. I remember it exactly like it was yesterday."

> "It makes me feel sick just thinking about the things that can happen."

"I recall feeling different from everyone and very lonely."

Or perhaps we struggle to relate to our child's situation:

"I was socially okay when I was a kid and still am."

"What's wrong with my child?"

"Where did my child get this from?"

Mixed up with this jumble of thoughts and concerns is the urge to blame:

"Why is the school not doing anything?"

"Is it those mean kids again? They are so out of control!"

"What kind of dysfunctional homes do these nasty kids come from?"

"We keep getting announcements about inclusion and diversity. What gives?"

And a small voice may even question your child's story:

"Can it really be *that* bad?"

"Isn't this just kids being kids?"

"Maybe my son just needs to toughen up a bit and work it out himself."

Once you get through the initial shock of learning that your child is unhappy and being targeted, self-doubt and concern set in:

"Why didn't I pick up on this earlier?"

"Am I losing touch?"

"What have I done wrong to raise a child who doesn't know how to fit in?"

"What am I supposed to do?"

"Should I step in? I don't want to be a helicopter parent, but . . ."

## MESSAGE TO PANICKY PARENTS: *NOT NOW*

The first thing you need to do is contain the clamoring fears, judgments, and opinions that well up inside you when your child finds the courage to tell you something is wrong. Avoid, as best you can, asking questions. Try not to convey that you are anxious and emotionally triggered. Those troubling thoughts that manifest as a nagging "voice" inside your head? Don't let them take over. Tell them calmly but firmly, "Not now." You are not denying or suppressing your very real concerns but rather simply directing them to take a back seat. One parent's mantra in such moments? "Not now. I am with my child."

This strategy helps you become more *present* to the moment, which is what your child needs most. When children are feeling shaky, vulnerable, and emotionally lost, they look for someone to *be there for them* at a time when others in their world are decidedly not.

I have gone into catastrophe-preparation mode many a time when one of my children has said, "Dad, I have some really bad news." But when I've been able to defer my reaction and focus on listening carefully to the details they provide about their situation, I've been in much better shape to offer loving presence and support.

## IS SOMETHING GOING ON?

Children seldom come right out and say they are being excluded, teased, or bullied. But their behavior can tip you off. Whether your child is an extrovert (friendly, outgoing, enthusiastic) or an introvert (shy, quiet, pensive), those natural characteristics become exaggerated if they are struggling socially. Children become *emotionally fevered.* They get upset more quickly and much more often than is normal.

**Extroverts Act Out:** Extroverts sweat it out. Their emotional response is to get hot-tempered, rowdy, noisy, angry, and larger than life. They push hard against restrictions and rules. They are, in effect, saying, "Get out of my way."

**Introverts Fall Back:** Introverts get cold and shivery. They pull back even further from relationships, and they become withdrawn, sullen, and stubborn. They are prone to recall and decry past hurts and problems—times when they felt undervalued or unseen.

**Concentration Changes:** Social stress can make it hard for your child to focus. You may notice a difference in the way they play; they become more vulnerable and reactive, or thin-skinned. Their ability to concentrate can plummet: they become easily distracted, flitting about from project to project, birdlike, never landing long enough in one place to make much progress. Alternatively, if they normally tend to bury themselves in tasks or projects, they may become hyper-focused and inflexible when they are upset, as they try to shut out the world.

**Transitions Become Harder:** Kids who are under too much social pressure are much more easily triggered during normal daily transitions. For example, younger children may refuse to leave a playdate, oblivious to the discomfort their tantrums cause their host family. And bedtime transitions, which were perhaps occasionally tricky before, become much more problematic.

**Controlling Behavior Spikes:** One clear sign that there is social trouble brewing? When a child tries to exert tight control over all aspects of regular family life. They may try to dominate play with siblings and become irate when things don't go exactly as they have dictated.

Other control issues manifest as problems with food and sleep. Your child may refuse to eat food they ate with minimal fuss before. Sleep may become so problematic that they absolutely insist you lie beside them until they fall asleep—which can take hours because their looping worries keep them wide awake.

Your child may try to dominate conversations and insist on having the last word. You may get calls from teachers concerned that they are talking back and having difficulty complying with simple requests. Alternatively, they may peel away from group activities at home or at school, preferring the relative security of solitude.

As we shift our thinking, we come to understand that our children are not simply misbehaving or isolating themselves. They are trying, desperately, to exert control over a world that is spinning out of control. Once we recognize that, our frustration can quickly give way to a deeper sense of compassion for what they are going through.

Even if your child commonly exhibits some of the difficult behavior described above, be on alert if it suddenly worsens dramatically. If their reactions become unusually intense and disproportionate, they are likely being teased, excluded, or bullied.

Without making it too obvious, see what you can find out from their friends' parents. Speak to their teachers. Observe their behavior around other kids. But most importantly, move in close. Spend time doing some of their favorite things with them. By doing that, you create a warm, shared space in which they are much more likely to open up to you about what is troubling them.

## STRENGTHENING FAMILY BASE CAMP

When life gets shaky for your child *out there*, in the world, it's important to make certain life *in here*, within the family sphere, is solid.

You may be tempted to direct your attention to what is happening at school or in the neighborhood, but what kids need most is for you to wrap them up in a great big puffy blanket of care and familiarity.

At some point, your child will have to journey out into a more difficult and demanding social environment—a world that can be cold and unwelcoming. In this book you will find a rich selection of stories you can read with them to support them on that voyage. However, the tools and strategies you collect from these tales will be much more useful and effective if you first devote time and effort to connecting with your child in a more conscious way.

One couple I met with, whose nine-year-old was feeling isolated at school, told me that their "increased daily care and attention provided her with a well-stocked base camp. Long afterward, when she was a teenager, she told us that spending all that time doing things she enjoyed with us, during that socially traumatic period, gave her the strength and confidence to face any challenges that arose in school."

The things you do with your child do not have to be elaborate or complicated. That's the beauty of it. When things are going wrong for a child and their lives feel out of shape, "normal" is exactly what they need. Go on bike rides or hikes with them. Set up a family game night, read out loud, or bake or cook a meal with them. Or launch into that tree-fort project that you've been putting off forever.

When one dad I worked with learned that his son Tommy was struggling to make friends in a new school, he asked Tommy to help him build a ramp in their driveway for Tommy's BMX bike. They enjoyed working together so much that they started to construct other equipment. Before long, several neighborhood kids joined in. Now, not only was the father spending more time doing things with his son that they both enjoyed, but he was also indirectly helping Tommy form new relationships outside of school. Armed with confidence buoyed by those new friendships, he had a much easier time making new connections at school.

When you spend more time deepening your connection with your child, you lift their spirits (as well as your own). Because at the very moment when they are feeling the most vulnerable, your actions convey a clear, unwavering message: "I see you. I value you. And I most certainly love you."

## STOP THE WORLD

We live in a time when myriad advertisers and multiple devices compete to capture our children's most valuable commodity: their attention. However, when your child is being picked on, it's important to hit the pause button, not just for screens and social media platforms but for all types of busyness that crowd and complicate their life.

When a child feels left out or is being teased relentlessly, the stress they feel doesn't merely affect one *part* of their life. It spills over their emotional riverbanks and floods into every corner of their life. This experience is not exclusive to children. We all know what it's like to be inundated with worries. But children aren't equipped with the proper defenses to handle the deluge. They haven't yet developed the executive brain capacity to see the big picture and keep things in context.

To help our children process what they are experiencing, we need to "stop the world." We have to create a space in which our children can speak, be heard, and be comforted. Stopping the world doesn't mean altering the healthy daily rhythms of family life. On the contrary, kids need more routine and familiarity in socially stressful times. Quite simply, we must put down the computer or put away our smartphone if our child wants to speak to us. Or even go so far as to take a mental health day away from our work in order to hang out with our child.

Some parents push back against the deluge of daily emails and texts by turning off notifications and making a sacrosanct promise not to look at their phone when their child is with them. Others choose to read their kid a story and tuck them in every night without fail. One father, who had a fast-paced, high-pressure finance job, told me he postponed a business trip in order to be at home while his daughter was going through a particularly rough patch. "I'd never done that before," he confessed. "But the time I spent hanging out with her and goofing around melted my heart." During that long, uninterrupted weekend they spent together, she disclosed things to him that he had no idea were going on. "It came out in little bits, here and there," he said. "As each day passed, she told me more." They decided to invite her mother over (the parents were divorced) to hear what had been happening and help them figure out how they could turn the situation around. Mom, dad, and daughter developed a solid plan that helped her resolve her social dilemma. "Authorizing myself to postpone my trip," the dad told me, "and spend all that time with my daughter was the highest-yielding investment I'll ever make."

## DIAL LIFE BACK

I have received countless calls from distressed parents despairing at the emotional toll teasing and exclusion have taken on their child. They ask questions such as "Can you help us give our son more confidence to join in?" or "Is there a way I can coach my daughter to stand up for herself?" Understandably they desperately seek the tools to deal directly with their child's problems. But before I talk about tools and strategy, I always say, "First we need to explore your family's pace of life to see if we need to dial things back a bit." (See "It's Life That's Bullying Me: Sophie's Story.")

There is little sense in pouring more water into a cup that is already overflowing. Sure, we can come up with commonsense strategies to help ease the teasing. But if life is moving too fast for the child—with too many activities and too little time to decompress—the tactics will not have a container to hold them. All that effort will become spillage and may well increase the child's feeling of hopelessness. The

question becomes, do we want to spend our time mopping up the spill or simply put our hand on the tap and turn down the flow?

My book *Simplicity Parenting* provides detailed strategies for dialing back the frenetic pace of family life. Here, in brief, are three strategies that will help strengthen your child's emotional resilience so that they can better face and overcome teasing, exclusion, or bullying.

### 1. Increasing Rhythm and Predictability

In a child's school life, transitions (arrival, departure, class change-overs) and recess are the times when teasing and other social confrontations are most likely to occur. They are also the times that are most changeable and socially unpredictable. There is really nothing that a parent can do about what happens in school because it's outside our control. But we can counterbalance that instability by making extra efforts to create a home life that is as secure and predictable as possible. It's important to know the big daily rhythms that provide the "when" things happen and the little rituals that give the "how" they are done. This creates a sense of security, allowing a child's nervous system to relax and revive. And its importance cannot be overstated.

### 2. Dialing Back After-School and Weekend Activities

Children who struggle socially need extra time to decompress. Cutting back on the number of playdates, after-school clubs, and weekend activities they are involved in will help alleviate their anxiety. One shouldn't stop everything, of course. Your child can remain involved in some activities that boost their self-esteem. But concentrating more on family-based pursuits (such as games, hikes, and home-centered projects) can have a calming, comforting effect. If they are used to a fast-paced life, they may initially complain that they have nothing to do. But boredom can be a gift. As they experience more downtime, children will search for things to do. And they will likely become more innovative and creative out of necessity. Becoming involved *in here* (at home), where it is safe and relaxing, is just what they need when they are not being seen or treated well *out there* in school, where there is a lot of social pressure.

### 3. Filtering Adult Information

We should moderate and filter what we say in front of kids, especially when they are being teased or excluded. Our children want us to acknowledge the social difficulties they are going through and may, of their own accord, bring them up. But we shouldn't broach the topic repeatedly ourselves. Every time these stressful situations are discussed, our children relive them emotionally. They reexperience the release of adrenaline and cortisol (the fight-or-flight hormones). We want home to be a sanctuary where they can seek support and relief. So try to keep things light and fun. You can check in with your child from time to time and let them know they can always speak to you about how things are going, but take care not to process your emotions and worries about their social woes in front of your child.

## AVOID JUDGING

When a child has laid their world bare to us, we need to treat them sensitively and respectfully. If we immediately demolish aspects of what they are going through with comments, advice, and judgments, they may become even more lost. It's better to reassure them by agreeing that what is happening is not fair and to offer to help them change what is going on by working out ways to deal with their situation. However, it is critical to withhold negative comments about the situation and the other kids who are involved. Judging those who are judging us is a toxic cycle that we don't want to model for our child.

### The Other Children and Their Families

Speaking harshly about the perpetrators of exclusion is not at all helpful. This is especially true if you demonize the children who are doing the excluding. Even though it sounds counterintuitive, children often worry about their parents "hating" the kids who are leaving them out. They may be secretly hoping that one day soon these same children *will* include them. And if that happens, they don't want to be stuck in between new friends and parents who don't like them.

Alternatively, your child may join you in labeling and psychoanalyzing the kids they say are tormenting them. This can make things worse if your child develops an image of these kids as monsters. That will make the situation scarier and more irredeemable. In other words, we need to help them avoid the emotional maze and find a straightforward path.

It is also tempting—in our effort to protect our child—to have concerns about or even "trash" the families of the perpetrators. But much of what we know about other families is either secondhand information or conjecture. And even if we are confident that our opinions are well founded and accurate, expressing them doesn't help our child feel more secure.

### The School

This is a tough one. We trust a school to keep our kids safe. When things go wrong, we tend to react strongly. We suffer from a toxic mixture of disappointment, anxiety, vulnerability, and anger.

Our anger is an emotional attempt to redress an emotional imbalance. Just like we tend to shout when we don't feel we are being heard, we often lash out at others when we feel hurt. When faced with an institution (the school) that we feel is ignoring or not addressing our concerns about our child's treatment by others, we can become frustrated or even enraged. Even though it is difficult, at such times we need to seek emotional balance. On the one hand, we want justice, but we will frighten our kid if we become enraged and react against a teacher or the school. And no matter what we feel, our child will still have to spend six to eight hours in that environment with the teachers or administrators we are railing against.

No teacher or school administrator is in the profession for the money or fame. A vast majority of educators care deeply about the children they teach and try to ensure that classrooms are socially healthy places. Most classrooms are safe. It is in buses, hallways, bathrooms, locker rooms, and, of course, during recess that problems tend to occur.

Because of this, it's better to be *inquisitive* when approaching educators rather than *accusative*. Yes, you need to get your perspective across. But teachers are very likely to have their own way of seeing things. I have been in countless parent-teacher meetings where there is an underlying tension about whose story is right—with both parties convinced that the other is not seeing the reality of the situation. I often ask for a pause while we "surface" this dynamic by saying to the parent or guardian, "No one knows your child in the family constellation as well as you do." To the educator: "No one knows this child in the classroom setting as well as you do." And then to both: "What a great team you make to work out how to address all the in-between places where the problem is coming up."

I feel compelled to add here that I have known of situations where a teacher's behavior is belittling and bullying, though this is rare. When it does occur, it is often unintended and unconscious. When it does arise, parents are well within their rights to raise concerns and insist on a thorough review, informing both the teacher involved and the administration. Nevertheless, the *inquisitive-vs.-accusative* principle still applies and helps us stay balanced and be better heard by those whom we are approaching to ask for help.

## CALLING IT WHAT IT IS

I use the terms *bullying* and *bully* less frequently as my understanding of the true dynamic of social conflicts develops. Most children I work with prefer the term *teasing*. *Bullying* is a heavily loaded word. Kids often avoid using it unless things are *really* bad. They may say it when they've heard adults use it repeatedly. However, when I talk to adults, the terms I prefer to use are *exclusion* or *hyper-controlling behavior*. In doing so, I don't mean to minimize the harmful nature of marginalization. But it is important to be more specific about the underlying motivation of the child who is doing the teasing.

Kids who hyper-control are looking for power. They seek it in a number of ways. They may, for example, try to derail classes at school, habitually draw attention to themselves, and attempt to dominate parents and other family members. (See "Truth Telling and Tattling: Emma's Story.")

Anyone who tries to hyper-control deserves to be understood. The use of the term *hyper-controlling* allows us to separate the child from their behavior. When we step away from judgment, we begin to focus on what's important: figuring out why they are overcontrolling. If the ultimate aim is for all the kids involved to shift out of an unhealthy dynamic, we need first to understand why these patterns of behavior are playing out.

If teachers or school counselors can use the term *hyper-controlling* when speaking to the parent of a child who is a central perpetrator of a teasing situation, they are less likely to meet denial or defensiveness. They are more likely to be able to work together on a plan that encompasses all of those aspects of the child's life in which boundaries and support are needed. In my counseling practice, I've seen many disoriented children who held on to life too hard in an attempt to hyper-control their environment. When we dialed back what was overwhelming them, they began to relax and unwind.

Some examples of effective support strategies for hyper-controlling kids:

- Offer help with academic learning.
- Dial back homework.
- Significantly increase rhythm and predictability in their lives.
- Cut out violent video games.
- Reduce screen time.
- Slow down the pace of life by reducing the number of after-school commitments.
- Carefully plan recess times and bring in student helpers from the upper grades to support healthier play and improved peer relationships.

I seldom refer to children who are teased or excluded as "victims" or "victimized." These terms suggest that they are passive and may suggest that they are somehow to blame for being "bullied." I prefer to speak about children being "targeted," "marginalized," or "excluded." An excluded child is being "dehumanized." While *dehumanized* is not a word that fits easily into a conversation with kids, the truth of it is undeniable and can guide our thinking. Children who are excluded or marginalized are being denied their basic humanity. It can become an unconscious habit for a group of children to see the marginalized child as being "less than," "not worthy," and ultimately "not as human as us." Clearly it is up to us to help our children see the humanity in all people. As educators and parents, we carry this as a sacred responsibility.

In all the hurt and complication of a social crisis in the lives of our children, we need, above all, to hold on to the vision that everyone involved has a right to be heard and a right to be treated like a human being. This may sound obvious, or even lofty and philosophical, but when you read through the stories in *Emotionally Resilient Tweens and Teens* with your child who is feeling left out or unseen, they will begin to sense that they are not alone, that there is hope, and that they can be valued for who they are.

# 2

---

# BELONGING IS A PROCESS, NOT A RIGHT

We want our children to be happy, kind, and strong. We send them off to school, to summer camp, or to be with friends, hoping that they will be welcomed and have a good time. Their happiness is predicated on being accepted into the group. We want them to develop a sense of belonging so that they can relax, knowing that their voice will be heard, their humor appreciated, and their essential character (quirks and all) embraced.

It's an understandable parental aim. We want our children to fit into a compassionate, accepting world. However, if we want (and expect) them to live in a state of permanent acceptance and harmony, we can inadvertently create problems. Children experience and grow so much more by working through and solving issues. It's the foundation of all learning—academic *and* social. To try to protect our kids from difficulties in relationships with friends and classmates, or to see these issues only as negative experiences that serve no purpose,

24

is to risk removing essential building blocks to the development of their emotional intelligence.

I witnessed the tension between the desire to be accepted and confronting the inevitable struggles that life brings at an initiation ceremony for boys in southern Africa.

The initiation process consisted of five distinct progressive steps:

### 1. Seclusion
First the young people were taken to a remote area where they experienced living alone for a week.

### 2. Endurance
Next, they were taken on a long, demanding journey in which they had to learn to work together.

### 3. Disruption
Then came a challenging period of preparation. They practiced for the ceremony during the night and slept during the day and were required to fast (drinking only water).

### 4. Change
When all was ready, the coming-of-age ceremony began. For two days and two nights, the young people took part in sacred dances. Each was given their "spirit name" and received gifts such as a milking goat and a small space to build a kraal of their own. This signified that new freedoms and responsibilities were now a part of their lives.

### 5. Belonging
Finally, the young men were led through an archway painted with the blood of a sacrificial animal. On the other side, they were given an adorned woven belt that symbolized their welcoming into the community of adults. They would now be allowed to attend tribal gatherings meant only for adults and take part in decision-making as

junior members of the community. They could also now call on the protection of the group were they to need it in the future.

ISOLATION/
SECLUSION

GETTING THROUGH IT/
ENDURANCE

DISORIENTATION/
DISRUPTION

A NEW ME/
CHANGE

BELONGING

While coming-of-age ceremonies differ according to culture and gender, many involve similar versions of these five stages of initiation. In 1983, when I was researching human-interest stories as I traveled through Southeast Asia, I attended the public part of a traditional female coming-of-age ceremony called the Ngraja Swala. As luck would have it, I was staying in a small family-run hotel close to the compound where a group of girls were cloistered as they were led through their initiation process. The hotel owner happened to be a central figure on the women's council responsible for leading the girls through their ceremonies. Each night, after attending the rituals, she returned to her hotel kitchen to prepare a meal for the hotel guests and her extended family. I would sit at the kitchen counter, chopping vegetables for her, and ask about their tradition. Being male, I was not permitted to attend most of the formalities, but my hostess provided me with a general picture of what girls in her culture had been taught in their coming-of-age ceremonies for countless generations.

After listening to her I realized that while ceremonies differ according to culture and gender, embedded within many of them are universal stages of initiation. At the heart of the process is what social anthropologists call *liminality*, the ritualized "in-between" state or disruption that the child must go through before being welcomed into the community as a young adult. While my hostess in Bali was not allowed to go into specific detail about this sacred female ritual, she spoke in broad strokes of a process that involved three stages:

- *Pre-liminal* or preparatory stage
- *Liminal* or disorientation stage
- *Post-liminal* or crossing-over-into-the-adult-community stage

The open part of the Ngraja Swala ceremony, which I attended along with the entire village, was a ritualized *post-liminal* celebration in which these newly minted young women were welcomed into the freedoms and responsibilities of the adult community. It was a joyful and colorful event in which every detail of the clothing, hair braiding, and dancing carried significant symbolic meaning.

What struck me most about these and other ancient initiation practices I attended and studied—all of which culminated in acceptance into the adult world as a new, mature member—was that, regardless of gender, they all involved perseverance through a long and arduous process.

What is the relevance of initiation for our kids in the wealthy Western world? The universal truth is that growing up—anywhere in the world—involves dealing with the five steps I witnessed in the

African coming-of-age ritual. Though only a small number of children go through such formal ceremonies in the West these days, all of our children experience the intensity of initiation in their social lives as they navigate the demands of social relationships.

The more I thought about it, the more I could see direct parallels between traditional tribal practice and what our kids go through as they work out their problems. I came to see intense relationships as our children's *social* rite of passage.

Initiation is about coming into your own as a person and rejoining your group or community in a new way. It's a crucial part of discovering who you are—and who you are not. For centuries this has been expressed through formal ceremonies and the preparations that accompany them. While this still has a central place in some families and cultures, all children have a similar opportunity for experience and growth when they go through intense social encounters.

Conflict is one of the most powerful experiences of this dynamic. When we help our children learn how to handle these uncomfortable or hurtful situations, we are supporting them as they become strong, resilient, self-directed young people.

Here's a brief overview.

**Isolation (Seclusion):** When you have problems with friends and classmates or are entering a new school, you can feel very lonely and have difficulty coping.

**Getting Through It (Endurance):** When you are left out, it can feel as though it's never going to end. A child needs help and support to "hang in there," move beyond the exclusion, and find ways to work with parents and peers to solve problems and reenter the group.

**Disorientation (Disruption):** Your world can turn upside down when things are going wrong with friends, classmates, or teammates on whom you have come to rely for company or connection. It's hard to know where you stand anymore, and you may feel miserable.

**A New Me (Change):** Getting through a problem that shakes up their life often requires that children dig deep inside themselves to find new capacities. With your support, they will emerge from their *social fever* with their *emotional immune system* boosted. And they will have changed and grown.

**Belonging:** After all that a child has gone through, there is often a period of time when they truly belong back in the flow of daily life with peers. Maybe it's with a different group of friends or the same group but in a new way. Life may be secure, fun, and safe, until it's not—and you *fall out* with your friends and, yes, you start the whole process all over again.

*Belonging* is just one aspect of the process, *and it can't last forever.* That's just not the way relationships work. We are constantly being asked to adapt, learn, and change. Very few friendships stay exactly the same without becoming stale or boring and fading away.

Friendships are best when mixed with a dash of spice for interest, a pinch of salt to draw out the flavor, and, of course, a teaspoon of honey—for sweetness.

## *Eldering*

But where are the modern-day elders in *our* communities? After all, it is the tribal elders who carefully guide youngsters in traditional coming-of-age practices like the one I witnessed. They nurture the tribe's traditions and work together for the good of the children. The answer is, of course, *us.* I'm not sure if that is good or bad news. Maybe it's both. But we are most definitely the elders in our society. As teachers, coaches, extended family, and, most of all, parents, we can step in and help our children through their social rites of passage.

The experience can become intense and uncomfortable for everyone. In fact, we often try to avoid the unease it causes us by either blaming everyone else involved or passing the responsibility to work things out onto the school. If we can hold back the urge to be accusatory, then we can also become more emotionally resilient alongside our children. We too have much to learn and can develop our understanding. We need to become involved—as guides and helpers—in our children's process of belonging, becoming, and belonging again. *Emotionally Resilient Tweens and Teens* can be a central part of the social foundation that helps you feel more confident to be an elder to the younger members of your own little tribe—your family.

## HARMONY ADDICTION

If there is one dynamic that can impede our children's growth, it is the widespread aversion to conflict in our society. We want every day to be a happy one. If we experience sadness, it is seen as something to be quickly pushed aside so we can get back to a life filled with joy. Nevertheless, accepting times of discomfort as a normal part of life can help us grow and become whole. If we can accept that occasional distress is a normal part of our children's lives, we can focus on helping them move through tough experiences rather than trying to avoid or push away the difficulties and challenges life presents to them.

A river's long journey to the sea will sometimes include tumultuous rapids, when the water squeezes through narrow openings between steep banks and cliffs. And there will be moments of calm and peaceful meandering. However, isn't it true that during times of turbulence, the water flows more quickly, covers more terrain, and carves out new paths? Likewise, when a child's life is unsettled, there is movement and possibility. In such turbulent social times, new ways forward can be forged that would not necessarily have developed in times of happiness and calm.

# 3

## BULLYING WITHOUT BORDERS

### *Cyberbullying*

About half of all peer abuse or hyper-controlling issues now involve some form of cyberbullying, and the numbers are on the rise. This trend is deeply concerning. But shouldn't we have expected far-reaching social consequences when we put some of the most powerful tools humankind has ever invented (smartphones, tablets, computers) into our children's hands while exercising minimal supervision?

Kids who are cyberbullied report that they feel scared and hurt, and they develop a negative self-image.[1] Here are more sobering cyberbullying statistics about our kids:[2]

25 percent engaged in self-harm
26 percent had suicidal thoughts
37 percent developed depression
41 percent developed social anxiety
60 percent of teenagers have been cyberbullied[3]

70 percent of teenagers have had rumors spread about them on-line[4]

20 percent of tweens (ages ten to twelve) have been cyberbullied[5]

90 percent of twelve-year-olds are using social media[6]

81 percent of kids feel it is easier to get away with bullying online[7]

## IN REAL LIFE VS. IN VIRTUAL LIFE

Because of the ubiquitous use of screens, we now use terms such as *in real life* (IRL) and *in virtual life* (IVL) to define and distinguish person-to-person communication and experience. What makes cyberbullying so much more damaging than regular exclusion?

### The Unknown

**In Real Life:** When you are being picked on, you know who the perpetrators are and can do your best to deal with them.

**In Virtual Life:** You may have no idea who is targeting you. It's human nature to be gripped by genuine fear when confronted with an unseen, unquantifiable threat.

### Bullying without Borders

**IRL:** It may be hurtful but the circle of people involved is mostly known. You can take a good guess at who the perpetrators are and who is seeing and hearing what is going on.

**IVL:** You simply cannot know what is being put out there about you and what social-networking apps are being used because of the multiplatform nature of the internet.

### It's Fast . . . Too Fast

**IRL:** Being left out used to be a slow-mounting process. As days passed, you could feel yourself becoming more and more of a social outcast. However, there was time to try to figure out what was happening and make corrections.

IVL: Your marginalization happens at the speed of fiber-optic light. The time you have to figure out what is happening is much shorter. Vulnerable kids, who know how quickly this can happen, become guarded and socially on edge, which in turn makes them even more likely targets.

## Cyber Whack-a-Mole

IRL: You can have reasonable hope that your life will settle down if you find a way to deal with the individual or group of kids who are picking on you.

IVL: While you're trying to deal with cyberbullying on one platform, another attack pops up on another app. You brace yourself for the next assault, but you have no idea what direction it will come from.

## Nothing Is Private

IRL: Embarrassment is something anyone who has ever been picked on remembers all too well. However, our feeling of *being exposed* has traditionally been limited to our immediate social environment.

IVL: Kids tend to be careless online and post a lot of information about themselves, and cyberbullies can grab these posts and photos and conflate and distort them. With so many children walking around with state-of-the-art video and camera equipment in their pockets (smartphones, GoPros, etc.), photos and footage of embarrassing moments can be uploaded and widely distributed within nanoseconds.

## No Place of Refuge

IRL: Kids can go home and wrap themselves in a blanket of normalcy—the familiar joys and annoyances of family life; they can take a long outbreath to quiet their nervous system, reset them, and ready themselves for the next day of discomfort.

IVL: There is nowhere to hide. As long as there is access to a screen (phone, tablet, computer), the threat lurks in every corner.

### It Comes After You

**IRL:** Kids who get bullied often figure out ways to navigate away from people and places where they are most at risk. Although it's far from ideal, they can take different routes or find times of the day when they feel safe.

**IVL:** Cyberbullies specialize in posting links to their cruel "work." Once your tween or teen is aware of the thread or platform where they are being teased, it is virtually impossible for them to keep from checking the site over and over to see what has been added and by whom. Many kids report that they can't stop themselves from looking even though they know what they see will upset them.

### Written in Permanent Ink

**IRL:** If you are excluded or even bullied, the problematic situation often fades with time. Even if you never forget, most people in your social circle will move on and have little memory of the difficult events you went through.

**IVL:** Once a photoshopped picture or demeaning comment is posted, it can remain *out there* indefinitely. It may be searchable years later by potential college admissions officers, employers, future friends, or partners.

### Schadenfreude: The Enjoyment of Someone Else's Suffering

**IRL:** There have always been people who enjoy watching others suffer. Passive colluding or *bystanderism*—in which other kids watch as a targeted person is emotionally or physically hurt, but do nothing—is quite common in bullying situations.

**IVL:** Children and teens who hyper-control and bully others are fed by the attention they attract. Because the *bystander* audience available to them when they cyberbully is so much larger, they are often goaded into committing ever more outrageous antisocial acts.

### The Digital Smoke Screen

**IRL:** There are always minor situations in which mean notes are passed around and rumors are spread. But it takes a more aggressive, hyper-controlling kid to actually *do* something that is noticed by others. After all, that is the point—to be noticed.

**IVL:** The antisocial script is flipped. Kids who cyberbully often prefer covert tactics, and they are much more likely to amp up their bullying tactics because they can hide behind online pseudonyms.

### Say It to My Face

**IRL:** It takes a certain kind of warped courage to say hurtful things to another person when they are standing right in front of you.

**IVL:** You can say anything you like about another person without having to witness the effect your words have on them. Not only do you not see the pain you cause but you also receive a stream of feedback (texts, messages, emojis) that encourages you to continue or even ratchet up the hurtfulness of your comments.

## WHAT TO DO

Most of the strategies detailed in *Emotionally Resilient Tweens and Teens* can be effective in dealing with online harassment. However, because the problem has become so toxic and widespread, we need to build a deeper and stronger foundation of emotional security under our kids.

If your child or teen is being cyberbullied, you must find a way to be even more skilled, serious, and supportive.

Though most of the advice provided in chapter 1 about helping your child deal with teasing, bullying, and exclusion also applies to cyberbullying, here is a brief overview through the lens of online harassment:

### Strengthen Family Base Camp

At the top of the list is your need to move in closer. Doing simple, fun activities together with your child or teen will counterbalance the negativity flooding into your family life via the internet. Your stead-fast, loving presence will provide your child with a buffer of safety and emotional security.

### Dialing Life Back Helps Everyone Involved

Cyberbullying moves fast. We need to do the opposite: slow life down for the child, tween, or teen who is being bullied. Take a high-altitude look at your child's life and see what can be dialed back. Reducing activities, commitments, and pressures will help them decompress from the intensity of a cyberbullying crisis. Then, once they get through this social challenge, they can pick up where they left off. Even though cyberbullying is not an issue in Sophie's story (see "It's Life That's Bullying Me: Sophie's Story"), the overwhelm that she deals with is central to helping susceptible children overcome the panic they feel when they are harassed online. Sophie learns that the frenzied pace of her life and the high expectations she and others place on her are what heighten her vulnerability and trigger her over-reactive behavior. Once she slows things down, she breaks the reactive cycle that caused her to feel like a target. When she recovers her resiliency, she makes friends and is able to face her challenges with burgeoning self-confidence. Every cyberbullied kid should learn to dial life back the way she does.

It's important to realize that the same is often true for kids who bully and try to dominate others socially. Such children and teens are also overwhelmed by the unrealistic demands placed on them. The main difference between the taunter and the targeted child, tween or teen, is that the former's default reaction is to attempt to hyper-control social situations. When their personal life becomes dysregulated, they grasp for whatever they can control, including other kids—especially ones who react openly and are therefore easier to manipulate.

### Bring It to the Surface

Kids tend to conceal the fact that they are being cyberbullied for two key reasons; these reasons are also why these attacks are underreported as compared with "traditional bullying."[8] First, children fear that their devices will be taken away from them and that they will be digitally *grounded*, even though they are the ones being targeted. Second, they fear that they will be labeled a "snitch" or "tattletale," which will trigger more widespread humiliation. Let your child or teen know that they will not be blamed. Reassure them that you will work on this social challenge together and that you will not do anything to further embarrass them.

### Stay Centered

Your child is very vulnerable and needs you to stay centered and remain in control of your emotions as they struggle with theirs. Because of the potentially severe mental health impact of cyberbullying, we tend to *lose it* and *freak out* when we discover what has been going on. All our protective instincts get triggered. But if you have to unload, do it with a trusted adult friend or relative, not in front of your kid.

### Keep a Record

Most cyberbullying leaves a digital trail. Take screen shots of posts, messages, or texts and print them out. One parent said that she and her daughter became digital detectives. They prepared a file to be used in evidence if needed. Astonishingly, cyberbullying is still normalized by some adults. But when they are presented with graphic, hurtful evidence, they will find it difficult to downplay the taunting and make excuses. In extreme situations, you may seriously consider filing a police report. Many states, provinces, and countries now have anti-bullying and anti-cyberbullying legal statutes. If you take this kind of action, providing evidence is essential.

### Involving the School

Perpetrators of cyberbullying are often the same kids who create hyper-controlling problems at school. Studies have found that over 85 percent of kids who cyberbully are also involved in traditional bullying.[9] It's important to realize that traditional bullies at school are three times as likely to engage in cyberbullying[10] and that many cyberbullies and cyber victims are also traditional bullying perpetrators and victims.[11]

If you decide to approach the school, remember that you are going to need their help. Try not to come on too strongly. Be assertive, *not* aggressive. Presenting them with printouts of online postings or message threads will awaken them to what is going on and strengthen their resolve to deal with the problem.

Nevertheless, here are two points of caution:

First, school officials may express concern but say there is nothing they can do because the activity took place during nonschool hours on devices that the school does not own. They may even point out that it is a police matter, not a school issue.

Second, you should check out how the school approaches social exclusion issues in general. If they have a harsh and punitive approach, you may not want to speak to them. Triggering a harsh response may put your child or teen in more danger of retaliation. However, if the school has a firm, clear, and restorative practice in place and walks the delicate line between not blaming and accountability, you can feel more confident that the problem will be well handled rather than potentially inflamed.

### Don't Get Put On the Virtual Witness Stand

In a traditional court of law, an attorney will question the defendant. But imagine a witness who has questions fired at them by tens or even hundreds of interrogators. That is the dynamic with cyber harassment. It is exactly what the targeted child or teen experiences. When you combine the number of online platforms available with the number of potential perpetrators and bystanders willing to "pile on" because they think they can hide behind cyber anonymity, you are looking at a waking anxiety dream. You feel an attack can come at you at any moment, from any direction, and you have no way to defend yourself.

The key is for your kid to avoid being put in that witness box in the first place. No one appointed these tormentors officers of the court. Your child absolutely does not have to answer their summons to appear. In Elena's story, Elena's life is transformed when she refuses to be questioned. She responds to belittling, racially tinged rumors, and cyberbullying by learning to deflect or diffuse her tormentors' attacks. (See "Rumors and Whispers: Elena's Story.")

### Being Okay with Who You Are

The internet is flooded with idealized images of gorgeous, immaculately dressed people doing very expensive and exclusive things. It's no surprise that regular kids try to emulate this "look" on their social-networking sites by posting pictures (often photoshopped) of themselves looking great and having a great time, surrounded by supercool friends. Captions further reinforce how cool and popular they are.

Emboldened by these curated images of their own *flawless, perfect* worlds, cyberbullies post distorted images or send demeaning texts about their victims. They act like self-appointed digital deities looking down upon mere mortals and presume they can exercise control over every aspect of their underlings' lives.

Your best response to all this hierarchical posing and fakery is to reject the entire construction. Help your kids see that who they are *is okay*—wonderful even. Point out how these images are meant to manipulate us into feeling dissatisfied and insecure about who we are and what we have. They are designed to make us feel small and diminished. Explain to your child, tween, or teen that being okay with who you are takes control away from your tormentors.

In Anika's story, Anika learns that changing who you are in order to be accepted by others exacts a steep price. When she learns that she can be cool *and* kind, her life changes. (See "The New Kid: Anika's Story.") In Destiny's story, Destiny learns how to cultivate her inner strength by developing a "self-talk" strategy. It is a powerful tool that enables kids to diffuse the attacks coming from the outside world by building their own inner power and centeredness. (See "The Shy Kid's Gift of Inner Strength: Destiny's Story.")

Finally, be open with your kids about your own difficulties when you were learning how to fit in. Kids love to hear stories about what we faced and surmounted when we were young.

But above all else, let them know how deeply you love them— quirks, mistakes, failures, successes, and all.

### Increase Real-Life Relationships

When things get hostile online, we need to help our kids pivot away from all that virtual toxicity. Help them find new activities, groups, and relationships *in real life*. A major shift is possible when a child who is rejected and attacked online finds even a minimal degree of acceptance with another person or group. In Joey's story, you will read about a boy who regained his sense of self-worth by finding friends who valued him in a completely different setting. (See "A New Group, a New Me: Joey's Story.")

Cyberbullied kids are especially wary of engaging in new relationships, so we need to proceed carefully. When consulting the mother of a cyberbullied boy we'll call Jack, I suggested that she find new outlets and activities for him. She tried to get Jack interested in visiting a BMX bike park, remembering how much he loved to ride and tinker with his bike. But he refused to go, reluctant to put himself out there. Rather than give up on the idea, she asked around and found a young man in a nearby town who ran a backyard bike repair shop. She spoke to the man about what Jack had been through and asked him if her son could work as his shop assistant. The young man put down his tools, looked her straight in the eye, and said, "Can he start today?" About a month after he started working in the shop with his new boss, Jack began to meet up with and go for rides with some of the kids who came into the shop to get their bikes fixed.

## BLOCKING, REDUCING & BREAKING FREE

The crucial first step is for your child to realize that their own reactivity is what inflames bullying, teasing, or exclusion. Sara's story illustrates how liberating it can be when a teen realizes that she has within her the power to cut off the oxygen that feeds the bullying flame. (See "How I Got My Confidence Back: Sara's Story.")

For online targets, however, there is an added dilemma. Smartphones are a primary communication portal for most kids. And because they are addictive, kids are extremely reluctant to curtail their use, despite the fact that it is through their own phones that their tormentors attack them. But there are three steps you can take to filter content in order to limit your child's exposure to cyber taunting rather than cutting off screen use entirely.

1. Block all IMs, texts, or emails coming from the kids who are cyberbullying your child, teen, or tween. Also block them on the social-networking sites your child or teen uses. And turn off all message notifications, because that interruptive sound alert can trigger your child's fear that something harmful is lurking online and *it just has to be* checked.

2. If your child experiences some relief from step 1, suggest that they go even further and shut down their social-networking accounts. Cyberbullies are relentless. They may

figure out ways to get around blocks. A thirteen-year-old who decided to step away from all social media posted and pinned the following comment across all the platforms he'd used: "You can say whatever you like, I can't stop you. I am not interested in what you are saying, and I am deleting this app as of now—goodbye." He left this comment up for a day and then shut everything down.

Kids may wonder, quite reasonably, if knowing what is being posted about them is better than walking around school completely out of the loop. However, time after time, kids have confided that after a few days, their concern begins to fade. Within a week or two they just don't care anymore. An eleven-year-old who had turned off her accounts told me, "That was one party invite I definitely did not mind turning down." "Maybe now you'll start getting some real invitations," I replied. She burst out laughing. "How did you know?" I *knew* because her anxiety was now firmly under control and her bubbly nature had resurfaced. Who wouldn't want someone like her at their party?

3. Consider a full breakaway from screens for three to four weeks. Think about it this way: After feasting over the holiday season, we often start the new year cutting back or going on a full-out cleansing diet. The same is true for kids who are cyberbullied. They have been force-fed a toxic digital diet for weeks or months. The best way to help them back to being themselves is to convince them to try a *digital cleanse*.

You'll find a very effective digital-diet program detailed in Dr. Victoria L. Dunckley's excellent book *Reset Your Child's Brain: A Four-Week Plan to End Meltdowns, Raise Grades, and Boost Social Skills by Reversing the Effects of Electronic Screen-Time*.

Another teenager I worked with told me that it wasn't until after she'd completed a digital detox that she realized how anxious she had become. "Every time I checked my phone," she said, "I could feel stress running through my entire body. You don't realize how wound up you have become until you break free from screens. The digital fast totally rebooted my nervous system."

How difficult was it for her to step away from all things digital? "At first it felt weird," she said, "but really, I thought it was going to be way harder than it actually was."

### Smartphone or Dart Phone

Bullying, teasing, and exclusion have always been problems. But cyberbullying has weaponized the act of dehumanization to a whole new emotionally devastating level. School programs that teach cyber civics have become essential. More and more, parents are questioning this new normal—wondering whether or when they should be giving children devices that give them unfettered access to social media. One parent-teacher spoke about the volatile virtual world her twelve-year-old lives in: "Cyberbullying is not a thing in our family because my kid doesn't have a phone. But I've seen too many kids hurt. It is seriously time to stop and think about what we are allowing."

The memory of sitting in an emergency room with parents of a cyberbullied tween who had tried and very nearly succeeded in committing suicide is etched into my soul. The mother had her son's phone in her hand. She had just read, for the first time, the vile comments and posts that had been wounding him for months. As she wept, she asked, "How could I have handed him this—this weapon of so much malice." Her husband tried to console her. "How were we to know?" he said. She shook her head and whispered, "We don't give guns to children. We just don't."

### Screen Creep

Working with so many caring, anguished parents whose kids have been cyberbullied, I have noticed one defining commonality: they have all experienced "screen creep" in their homes. They started off with the rationale that computers should be allowed in their kids' lives and homes because they are necessary *tech tools* they need for schoolwork. However, all too soon the tool becomes a *tech toy*, used instead for video watching and gaming. The final step is when the screen becomes a *tech talk* device. That's when texting, messaging, and social media, with all the associated notifications and content, prove to be a Pandora's box filled with very real dangers and emotional exposure.

Be on the alert for screen creep. With every social-networking app you allow your kids to download, every video game or console you buy for them, every moment you let them do "just a little bit more," your child becomes more vulnerable to cyber abuse. Making *screen-time* boundaries is a good start, but if we are to be proactive about preventing cyberbullying, we need to take a conscious look at *screen content* and trust our instincts when we find things that just don't feel right.

As you can now see, cyberbullying truly is *bullying without borders*. It can flood into our kids' lives and our private homes with almost unstoppable force. But it doesn't have to be that way. We have a choice to make. A powerful one. We can coach and support our kids to develop the strategies they need to channel and deflect this grim digital deluge. If they do, they will not only break free from cyberbullying but also uncover an inner strength that will help them navigate the ever-increasing presence of virtual communication as they grow up and move out into the world. And they will have the tools they need to become responsible cyber citizens.

# 4

---

# "I CAN HELP. I AM HERE FOR YOU."

By the time our kids approach us with their problems, they have likely tried a bunch of things to deal with the exclusion they face. We tend to jump in with suggestions such as "Just walk away" or "Just ignore them." (See "Stop Pushing Me Around: Michael's Story.") However, it's so important instead to ask about and recognize their efforts, even if they didn't work. When we make flat suggestions before hearing them out, our kids lose confidence in our ideas. And when we use words such as *just*, we make it sound easy. It's not. Make sure your tone or attitude doesn't make your child feel incompetent or even more *like a loser* than they already feel.

## AFFIRM YOUR CHILD'S EFFORTS

Here are a few helpful comments and questions you can use:

- "Sounds like it has been hard."
- "Has it been going on for a long time or just a little while?"

- "Have you tried some things to work it out, or is it hard to think up ideas like that?"
- "Sounds like you have been brave."
- "Knowing what to do when you are left out is not easy."

Try to have a kind and attentive but matter-of-fact tone. Getting this right is important. You don't want to sound dismissive, but you also don't want to sound too sentimental and over-involved, because your child may close down if you get into their space. Just be you. Speak in your normal voice. That is the best way to reassure your child that they are being heard and are safe when they are talking about it with you.

## CAN YOU HELP ME UNDERSTAND . . . ?

An effective question with which to begin an exchange with your child is "Can you help me understand what's been happening?" Children love to connect when the request is genuine and they feel safe. By beginning in this way, you open up the possibility for a meaningful conversation. You are signaling to them that you are present and ready to listen rather than talk. Children who are being picked on or left out need to be listened to because they feel the world does not value their voice. Also, this opening question is both practical and compassionate, making it clear that they know their dilemma best and you very much want to understand.

## SMALL STEPS VS. ONE BIG,
## LONG CONVERSATION

Children *really* dislike it when we "go on and on." They may occasionally want to have a long and in-depth conversation, but much more often, particularly when speaking about a troubling situation, they like it when we keep it brief and spread out such a conversation over a few days. This gives them space to breathe and keeps them from feeling as though we are trying to squeeze information out of them. It also gives you a chance to pause, calm down (if necessary), and consider what is essential.

Choose your time carefully. We all know that there are good and bad times to talk to a child. They might need to speak with you away from siblings because they are embarrassed, or they might have the kind of relationship with a sister or brother that makes it easier for them to open up when their sibling is present. As one mother said, "Parenting is the art of lying in wait for the right time." Some parents find it best to be doing something while having the chat: making the bed together, unloading the dishwasher, taking a short car trip.

Here are a few examples of comments and questions you may find useful:

- "Is it okay to talk about this just a little bit?"
- "We don't need to talk about this for long if you don't want to."
- "Let's make the bed now and you can tell me as much as you want to about what's been happening."

You might even want to give your child a heads-up that you will not "go on and on." When you do that, you are doing what I call "advance paving" of the path you will walk together in the coming days or weeks. One effective way of doing this is to say, "I don't want to go on longer than is good for you, so I'd like to check in from time to time over the next days/weeks and we can chat. Sound okay?"

## IT'S ALL ABOUT EASING REACTIVITY: UNCOVERING THE TRUTH

In my school years, I was one of those quiet yet feisty kids. I tended to hover on the outer edge of social situations until I felt comfortable joining in. I was good at games and sports, which often gave me a kind of immunity to being picked on. However, I watched with interest and empathy the children who repeatedly got teased and left out. It made me sad, uneasy, and puzzled that they had to endure this kind of treatment. I also observed others on the playground who—despite their obvious physical and cultural differences—deflected mean comments, stayed in the game, and found friends. The key to their success? They didn't *react* to taunting. And they did this in a handful of ways that drew my attention.

The main thing I noticed was that they didn't display anger or fight back aggressively. They kept their cool and stood their ground. I admired their courage and wanted to figure out how they did it. Here are some of the things I noticed:

- Some kids would agree with an insult or jab: "Yeah, I know I'm not that good at running, but I still like playing."
- Children with a good sense of humor would make people who tried to tease them laugh. One boy I knew had a peculiar habit of walking up on his toes; he was told derisively that he was an airy-fairy ballet dancer. So the next time he played four square in the schoolyard, he pirouetted or twirled after hitting the ball. It cracked everyone up. His would-be tormentors shook their heads and smiled—and stopped teasing him.
- Some kids would respond by repeating a bland phrase—"So what?" "Whatever." "Heard it before."—every time a mean comment was made.
- One really effective strategy I noticed was to simply state the obvious by saying something like, "Go ahead. I can't stop you saying that." One classmate whose family had emigrated from an Eastern European country would say with a shrug of his shoulders, "It's a free country." This noncombative approach struck me as particularly effective. Not only was he saying something that was true and therefore irrefutable, but he was also relaxed and matter-of-fact about it. His attitude and man-

ner drew others to him. I figured it was because they felt safe in the company of someone like him.

Later in my teens, I joined an elite youth soccer team. We played in front of large crowds, with scouts from top-ranked teams present, and there was intense pressure to win. Players often "trash-talked" their opponents to try to throw them off their game. They would say some pretty horrible things. It was hard to ignore, but armed with the strategies I had observed over the years, I'd either state the obvious—"Go ahead. Say whatever you like."—or crack a joke about what was being said: "Yeah, I sure messed that up. Probably best to kick the ball when it's actually there." This not only deflected the mean or sarcastic comments but often made my opponents laugh. They'd smile and say "Good job" when we shook hands at the end of the game. I made some pretty good friends among the players of the teams we played against. We even started hanging out before or after our games in spite of the fact that they were supposed to be *the opposition*.

When I became a teacher and school counselor, I started teaching children these ways of dealing with teasing. But it was also clear to me that the issue needed to be approached from the other side. Our school needed to take exclusion issues seriously.

When I became an outside consultant, I developed, with the help of students, a school-wide anti-bullying program called the "Social Inclusion Approach" (SIA) and introduced it to thousands of schools over the next thirty years. This approach (which is featured in "Standing Up and Speaking Out: Darpan's Story") has led to systems whereby older students are trained to intervene and ease potentially difficult situations in the corridors and playground. The Student Social Action Committees, as they are known, have been very helpful in making the playground culture more inclusive by building willingness among children to reach out for help when social tension arises, so that older kids can engage in on-the-spot problem-solving.

This type of work is critical because unless targeted children are coached and cared for by older kids, teachers, and particularly parents, and taught tools they can use to help them learn to stand up for themselves, they will feel vulnerable, helpless, and reliant on "the school." And while it is essential that schools develop processes to help prevent and deal with bullying, the fact remains that so much teasing and exclusion happens outside the scope of the teacher's supervision. We must teach children who are being marginalized to become more self-reliant in those situations. That is why we have presented practical strategies in the ten peer-narrated stories in this book.

### How to Speak to Your Child about Reactivity without Making Them Feel Bad

If your child is being picked on, it is important to help them realize that is not happening because of their body shape, appearance, mannerisms, or abilities. This can be hard for them to grasp because that is what they are being teased about, so they naturally believe it is the cause of their troubles. (See "How I Got My Confidence Back: Sara's Story" and "But What If It's True? Daniel's Story.")

I remember talking to a ten-year-old I'll call Tony, who was convinced that he was being teased because he couldn't hit the ball well in the daily game of T-ball. Tony clearly wasn't a strong batter. But when I asked him if there were other children who also weren't good hitters, he matter-of-factly replied that there were five others. He listed them by name and informed me that he wasn't exactly the worst. I asked him if all five of the other "bad hitters" were teased. He named one who was teased a lot and four who were not. Then I pressed him about why he thought that four weak hitters were never teased, while he and the one other boy were taunted and put down.

Tony was silent for a minute. He tried to figure this all out. Then he asked, "Do you think it's because Jaden and me get really mad and shout back at them, and José and Mia and the others don't?" I nodded slowly. "Yesterday," he added, "Mia swung so hard she spun around and fell over. She lay back on the grass and shouted out for us to call an ambulance. Everyone laughed." (See "But What If It's True? Daniel's Story.")

"Okay," I said, "what would have happened if you had missed the ball like that?"

"Oh! They would have called me all kinds of names." Tony was on a roll now. "And I would have got embarrassed and shouted back at them or stormed off. I threw the bat once."

"Did that make them stop?" I asked.

"No-oh," he said. "They laughed even harder and said even worse stuff."

I gently suggested that he was not being taunted about his T-ball batting skills. At first, he looked confused. He had always believed that this was the crux of the problem. But he eventually agreed with me because of the simple fact that four kids were at least as bad as he was, but they were never teased. It was finally dawning on him that the teasing wasn't triggered by his lack of skill but by his *big reaction* to their taunts.

I have led countless children through this kind of conversation, and it is hard to look at their faces when they realize the truth. Many felt that they were to blame. It's very important to move in quickly to assure them that they have been brave and done the best they could, that most certainly they have nothing to be ashamed of. In fact, they have now uncovered their superpower.

When kids like Tony finally realize that they inadvertently empower their tormentors when they react in anger, hurt, or fear—and that when they don't react outwardly, they keep their power for themselves—they begin to shift the dynamic. One young teenager put it perfectly: "I've been putting so much wood on *their* fire that *I've* been getting burned and they think it's fun. They're not gonna get no more wood from me." Another kid told me, "It's weird because the more I get mad, the bigger *they* get, and *I* just end up feeling really small."

## I CAN HELP. I AM HERE FOR YOU.

Above all else, children need hope when they are disheartened because their social lives seem desolate. You have created space, tried to be present, done your best to provide a safe home base, and listened deeply. And they now understand that their superpower is their ability to control their reactivity. But what can they actually do to make this stop?

### We Have the Tools

A simple, clear statement that you can show your child how they can stop the teasing will provide them with relief and renewed confidence. You can say this with quiet certainty. Why? Because you will work together using the effective stories of trouble and triumph that are laid out in *Emotionally Resilient Tweens and Teens*. The stories will provide you with many ideas that will help you and your child turn things around.

### Ask If They Want to Know about the Tools

This may sound obvious, but it's important to knock on the door when a child is troubled. Asking to be let in sends a clear signal of respect and empathy. If you have followed the advice given here and built a solid foundation, few children will reject your offer of help. We need to "connect before we direct,"[12] and if the connection is not strong enough and they only crack the door open, don't worry. Back up and figure out what you need to pay attention to in order to address their hesitance.

### Many Other Kids Have Used These Tools

When a child is worried because nothing has worked for them, they will really light up when you tell them that many kids have used these stories and strategies to stop teasing, exclusion, or bullying and even learned to make new friends. Thousands of kids around the world have learned to stand up and be strong—and they can too.

### Plan and Practice Together

It can be a little daunting for a child when you tell them that they must learn some new strategies. Assure them that you will help them make a plan, that it won't be complicated, and that together you'll choose an approach that is doable and feels natural.

Next, let them know that you will practice with them at home before they have to use the new strategies at school. Tell them it's like learning lines for a play. You have to memorize lines and know where you will speak them on stage. At first, when they are rehearsing, they might feel a bit strange. But after a little while, they'll get the hang of it and sound believable—as if they really are speaking for themselves and not just like a character in the play. For example, let's say your child has listened to one of the stories in which a character repeats a few simple phrases over and over when trying not to react to teasing. They decide to say "Heard it before; boring" when they are teased about being a slow runner.

The next step is for you to tell them that at least three times each day for the next few days, you will try to catch them unaware and call them "turtle," "slowpoke," or some other name the kids at school have been taunting them with. Your child will then practice saying "Heard it before, boring" without visibly reacting. You do this together until they feel ready to use their comeback at school.

### It's Our Secret

A mother and a daughter (call her Gia) worked out a strategy to deal with nasty rumors that were being spread about her on her soccer team. They discussed how Gia could break out of the pattern of being forced to defend herself. They workshopped her "lines." After sifting through bad ideas and laughing at failed attempts, they came up with "Who made you the rumor police?" They practiced how she would say it each night to make sure it was just right. (See "Rumors and Whispers: Elena's Story.")

After her soccer practice later in the week, Gia climbed into her mom's car. "I did it!" she exclaimed, elated. "I asked Emma," the soccer team's gossiper in chief, "who made you the rumor police? 'I did,' Emma said. 'What are you gonna to do about it?' And you know what came out of my mouth then, Mom?" Gia told her mom giddily. "I said, 'Oh, did I miss the vote for police chief?' We never planned on *that* line. I guess I was inspired! But *the very best part* was that some of the girls laughed out loud and talked to me just like they used to, before Emma started all this horrible stuff."

What pleased Gia's mom the most about the situation was that Gia felt so validated. "She and I worked out a strategy together," Gia's mom told me. "But she executed it all by herself. That made her feel self-confident." Which indeed she was!

## ENCOURAGING PARENTAL PERSEVERANCE

When you approach your child about their social difficulties, you may get the brush-off. Kids often think they "get it," and they react defensively when you approach them. "I know all this stuff!" one tween we'll call Diana told her mom. Her mom had suggested Diana read Sara's story, about a girl who gives a clique she is eager to join too much power over her, until she learns how to stand up to them without overreacting. (See "How I Got My Confidence Back: Sara's Story.") "I can figure this out on my own!" Diana insisted. Her mom, who I was counseling, was stymied. "How can I help her," she asked, "when she rolls her eyes at everything I say and throws up a dismissive wall to shut me out?"

The truth of the matter was that Diana clearly couldn't handle the situation on her own. Kids often can't. They are right in insisting that they recognize the principles of these commonsense strategies to combat teasing and exclusion. However, they clearly don't know how to turn their thoughts into action with any consistency. If they knew how, they wouldn't be so socially tangled up. Nevertheless, it's not surprising that some kids push back when their parents offer to help. They have become practiced at being defensive and will try to conceal their vulnerability.

What you can do in such situations is assure the child, tween, or teen that you believe they know this way of dealing with taunts or exclusion. You just want to ground their good insights in an everyday strategy that can help them put an end to the unfairness they are experiencing. Diana's mom quietly insisted her daughter read the story. When she finished, Diana was silent. She clearly had seen her own struggles reflected in Sara's friendship woes. Soon after, she was able to talk things over with her mom and eventually improve her social situation.

Let your child know you want to check in with them briefly every couple of days to go over how the strategies they read about in this book can help. Promise to keep the conversations brief and practical. If they push back against the strategies you suggest, don't be deterred. When a kid says, "I just want to be left alone," that is precisely the time when they desperately need someone who cares deeply for them to remain close. This is especially true when exclusion and isolation are at the heart of the social problem. No matter how prickly or sullen they get, they need us to remain emotionally present—and walk beside them with patience and persistence.

*Part Two*

---

# YOUR
# TEN-STORY
# TOOLBOX

In the next section of *Emotionally Resilient Tweens and Teens*, you will read ten stories that provide you and your child, tween, or teen firsthand examples of peers who've been through it all and learned how to take control of their own lives. They are fellow students— older teen mentors who have struggled with teasing, subtle social exclusion, or bullying and become masters of their own destinies rather than remaining mired in victimhood and tormented for months, sometimes years.

## WHY ARE THEIR STORIES SO EFFECTIVE?

Why are the stories of these teen mentors so effective? Because they offer your child critical social skills and strategies to help them navigate these ten common challenges of teasing, exclusion, and bullying:

1. Figuring out why you are being teased.

2. Finding a new attitude when dealing with social exclusion or bullying.

3. Handling rumors.

4. Dealing with physical needling and bullying.

5. Navigating online exclusion and cyberbullying.

6. Understanding the difference between tattling and truth telling.

7. Standing up for others without making things worse for yourself.

8. Making *real* friends.

9. Bringing social/cultural change to your friends and your school.

Our ten teenaged narrators write about the difficult experiences they went through in school—times when they were excluded, were made to feel invisible, had rumors spread about them, faced cyber-bullying, were physically pushed around, or simply just didn't know how to fit in.

In each story you'll read about a real-life problem and hurt feelings of the person being picked on. You will also learn the different ways they try to make the teasing or bullying stop. You may recognize strategies they used that didn't work for your child. Or you may sympathize with them when you hear about people who tried to help them but made things worse.

However, the kids in these stories eventually found someone (parent, teacher, cousin, or classmate) who helped them work through their problems without interfering or embarrassing them. Your child, too, can find someone they can trust to look through these stories with them and coach them through their difficulties—someone like you, your spouse, or even a close relative or family friend.

Each storyteller discovered a new way to see why they were being targeted and what was *really* going on. The key moment came when they realized that their own fears and reactions were what gave the teasers control over them. Everything changed when they were able to figure out how to stand their ground, be strong, gain respect, and make new friends.

Many parents and kids have used the strategies laid out in this book to break free from the teasing trap. Some suggestions could be perfect for the situation you and your child find yourselves in. If so, test them out right away. Or your child may need to tweak a strategy a little before they can apply it to what is happening to them.

Pay special attention to the specific tactics each teen used to resolve their social challenge. Whether it's Sophie, who realized she had to dial things back in her fast-paced life; or Michael, who learned how best to handle physical bullies; or Elena, who dealt with rumors and cyberbullying—each problem has a practical solution that your child can learn about here and use to deal with their own difficulties.

You'll probably find the last story one of the most inspiring because, at first, Darpan—who himself overcame teasing in elementary school—quietly defends younger children who are being picked on. When kids and teachers in his school notice his small acts of kindness and inclusion, they ask Darpan to help more kids. Eventually a motley crew of high-school students band together to change the culture of the entire school. In doing so, Darpan and his friends find a whole new place within themselves that gives them and other kids throughout their school the strength to stand up and speak out—openly. And most importantly, they find a place within themselves where they can truly feel that *I am me . . . and that's okay!*

# 5

---

# THE NEW KID

## *Anika's Story*

It's not easy to stay true to yourself when you are trying to make new friends. Anika's story explores the tension that arises when you cross the line and give up too much of yourself in order to fit in with a group of friends.

All kinds of subtle characteristics define a group. The more people in the group, the more complex the social math gets. A group may dress in the same way, use similar terms, prize certain possessions, use private social-networking groups, follow the same set of influencers (actors or musicians), and engage in the same activities (sports, drama, etc.). Friendship groups tend to have their own way of seeing the world too: a collective outlook about what's funny or cool and what's decidedly not. And it can become critical to align with the dominant group identity if you want to be "in."

Kids learn to compromise when they join a group. But it can be hard to balance your own way of being with the accepted behavior of the group. The middle-school years present particular challenges because it is during these years that children emerge from their "little kid" cocoon but are certainly *not yet* young adults. These are the "tween" years, when kids begin to form their own social personalities. Many lean hard into the comfort of friendship groups to establish their identities.

However, you can give up too much in order to fit into a group. When you do that, you often feel uncomfortable. You may even be pressured into doing things that really don't feel right.

## POINTS OF UNDERSTANDING

- Feeling lonely and left out is subtle yet strong.
- The way we treat other people defines us.
- Changing the way you look on the outside to fit in doesn't change how you feel inside; a façade that feels wrong is hard to maintain for very long.
- Friendships based on exclusivity and putting other people down often sour or backfire.

## POINTS OF HOPE AND LEARNING

- We shouldn't have to change or cover up who we are to please others.
- There are people who will value you if they are given a chance to get to know you.
- Being cool *and* kind is possible and will lead to deeper and longer-lasting friendships.

We all long for independence in our younger years, yet a certain amount of compromise is needed to be part of most friendship groups. Anika's story illustrates that it's not worth conforming to behaviors that don't align with your beliefs—and you can actually make good friends while remaining closer to your own values.

*My name is Anika. I'm eighteen. This is a story about what happened to me when I started at a new school in seventh grade. What I learned from that experience has been very important to me—growing up these past six years—and I want to share it with other kids to help them make better choices when they struggle to fit in at a new school. I was young and immature back then, and I just wanted to be well liked and popular. But I went about it the wrong way. In order to fit in, I changed who I was and tried too hard to please others. I turned into a person I could hardly recognize and didn't like at all.*

When I was twelve, my mom was offered a job in Wisconsin. Since my dad worked from home mostly, our parents decided to move the family from Minneapolis—where my younger brother Tommy and I had lived our entire lives—to Madison. We were not happy about this at all. Tommy and I had lots of friends, and I had just gotten used to being a middle-schooler in Minneapolis.

Starting seventh grade at Clear Rock Middle School in Madison meant starting over—*again*. But this time I didn't know a single soul. I wore jeans and a light-blue pullover on my first day: casual and low-key. That's been my MO forever. I guess I take after my mom, who is super modest and chill. Don't get me wrong—she can be willful and firm when she needs to be. But she's basically a kind, calm person. Never overbearing. I like that about her.

I kept mostly to myself that first day, though I did answer two questions Miss Jones, my new English teacher, asked me. She's super nice and genuine. I liked her the second I saw her.

At lunch I sat down alone.

"Hi. I'm Danielle. Can I sit here?"

"Sure," I said.

"You're the new girl, right? Anika?"

"Yep. That's me."

"You nervous?"

"A little bit," I confessed. "Are people nice here?"

"Pretty much. No one is, like, awful."

"Who are *they*?"

I nodded to four pretty girls who were chatting away excitedly across the dining room. Several boys orbited them, vying for their attention.

"Oh. That's Bea and Co.," Danielle replied.

"Bea?"

"Bea-trice," she said. "She kinda runs things around here. With her are Kiara, Skylar, and Avery. They are about as close to an "it" crowd as we have here at Clear Rock. They're pretty cool."

"Well, thanks for the 411."

"You're welcome, Anika."

That first week, Danielle and I hung out pretty regularly. We sat together at the cafeteria and met up after school twice. But the next Monday, as I was headed over to sit with her at lunch, someone called out to me.

"Anika!"

I spun around. It was Bea.

"Hi."

"You're cute!" she said. "In a wholesome, homespun kinda way."

"Thanks."

"Come sit with us."

"Okay."

Bea and the others invited me to sit with them at lunch every day that week. We talked about everything: clothes, movies, teachers, boys. Bea had fixed opinions about everything and everyone, which no one ever contradicted. And Kiara and Avery did anything she asked them to. Skylar was less spellbound, but she clearly enjoyed being in Bea's clique. Bea was just someone you wanted to be around; someone you wanted to approve of everything you did. I could see why she was the most popular girl at Clear Rock. And I was so excited to be included that I completely forgot about my fledgling friendship with Danielle.

## MY POPULAR-GIRL MAKEOVER

"Don't get me wrong, Anika," Bea said, one day after school. "You can totally get away with it. But your wardrobe needs a total makeover."

"Really?" I asked, wishing I could disappear instantly.

"Don't be silly, darling," Bea added. "I can totally fix you."

"Bea's right," Kiara said. "She's a total pro at this. She absolutely transformed Avery last year."

"What about you, Kiara?" Avery shot back. "You certainly weren't Little Miss Wisconsin in sixth grade yourself!"

"Quit bickering, girls," Bea scolded. "We have work to do. Come over to my house tomorrow, Anika, and we'll get started."

"Okay," I gulped.

Bea and I had a great time at her house after school the next day. We dressed up in all kinds of different outfits. Some were Bea's. Some belonged to her older sisters. We even snuck into her mom's closet and tried on some of her cocktail dresses. Bea set aside several tops I could borrow to wear at school for the next few days. I stuffed them in my schoolbag and changed into them each morning at school. I basically wore whatever she told me to. I was so worried that she would suddenly wake up and realize I just didn't fit in with her, Kiara, Avery, and Skylar that I agreed to anything she proposed.

I also started hassling my mom to take me shopping.

"Take me to the mall, Mom," I pleaded. "I *really* need to get a new outfit."

"Why, honey? We just got you a bunch of really nice back-to-school clothes."

"I need something different. Something that works."

"Oh boy. What's his name, Anika?" Mom said, making her funny face.

"Oh my god, Mom! There is no *boy*. It's just—school is different here."

That Saturday, Mom and I went shopping all afternoon. It was awesome. When we were finally done, I had a new pair of tight-fitting capri jeans and tops that made me look, well . . . *hot*. I felt kinda bad because I'd really pressured Mom into getting them. We are not wealthy by any stretch. I knew well we could barely afford all this stuff. Mom worked full-time and Dad had just started working a second job. We were doing okay, but money was always tight and we had a budget we needed to stick to.

My little brother Tommy had been lobbying hard for new cleats he could use when he joined his new soccer team. I wondered if these purchases would mean he could not get them.

That night I overheard my parents talking when I passed by their bedroom door.

"What about Tommy's cleats?" Dad said.

"I guess he'll have to wait," Mom replied.

"Do you think that's fair?"

"Honey, she's in a new school," Mom said. "She's desperately trying to fit in."

"I guess the move's been a little tough on all of us," Dad conceded.

"I just couldn't say no," Mom said softly.

I was so glad Mom hadn't, even if I felt a little guilty about Tommy.

The next day I wore my new outfit to school along with a bit of Mom's blush and eye liner I snuck.

"You look killer!" Bea said.

"Such a hottie, Anika," Kiara added.

Avery smiled, motioning for me to twirl, then nodded approvingly.

I floated into English class feeling like a Hollywood starlet.

"Is that you, Anika?" Miss Jones asked. "I hardly recognized you!"

"Yes, Miss Jones. Just little ole me," I replied. I felt great, but a little weird too. Was this really me? All showy and seductive? When I turned around, I caught Jason Cheney gawking at me. I stuck out my tongue at him playfully. He laughed.

"OMG!" I said to Avery. "Guys who'd never noticed me before are checking me out."

"Like I told you," Avery replied, "Bea's a sorceress."

Along with my new look and my new friends came a group attitude I wasn't used to. Cool girls like Bea and Kiara never raised their hands. Instead, they giggled a lot and rolled their eyes when others spoke. I had always been a serious student. I *loved* English—reading, writing, and talking about books in class or anywhere else. And Miss Jones was super nice.

When Miss Jones asked me a question about the theme of greed in John Steinbeck's novella *The Pearl* in the middle of class, my brain almost burst with ideas. I had just reread the entire book the night before for class. But instead of answering in full sentences all that I knew, I mumbled a lame know-nothing response. I was as shocked by my answer as Miss Jones was. I'd suddenly been overcome by a wave of fear. I didn't want to appear too eager or smart and outshine my new friends.

As we walked out at the end of class, Miss Jones stopped me.

"Can you stay after class for a minute, Anika?" she asked.

"Sure," I replied. "I'll catch up with you guys in a minute."

Bea rolled her eyes, turned on her heels, and walked out. But I could see the four of them hovering outside the door.

"You are such a capable student, Anika," Miss Jones said. "Your homework is stellar as is your reading log. But I get the feeling you are holding back in class for some reason. I know you read this assignment."

"I'm sorry, Miss Jones," I said, turning crimson. "It's just—I couldn't think of what else to say."

"Well . . . your writing assignments are very creative," Miss Jones said, filling in the awkward silence.

"Thank you, Miss Jones."

"It's good to have new friends, Anika," she added, "but there's got to be a bit of a balance. Friendships shouldn't keep you from being you, from exploring your interests and doing your best at what you love and are good at."

"Yes, Miss Jones," I said demurely.

"You are a very promising writer. I know the school year has just started but I've got a hunch this could be something you take somewhere in life. If you really work at it."

"Really? You really think I'm a good writer?" I replied excitedly. "That I could *be* a writer?"

"Well, Anika, there is only one way to find out," Miss Jones replied. "You've got to go for it. Don't hold back."

"Thank you, Miss Jones." I felt excitement stirring inside me. Wow. That would really be truly amazing. I'd always hoped I'd be good enough to be an author one day.

"Come on, Anika. Let's go!" came the peevish call from the hallway.

"Thank you, Miss Jones," I said, embarrassed. She smiled and motioned for me to go. As I left the classroom, Bea, Kiara, Avery, and Skylar encircled me.

"What was that about?" Bea asked.

"Are you in trouble?" Kiara chimed in eagerly.

"No. no. It's nothing," I replied. "It was kinda stupid. She thinks I'm really into her class." I rolled my eyes.

"Oh my god!" Bea exclaimed. "That's such a joke. It's soooo boring in there."

"Exactly," I said.

But I felt like a total fake. Why had I just said that? I loved writing. I loved English. And so far, Miss Jones's was by far my favorite class.

Looking back on that day, I realize that was when I started losing my way. I felt uneasy inside. I didn't understand it then, of course, but I was trying way too hard to be someone I wasn't.

## MIRROR IMAGE

That afternoon when school let out, I spotted my mom waiting for me in her car as I headed toward the buses with Bea, Skylar, and Kiara.

"OMG! My mom's here!" I said.

"Are you serious?" Bea replied.

"I thought you take the bus," Skylar said.

"I do. I have no idea why she's here."

I freaked out. I was wearing a supertight, low-cut tank top Bea had loaned me. Mom had never seen me dressed like this. She spotted me, smiled, and waved me over. As I got closer, though, I saw her face change.

"Anika? Anika!" she called out. I held my backpack in front of me to conceal what I was wearing, but it was clearly too late. For a second, I saw myself through my mom's eyes and I felt *really* uncomfortable. It was clear how shocked she was—way too much was showing.

As I got closer to the car I realized, to my horror, that Bea, Kiara, and Skylar were still with me. They giggled and chatted loudly.

"Did you see what Danielle was wearing?" Bea said.

"She looks so lame," Kiara replied.

"Yeah. What is she, Amish?" I said, forgetting my mom for a second.

Everyone laughed fitfully.

"God! Don't people ever get it?" Kiara said. "No one should be allowed to leave their house dressed like that. There should be an alarm that buzzes if you do."

"Bye, Anika," Bea said sweetly when we'd reached Mom's car. I waved at her and the others and slipped into the passenger seat.

"Hi, Mom!"

Mom didn't respond. She just stared at me *like I was a foreigner.* She must have thought I'd turned into an alien or something. It's not that our family is prudish or anything. We just didn't dress or walk or talk the way my new friends did. Come to think of it, I don't recall my mom ever saying anything mean about another woman. And all she heard us do was diss another girl.

At that moment my mom was like a mirror, reflecting my new petty, mean-girl self right back at me. I didn't like what I saw at all. Mom didn't say much of anything on the drive home. She never did at such moments. But what she didn't say nearly deafened me. I felt so ashamed.

The second I got home I raced upstairs and changed. Lying on my bed, I wondered if it was just me. Did Bea, Kiara, Avery, and Skylar have similar thoughts? Was it true that inside we are one way and outside totally another? I guess that's the case to some degree for everyone, and that's okay. But when who you are on the outside doesn't match up at all with who you are on the inside, you start to feel really weird. Mom seeing me in total mean-girl mode made me feel hollow inside. I was a total fake. A liar. But I liked Bea and the others so much. They were cool. Boys fawned over them. When I was with them, everyone looked up to me. Everyone wanted to be like us. And that made me feel so good.

The next few weeks were a whirlwind. Guys I didn't even know wanted to talk to me. Girls asked me for advice. I got invited to three different parties. And borrowing outfits from Bea and Avery—who were my size—became a daily makeover strategy.

One day, after Friday assembly, Danielle approached me.

"How are things going?" she asked.

"Great!"

"You seem to be fitting in pretty well here now," she said.

"Yeah. Everyone's been really nice to me," I said. "Listen. We're going to Five Points Mall right after school. You wanna come with?"

"Do you think they'll be okay with that?"

"I don't see why not," I said. "Meet us at bus pickup."

When school was out, Danielle walked over to where Bea, Avery, Kiara, Skylar, and I were gathered.

"Hi, Danielle," I said warmly.

"Hi, Anika," she replied, smiling.

Bea looked her up and down, then paused. We all went silent.

"Yes? May we help you?" Bea said coldly.

Danielle bit her lip. Her eyes started to water.

"I—uh—Anika—," she sputtered.

Bea cut her off with a dismissive hand gesture and everyone spun around in unison and walked away. I hesitated.

"C'mon, Anika," Bea barked from a few yards away. Then she turned to Avery. "Can you believe that girl?" she said. "Who does she think she is? Her dad's, like, a plumber or whatever, isn't he?"

Everyone laughed.

I felt awful about how they'd treated Danielle. What did it matter what her dad did for work? She was funny and nice. There was nothing to dislike about her. I wanted to talk to her—to apologize. But I also didn't want to end up frozen out. So I said nothing and followed.

## THE CLIQUE GOPHER

A week later, as recess ended, I went into Mr. Swensen's classroom to look for my lost pencil case. The light was off, and no one was there but me. As I walked past Mr. Swensen's desk, I spied a folder marked "7th Grade Algebra." I don't know what got into me, but I stopped and opened it. Inside I discovered a master file of next week's test, with all the answers written in. I dropped the folder and rushed out into the hallway where my classmates were starting to gather before our next class.

"Guys, guys. You won't believe what I just saw!" I said, shaking.

"What?" Bea asked.

"Next week's test! With all the answers."

"Well? Why are you standing there?" Bea hissed. "Go in and get it. We'll keep watch."

I slunk back in and reopened the folder. Then I took snapshots of each of the five test pages with my cell phone, closed the folder, and rushed back out into the hallway.

Bea hugged me.

"You're awesome," she said. "Text us the pages!"

Two days later, the five of us were called into Vice Principal Sanchez's office.

"A serious situation has been brought to my attention with regards to next week's seventh grade algebra test," Vice Principal Sanchez said.

We glanced at one another but no one uttered a word. After a long pause, he spoke again.

"Anika, is there anything you want to tell me?"

"I, uh, why me?" I asked.

"You tell me, young lady," Vice Principal Sanchez replied.

"But we *all* did it," I said, desperately searching my new friends' faces. "You guys asked me—"

"That is soooo not true, Anika," Bea cut in. "I can't believe you just said that."

"Well," Vice Principal Sanchez said, "you *did* all have it sent to you."

"But we didn't ask her to," Bea insisted.

"Yeah! Why should we be blamed just for getting something sent to us?" Kiara added.

I got a zero on the test and was not permitted to take a makeup like Bea and the others did. But at least I wasn't suspended or expelled. I was a straight A student who had never been in trouble before. And we'd been caught before we actually took the test, which turned out to be a good thing. Because if we'd taken it and cheated, we would have been much worse off.

It was Skylar's mom who'd discovered what we'd done and turned us all in, including her own daughter. She had walked in on Skylar staring at an enlarged photo of one of the test pages on her laptop and grilled her about it. Skylar caved pretty quickly and showed her mom our group text. There it was for everyone to see: five photos of the master copy of our next math test, sent from my cell phone number to Skylar's, Bea's, Kiara's, and Avery's. We were so busted.

I felt horrible. I'd never cheated in my life. That just wasn't who I was. Mom and Dad were shocked and furious. They grounded me for a month—another first.

## PERSONA NON GRATA

At school I was assigned forty community service hours—cleanup at the cafeteria and on the grounds, and other odd jobs that kept me after school four days a week. Worst of all, Mr. Swensen told me that I'd have to work super hard and do really well for the rest of the term just to pass the class and avoid having to retake it in the summer.

I also got the deep-freeze treatment from the others. No one said anything definitive, like "We're done with you." But they basically ghosted me. No one answered my texts or DMs. And at school it was like I didn't exist. Whenever I walked toward them, they turned their heads or walked way.

At one point, in the cafeteria, I spotted the four of them giggling excitedly. "This is my best chance," I thought. "They all seem to be in a good mood." When I went up to them, they suddenly went silent.

"Hi," I said.

They all just stood there staring at one another, saying nothing.

But the message came in loud and clear: "You're not wanted."

I walked away trembling, wishing the ground would open up and swallow me whole. I wasn't just being shunned; I'd been banished. Being frozen out by Bea and Co. so publicly made it unquestionably clear to everyone else: "Stay away from Anika. She is not cool." No one else talked to me.

I was so lonely. Maybe I'm being melodramatic, but it was one of the worst weeks of my life. I'd given up so much to be accepted by Bea and Co. that now, without them, I felt like a total zero. There was no place to go and no one to hang out with. I'd hit rock bottom.

The following Monday I was sitting in the library—the only place I felt relatively shielded from rejection now—when I spotted Danielle coming in with one of her friends. I hadn't seen Danielle around campus much during free time for a while. I wondered if maybe this was where she hung out most of the time, keeping a low profile.

She walked right up to me and said, "Hey, Anika. I heard what happened in math. Are you okay?"

"Not really," I replied. "They blamed me for everything, even though they egged me on."

"I figured as much," she said. "That didn't sound like something you'd ever do."

"I did do it, Danielle. I stole the answers. But you're right. It's not me at all."

I met up with Danielle later that day at bus pickup. She shared her granola bar with me as we talked about her music and my writing. She was so funny and sweet. She made me almost forget everything that was going on.

A couple of hours later I got a text from her: "See ya tomo, girl!" Just four words but what a difference they made. I had a friend again. I felt almost semi-normal. And with Danielle, I knew I didn't have to put on a cool-girl act. I could just be me.

Don't get me wrong. I still missed being one of the "it" girls. We were cute and popular. Every girl wanted to be us. Every boy wanted to hang out with us. And I craved that feeling of belonging and being at the center of everything.

Maybe I was foolish, or too hopeful, or just a glutton for punishment, but a few days later, at recess, I approached Bea and Co. one more time.

"Hi, guys," I said hesitantly.

Utter silence.

After an almost interminable pause, Bea looked me in the eyes as her hands slid up onto her hips.

"Yes? Can we help you?"

"I . . . uh—," I stuttered. I couldn't think of what else to say.

"Fascinating," Bea replied, then turned on her heels and walked away, Kiara and Avery in tow.

"Doesn't she get the hint?" Bea said, just loud enough for me to overhear. The others laughed. Everyone except Skylar, who just stood there looking a little sad.

"No, I don't," I said loudly. "Not really. Whatever. I'll be fine." I swung around and walked way, feeling shaky but glad I'd stood up for myself. I felt like I'd been true to myself for the first time since school started.

But my heart sank when I saw they'd turned the corner. That was just about the meanest thing they could do to me after I'd been a real friend to them—act as if I was worthless. A nothing person. It was also pretty much exactly the way Queen Bea had treated Danielle when she had tried to join our group the first week of school. God! We'd all acted like such spineless, pliant little Bea-ettes. Danielle had done nothing to deserve such a cruel brush-off. Well, I figured, if Danielle could handle heartless public rejection, then so could I.

At home that night, I wondered why Skylar hadn't joined in with the others. Then I thought some more. And honestly, I couldn't remember one time when Skylar had been mean or harsh the way Bea, Kiara, or Avery could be. Skylar was an integral part of the group, but she got quiet when the others got mean. I guess I'd just gotten so caught up in things that I hadn't noticed this before.

## STARTING OVER: ONE FRIENDSHIP AT A TIME

I decided to figure out a way to talk with Skylar the next day, one-on-one.

The moment came in advanced Spanish class, which we shared. Everyone else from the group was in the slower Spanish class.

When Skylar entered the class, she walked by my desk and said, "Hi."

I felt a surge of hope. "Hi," I replied.

I guess I wasn't totally invisible after all.

At the end of class, as I was packing up my books, I noticed Skylar hanging back. When I was about to leave, she came up alongside me.

"Look, Anika. I don't agree with what Bea and the others did. It wasn't fair. And really, it wasn't true."

"That's okay, Skylar," I replied.

"No, it's not. I feel really bad about it. And about a lot of other things too."

"What's that?" I asked, pointing to a pad with a half-visible drawing on it poking out.

"Oh, just a doodle of mine."

"Can I see it?" I asked.

"Sure."

"Whoa. That's way more than a doodle. That's beautiful." She'd drawn a picture of three horses galloping across a field.

"I didn't know you were such a good artist!" I said.

"Thank you, Anika," Skylar replied, beaming. "It's just a hobby. Takes my mind off of things. Do you want to get away from all this crazy school stuff and come over to my house tomorrow?"

"I'd love that," I said. "Hey, you okay if we invite Danielle too?"

"Definitely."

"I really like Danielle," I added. "And I don't like the way we all treated her."

"Me neither."

I discovered that Skylar wasn't at all exclusive about her friendship. She was definitely part of the Bea crowd, but she was also okay hanging out with me and Danielle. She didn't let Bea lord it over her like the others. I really appreciated her free-spiritedness.

One day I asked her outright: "How do you do it?"

"Do what?" Skylar asked.

"Hang out with the cool crowd without getting swallowed up in all of it? With being popular and all of that stuff?"

"Well, it's not always easy," she confessed. "But a few things have helped me along the way. Some I learned on my own. Others, my older sisters told me. Or my mom."

"Like what?" I asked.

"I like being with Bea and Co. But when they get snarky or mean toward other kids, I don't join it. I don't like putting other people down. It makes me feel bad."

"Me too!" I said.

"Also, we all dress kinda alike, you could say, but I make sure to keep my own style too. Like my scarves."

"I love your scarves!" I said.

"And my mom tells me and my sisters one thing, over and over: 'You don't have to choose.'"

"What do you mean?" I asked.

"You can be part of a group and also be friendly with other people. If Bea told me I wasn't allowed to speak to other people, I'd be so over her. I wouldn't let her or anyone do that to me."

"Yeah, you're right. That doesn't make any sense at all."

"And another thing. I like doing the stuff we all do together, as a group," Skylar said. "But I also like doing other things. Like you. You're so good at sewing. Those guys don't sew at all. But that doesn't mean you shouldn't sew. Right?"

"Definitely not," I nodded.

I really liked the fact that Skylar could be such a dedicated friend to Bea, Kiara, and Avery, but she also held her own so well. She didn't seem to need to change who she was in order to fit in better with them. She held on to her own values, things her mom and older sisters had taught her. And that kept her cool and kind rather than cool and cruel, like some of the others. I learned so much from talking to her and from the way she treated people.

Anyway, from that point on, things got a lot better at school. And even though Skylar ended up at another high school—and we are both headed to college now—we've stayed in touch all this time. I don't see Bea, Avery, or Kiara at all. But as strange as it might sound, I don't hold any grudges against them. I hope they are doing well too. We were all kind of young and foolish.

Middle school can be tough. And sometimes we do things we regret later. I certainly did. I wish I'd been stronger and stayed true to myself from the beginning. But that's okay too. Because in the end, I figured out that when you follow your own path, you end up where you are supposed to be.

And Danielle? We're still best friends.

To all newbie middle-schoolers who feel that their inside and outside worlds are drifting too far apart, here's my simple advice: Take risks. Try to make new friends. But also stay true to yourself. And if a friendship fades—as hard as that may be—it's for the best. And if it doesn't, cherish it. You know you've found someone who likes you for who you are and not who they want you to be. Whatever you do, don't get swallowed up by a clique. Look for someone you can connect with, and with time, attention, and care, build up a true friendship.

---

This story was about . . .

- Feeling lonely and left out
- Not changing who you are to please others
- Doing what you love, not what everyone else does

Anika tried too hard to please others in order to fit in at her new school. But changing who she truly was made her feel lost and lonely. She learned from a friend how to hold on to her own values: how to be cool and kind—rather than cool and cruel.

# 6

---

# BUT WHAT IF IT'S TRUE?

## *Daniel's Story*

Kids who seek power tend to single out those who are different. There are, of course, a wide range of reasons kids are targeted—chief among them are mannerisms, appearance, and body shape. It's not surprising that when a child is teased about something they can do little about, such as their weight, they assume that because the hurtful taunts are based on "truth," they're helpless to change things. Such feelings can trigger a troubling spiral of insecurity and hopelessness.

If a child, tween, or teen is different in any way, they need support to understand that no one has the right to marginalize and stereotype them.

### POINTS OF UNDERSTANDING

- Being teased is not about truth; it's about power.
- Although it can be painful to be singled out for your difference, that is not what the teasing is really about.

- There are many kids with differences who rarely get teased.
- Defending yourself by overreacting often makes the teasing worse.
- Some kids enjoy having mean fun at the expense of a vulnerable child.

## POINTS OF HOPE AND LEARNING

- Deflecting verbal taunts by agreeing with the obvious is one way to leave taunters with nothing to tease about.
- Humor is a surprisingly effective strategy for defusing put-downs. It can also prompt bystanders to laugh, which disempowers the teasers or bullies.
- The ability to laugh at yourself is a sign of inner strength.
- The "Yeah, I know . . ." solution is not complicated.
- With these strategies, it is entirely possible to shift from being targeted to making friends.

When a child is being targeted for something they can't change about themselves, it is important to help them realize that there is a solution to their seemingly impossible situation. The two key changes they *can* make are rejecting the belief that they are being picked on about what is "true" and controlling how they react or respond in the face of their tormentors.

-------------------

*My name is Daniel. I'm nineteen. I'm a sophomore in college now, studying psychology and history. I chose those subjects because I like to figure out why people behave the way they do—what motivates them to act in certain ways and how what happened to them in the past shapes the way they handle things in the present and future. I wrote this story about some rough times I had in middle school because figuring out how to interact better socially with other kids back then is what saved me. I'm hoping if I share what I went through, maybe I can help other kids learn to cope with teasing or bullying, or better yet, prevent it from happening to them in the first place.*

*No one should have to go through what I did. But the fact is, a lot of kids do. What they may not realize is that it doesn't have to be that way. It took me a while, but I finally figured out that the reason I felt powerless when I was teased was because I believed that my tormentors were right. What they said about me was basically true. So how could I refute it and defend myself? Then I learned from another kid that teasing is actually not at all about what is true—it's about how you react. If you get upset easily and expose your vulnerability to other kids, you become powerless in the face of your tormentors. What you need to do is get to the point where you have some control over how you react—even when what people say to you is painful. That helps you become stronger and better at handling mean behavior.*

When I was little, my dad and I spent a lot of time together. We lived in Bangor, Maine, where winters can be pretty fierce. In his spare time, my dad liked taking apart engines and rebuilding them. And I liked to watch and help him when it was too cold or stormy to play outside. We'd spend hours and hours on Sundays and during holidays in our garage tinkering with a beat-up 1957 Ford pickup and a 1967 Camaro, which he called his twins. He often joked that he had three kids. Me and "the twins."

Dad and I are similar in many ways. We have the same goofy sense of humor, we are both pretty easygoing, and we are both big. That's the one thing I wish I hadn't inherited from Dad. He's smart, strong, and kind, but he also tends to put on weight really fast.

I was big back when I was younger—really big. Things changed for me somewhat when I got to high school. I got into fitness and sports, where my size became an asset rather than a liability. I did a lot of physical training. I'm still a big guy—like my dad—but now I'm a lot stronger and faster, not pudgy and roly-poly like I was back in middle school. I guess that's just the way my dad and I are built. If I stopped working out and playing today, I figure I'd balloon pretty quick.

But middle school was brutal for me. Hardly a day went by without someone poking fun at my size, my body type, the extra pounds. It was constant. The only school days I remember fondly as a kid were back when I was too young to notice or care. That was a blissful time. When you are little, nothing really matters. You just want to have fun and horse around with friends. You are oblivious to differences in weight or looks.

People say little kids are naïve, but I think they are just free-spirited and untainted. Our neighborhood was a motley mix. So was our elementary school. But back then, being skinny or tall or fat didn't factor in at all. We lived in a private bubble where everything was boiled down to the essentials. All that mattered was being fair and having fun.

I didn't wake up to the fact that everyone was different, that some folks were poor and others came from faraway places, or that being "too fat" or "too small" or "too anything" was at all important. I didn't really see myself as different from any of the other kids until third grade. That's when it started, one day at recess.

It was the first week of school. We were playing tag and two fourth graders—Larry and Kevin—made me "it." Then they ran around just out of my reach and laughed and taunted me.

"You're way too big," Larry said.

"You'll never catch us, blubber boy," Kevin added.

I chased after them as hard as I could, but it was impossible to nab them. They mocked me relentlessly for being slow and clumsy. Truth be told, they were quick and athletic. And I was, well, overweight.

They could see I was exhausted and upset but that didn't stop them. In fact, they just got meaner.

"This is boring," Kevin called out.

"Yeah, Daniel's never gonna catch us," Larry said. "He's just too slow and fat."

"You're so big you should have your own zip code, Daniel!" Kevin quipped.

Everyone laughed. Then the bell rang, and kids started going back into class.

I just stood there, gasping and feeling weird. No one had ever said anything nasty like that to me before. Their comments burrowed themselves deep inside me. Their taunting voices were still echoing in my head when I got home from school. I was really confused. I'd never thought about myself that way—as fat. No one ever singled out me or anyone else or made fun of me like that before. No one really cared.

I went up to my room, closed the door, and sat on my bed. I hadn't taken much notice of mirrors or cared about them before. I sat there and stared into the full-length mirror on the inside of my door. All I saw was me. Just me. Daniel. But then I looked more closely. And suddenly there he was—the pudgy blubber boy who couldn't catch anyone in the schoolyard.

## PUSH-UPS AND PUT-DOWNS

By fifth grade things had gotten really bad. The teasing continued nonstop. And nothing I did helped. So I kept to myself mostly. I didn't go out for any sports teams even though I played catch with my dad and some of the younger kids in my neighborhood. When I started sixth grade, I was determined to end this nasty treatment for good. I showed up at school the day after Labor Day wearing loose-fitting, baggy clothes—cargo pants and a hoodie that were at least a size too big. No one seemed to notice me or care, so I figured that was a good start.

The next day we had gym for the first time that year. Everyone crammed into the locker room to get changed into our mandatory gym garb. As I was putting on my gym top, I noticed a kid gawking at me. He didn't say anything, he just stared.

Mr. Watson, the gym teacher, met us at the door to the gym and instructed us to form a large circle. "Oh boy," I thought. "Just my luck." Mr. Watson, who we all called Coach W., was not your average, balding, middle-aged history teacher who doubled as a gym teacher. He was one of those hard-core fitness freaks with a ripped body and an intense, upbeat personality. The "Let's go," "You can do it," take-no-prisoners type.

"Okay, guys, here's the deal," he called out. "No matter what we do, we are gonna get in shape this fall. I don't care if you are an athlete or a mathlete. Sound mind, sound body. Let's do this!"

His enthusiasm was met with a few groans and guffaws. But a lot of the kids seemed into it too.

"We'll do dynamic warm-up exercises and some strength and conditioning," Coach W. said. "Then games for the second half of class. You gotta earn it, people." He had us do jumping jacks and squats and running in place.

"Now I want you guys to do three sets of five push-ups and then three 1-minute planks. We'll start out small today and work our way up."

Some of the boys got down and pumped out perfect push-ups. Others struggled and contorted their bodies but got up and down. As hard as I tried, I couldn't get up off the ground. My arms just couldn't lift up the rest of me.

The girls did their push-ups from their knees.

"Okay, guys, listen up," Coach W. said. "We build up our strength over time with repetition and effort. He looked straight at me. "If you can't do straight push-ups, start on your knees."

I tried to do them from a kneeling position. It worked a lot better. But as I worked through my third set, three of my new classmates, including the kid who'd been staring at me in the locker room, started fake cheering for me.

"Yeah, big guy, you can do it!"

"You go, girl!"

"Nice finish!"

A few of the girls joined in too.

"That's enough, guys," Coach W. said. "Who's up for some basket-ball?"

Back in the locker room when gym was over, they started in again.

"Hey, Jeff, check this out!" It was the kid who'd been staring at me earlier.

"What's up, Tommy?"

"Yo, lift up your shirt, Crossfit," Tommy yelled, as he rubbed his flat stomach. "I want Jeff to see that six-pack of yours."

I turned beet red.

"What did you call me?"

"Crossfit!" Jeff repeated. "I love it!"

"That's not my name," I said.

"We christen you Crossfit!"

"My name is *Daniel*," I growled.

"Hey, everyone. Meet Crossfit!" Tommy said.

"All hail, Crossfit," Jeff intoned.

A chant went up. "Crossfit! Crossfit! Crossfit!"

There was nothing I could do. I finished changing and got out of there as fast as I could. I didn't want them to see me cry.

The nickname stuck. Everywhere I went that week I was Crossfit. At first I didn't understand the barb. But then I looked it up. CrossFit was high-intensity interval training; a type of strength and conditioning exercise for athletes and fitness buffs.

It stung every time I heard it, which was at least a dozen times a day. Tommy and Jeff would mutter it under their breath before I answered a teacher's question. Or they'd yell it across the hallway or cafeteria. And they weren't the only ones.

"Daniel, what's wrong?" my mom asked at the dinner table one evening about a month into the school year. "You look kinda down."

"I'm fine, Mom."

"Where's my favorite goofy guy?"

"I'm fine!"

"No you're not, Daniel. Come on. What's going on? Tell your mom."

"Do you think you could homeschool me?"

"Daniel! Is sixth grade that bad?"

"Yeah, well, everyone is on my case."

"About what, sweetie?"

"It's embarrassing."

"You can tell me anything, Daniel."

"Come on, Mom. What do you think?"

"I don't know, Daniel. You tell me."

"About my body. I'm fat, Mom. And there's nothing I can do about it. What's worse is what they say is true." I was sobbing. "They're right. I *am* fat."

"Oh, honey!" Mom said. "We love you just the way you are!" She hugged me for what felt like forever. Then she said, "Daniel, just ignore them. And they'll move on to something else. Okay?"

I didn't respond, but my heart sank. If that was all my mom could come up with, I was in serious trouble. I'd tried that strategy for years. I'd ignored the taunts, the body-shaming one-liners, hoping my classmates would get bored or tire out. I'd willed them to stop. I'd even wished they'd find some other hapless target to sink their claws and fangs into.

Mom was clueless. Ignoring bullies never works.

The next week was particularly bad. Tommy and Jeff kept coming at me. On Friday, in between classes, I opened my locker and a mountain of junk food poured out.

"Crossfit! You oughta go easy on that stuff," Tommy, who was behind me, said. "Remember what Coach W said: you are what you eat."

Everyone around us cracked up as I spun around.

"How'd you do that? How'd you get into my locker?" I stammered, fighting back tears.

"Whoa there, big guy," Jeff said. "Just a friendly prank. Nothing to get all riled up about."

On Saturday, Mom, Dad, and I went to my cousin Anthony's house. He lives about fifty miles south of us straight down I-95. He's my dad's older brother's kid. He was a seventh grader back then, and pretty big, like me. I guess it must run in the family. But his weight didn't seem to bother him that much and I wondered how he dealt with it.

After lunch we walked over to a pond down the road from his house where we liked to catch frogs and skip rocks.

"Hey, Anthony," I said, as I searched the ground for a round, flat stone I could let fly. "I was wondering, what would you tell a kid—a friend of mine—who is being bullied a lot at school?" I found a good stone and let it rip. One, two, three . . . eleven hops total.

"Good one, Daniel," Anthony said.

"Like, how he could make other kids just cut it out?" I added

"Good question," he said. "Is it one kid or a bunch of them?"

"Pretty much the whole class."

"But is there, like, one jerk-off who riles everyone up?"

"You mean, like a ringleader?" I asked.

"Yeah, I guess." Anthony let his own stone fly. Six quick hops before it sunk.

"Two of them, I guess."

I thought of Tommy and Jeff. They had started the whole thing. Everyone else kinda followed their lead.

"My advice?" Anthony offered. "Pick a time and place when everyone's around except adults and go after the worst one. The one who's most in your face. Sometimes you gotta just stand up for yourself, you know what I mean? If you fight back strong, everyone else will think twice about bothering you again. Bullies like easy targets. That's what I'd tell your friend." He pointed at a tree twenty feet away from us.

"Let's see who can hit that tree three times from here first, Daniel."

"You're on!"

I thought about what Anthony suggested. I'd never tried anything like that. It was kind of scary. But I was so fed up with the way things were that I felt like I had nothing to lose. Still, I kept postponing my planned confrontation. Then one day at recess, two weeks later, things fell into place unexpectedly. A girl in our class got hurt and both of the outdoor recess monitors rushed over to help her. Tommy, Jeff, and a bunch of others were all clustered together around the corner from the main area, mostly out of sight. I walked toward them.

"Hey, guys," Jeff said, "can you feel the ground shaking?"

Everyone laughed and looked at me.

"Why don't you say that again, Jeff—to my face," I said, surprised at how loud and unwavering my voice was.

"Whoa. Look who woke up and got tough," Jeff shot back.

But I could see he was shocked. I walked toward him.

"Hey, what are you doing?" he yelled, as I grabbed his shirt and shoved him backward. He stumbled and fell, and I toppled over him.

We rolled over on the ground and Jeff squeezed out from under me. Next thing I knew, he was on top of me, and he punched me hard in the mouth. It stung, but I was so angry I shook him off of me and stood up. As he got up, Jeff grabbed at me. He got a fist full of my oversized T-shirt and yanked it up. Now my shirt was pulled half over my head and I couldn't see. But I could feel my oversized jeans sliding down around my thighs. Everyone laughed.

"Maybe next time you decide to be a hero, you'll think twice, fat boy," Jeff hissed. "Wasn't that pathetic! Let's get outta here, guys."

As I adjusted my shirt, I watched him shake his head and walk away.

"Did you see all that jelly belly jiggling out in the open?" Tommy said.

Another round of chuckles as they all turned the corner.

Now I was alone, still gasping for air. So much for taking a stand. I felt worse than ever. Tired, beaten, and worst of all, totally humiliated.

I moped about the house on Saturday and Sunday. Mom kept asking me, "Are you okay?" Dad didn't say anything. I could tell he was worried, but he wasn't the prying type. On Monday morning I told Mom I wasn't feeling well. She let me call in sick. Tuesday too.

Back at school on Wednesday, I skipped recess. I went to the library instead. On Thursday I volunteered to help our teacher in the classroom so I could stay in. On Friday I asked to see the school nurse. I was just trying to make myself invisible and make it to the weekend. But I knew I couldn't hide forever. And I was running out of ideas about how to skip recess and lunch in the cafeteria.

Later, during history class, I noticed an awkward silence.

"Daniel? Daniel!" Mrs. Blake exclaimed. "Are you paying attention?"

"Sorry, Mrs. Blake," I stammered.

"Can you answer the question please?"

"What was the question?"

Everyone laughed.

"Way to go, Crossfit!" someone muttered.

"Moving on, kids," Mrs. Blake said. "I want you all to finish the reading and answer the three questions in the chapter workbook."

## RECESS TARGET

I couldn't believe I had spaced out in history—my favorite class. But all I could think about was how I was going to survive five recesses the following week.

That night I sat on my bed and cried. I was really stuck. Things just kept getting worse. Covering up and concealing my body hadn't worked. Ignoring everyone, my mom's suggestion, just provoked them to come at me harder. And Anthony's solution to fight back had made everything ten times worse. The more I tried to disappear, the more visible I became. It was like I was in one of those sub-Saharan Africa documentaries my dad loved to watch. I was that wounded stag at the back of the pack and all the hyenas were zeroing in on me, the slowest target, the weakest one, following my trail of fear.

The next week things shifted a bit at recess. Due to a scheduling conflict, the seventh grade got lumped in with the sixth grade. That meant there were twice as many kids out there running around, playing ball, or just sitting in clusters talking and laughing. It worked out well for me because Tommy, Jeff, and the rest of the kids who ganged up on me were busy hanging out with the older kids, trying to impress them. I mostly kept to myself.

I noticed a seventh grader named Henry sitting with two girls at the edge of the courtyard fence. He was a big kid, just like me. Bigger actually. He seemed like he was having a good time. So were two other plus-sized seventh graders. They were playing ball with some other kids. I could tell they were slow. But nobody got on their case. For the next few days I kept an eye on all three of them during recess.

I started to wonder, "Why were these heavyset kids not targeted?" Henry was visibly more overweight than I was, but he seemed to get on pretty well socially with everyone. On Thursday, as he walked across the courtyard during recess with a friend, one of my sixth-grade classmates, who was playing kickball with Tommy and Jeff and some of the more athletic seventh graders, called out, "Hey, Henry! You got it all hanging out there, don't ya? You gonna make it to lunch?" A couple of kids chuckled. All Henry did was shrug his shoulders.

"How you guys doing?" he addressed everyone, smiling. The kid was silent. A seventh grader piped up: "See you in bio, Henry." Henry waved at him and walked away.

The following Monday was the dreaded all-middle-school field trip. I'd considered calling in sick. Being out there on my own with everyone playing sports and having fun was not something to look forward to. The teasing at recess had abated because everyone was distracted by having all the seventh graders mixed in with us. But during class and in the hallways Tommy, Jeff, and their buddies would turn up the volume on their nastiness.

That morning, as our class got on the sixth-grade bus, I hung back so I could position myself in relative safety, sitting up front across the aisle from two teachers. But I worried that when we got to the park I'd have nowhere to hide.

When we arrived, most of the kids started horsing around with a Frisbee or playing ball. I quickly withdrew to a shady area where I found a tree to sit under. There I spotted Henry sitting cross-legged, having something to eat, as he often did. I sat down next to him.

"Hey."

"Hey, Henry."

"How are things?"

"Okay, I guess."

"Want some peanuts?"

"Thanks, man. Henry, can I ask you a question?"

"Shoot."

"How come no one ever really gets on your case about . . . you know—"

"My size?"

"Uh, yeah."

"Well, people did a few years back," Henry said.

"Really?"

"Yeah. Well, it used to bother me a lot. But everyone in my family is big and there's not a lot I can do about it. I'm not gonna show my feelings to mean kids who don't really care about me anyway and aren't my family or friends."

"I guess not."

"Look, Daniel. It's not about being big, four-eyed, or having a crooked nose."

"What do you mean?"

"Well, it's like this. I've been watching you for a few weeks now, okay? What it is—it's how you react. Remember when you got into that fight?"

"Don't remind me."

"I thought you were really brave to do that."

"Really?"

"Yeah . . . but it was kinda dumb too," Henry said. "The key is not to let them know you're upset."

My conversation with Henry lasted less than five minutes but it changed everything. Here was a kid everyone considered "fat," who had figured out how to cancel out all the teasing and bullying that was directed at him. There were three kids in the seventh grade who could be considered overweight. None wore targets on their backs like me. I was the only heavyset kid in the sixth grade and I was constantly under attack.

What Henry taught me was that all that teasing and taunting was not about what was true. I wasn't being mistreated because I was fat or wore glasses. I could have been skinny, poor, or even bucktoothed. Any of those things could be true, but none would explain why my classmates were so nasty toward me.

But because there was truth to what they teased me about, that's what I focused on. That was my big mistake. It being true that I was "fat" concealed a more important underlying truth: the teasing wasn't about my body shape at all. That was just the launching point. What kids grabbed onto when they started in on me, what it was really about, was the intensity of my reactions. And the fact was, I believed that I was being teased because of who I was—because of me—and not because of how I behaved.

For years I'd totally misunderstood what was going on. I was too reactive—I got upset too easily. As soon as I realized that it wasn't about what was *true* but rather my *reactions*, everything changed. From that day on, things started to get better.

At least now I could devise a strategy of some sort. I decided to test out my newfound wisdom the very next day at school. But no one got negative with me all day. As weird as this might sound, I was actually disappointed no one taunted me because I was so fired up. I wanted to test out my plan.

On Wednesday, things were back to normal. At recess, Tommy, who was with Jeff and two other classmates, walked past me and let loose with "Hey, Crossfit! Have you put on a few pounds since Monday? You're looking the very definition of rotund today!" He chuckled, marveling at the sophistication of his own joke.

"Yeah, I know," I replied. "My mom's StairMaster broke down yesterday. It's completely thrown off my fitness regimen. Don't blame me. Blame the machine." I smiled at him. He looked puzzled, then he turned to Jeff and said, "Let's ditch this loser and go play some ball," and walked away.

Later at the cafeteria, Lisa and Tanya, who were good friends with Tommy and Jeff, passed my table. Lisa glanced at my tray and did a double take.

"That's quite the feast you have there, big boy," Lisa said. "Right, Tanya?"

"Yeah, I know," I replied. "It's a lot for one person, right? You want some?"

"No thanks," she said curtly. As they moved away, I caught a smile forming on Tanya's lips, which she quickly suppressed.

Later that afternoon, just before math class, Jeff, who was leaning against a row of lockers, started in: "Where'd you get those jeans? In the adult section at Macy's? Are they XL or double XL?"

"I know, right?" I said, shaking my head in agreement. "It's a pain but I have to spend at least two days each month with my tailor getting everything refitted."

The bell rang, ending my conversation with Jeff abruptly. But I glanced over at him. He was staring at me like I was some endangered Costa Rican parrot.

I heard someone cracking up behind me. I turned around and saw Henry grinning as he walked by. He gave me a thumbs-up.

The next day at gym, Coach W. had the class doing warm-up sprints.

As I started my turn, Tommy yelled out, "You run like a turtle, Crossfit!" Everyone laughed.

"You're right! I know . . . ," I called back. "I'm as slow as molasses."

I slowed down and pantomimed slow-motion sprinting. That silenced Tommy, who didn't lob another put-down my way for the rest of the day. But others laughed.

"Good one, Daniel," I heard someone say.

My new response to teasing was working wonders. I realized I didn't even need to think up complicated comebacks. All I had to do was start each response with "Yeah, I know" and end it with a variation of the words the teasers slung at me, or something light and funny, if it came to me. When I did that, the kids who said mean things stopped cold. Their insults lost their zing. And their snarky follow-up comments had nothing to latch on to.

For the next couple of weeks, Tommy and Jeff continued to taunt me, and I kept up my lighthearted, underwhelmed responses. Soon I was able to shrug off pretty much anything my tormentors tossed my way. And I could tell they weren't all that into it anymore. The teasing started to taper off. An entire day or two would go by without a single put-down.

My other classmates stopped treating me like a pariah to be shunned at all costs.

Henry and some of his friends—cool girls from the seventh grade—would stop and talk with me in the hallways. Kids in my class noticed this, and a few of the sixth-grade girls started smiling and acknowledging me too. Tanya sat down next to me at lunch one day and we talked about our favorite books and movies.

The next day, when I walked out into the playground at recess, I saw her and Lisa talking with Jeff. Then Jeff came toward me. I tensed up instinctively, steeling myself for another fat-boy zinger.

"Hey, Daniel," he said "We need another player for kickball. Can you join us? Can you play first base?"

"Sure." I said, smiling to myself.

Henry was right. If you paint a target on your own back, you'll get shot at. As soon as I stopped taking myself and everyone else so seriously, the arrows stopped flying and life got a whole lot easier.

---

This story was about . . .

- Understanding that being teased is not about truth, it's about power
- Learning when to agree and respond with humor
- Diffusing disputes and making friends

Daniel felt powerless because he believed that what his tormentors said about him was basically true. When he learned that teasing is not at all about what is true but about how you react, and he gained better control over his reactions, everything changed.

# 7

## HOW I GOT MY CONFIDENCE BACK

### *Sara's Story*

Exclusion is mostly about control—a desire to dominate others, which takes many forms, but at its core is a need for power and control over others.

Nothing much can change a situation until we truly understand why one person seeks to belittle another. It may seem complicated, but Sara's story breaks this down and makes it clear.

In her story, kids engage in cyberbullying. But we need to keep in mind that while cyber teasing can be more hurtful and widespread for the child being picked on, the aim is the same as in any other bullying situation. Whether in person or online, it involves hyper-controlling kids targeting others.

### POINTS OF UNDERSTANDING

- The key to defending yourself is learning how to temper your reactions.

- The teasing is not about something personal, such as the way you look or talk; it is about gaining control over you by forcing you to overreact.
- The more you get upset, the more power you give away.
- Trying to fit in by giving up who you really are truly doesn't work. In fact, it only gives the kids who are excluding you more control over you.
- Not everyone feels it is okay. Kids who get caught up in a teasing situation are often uncomfortable, confused, and don't know what to do about their role in the meanness.

## POINTS OF HOPE AND LEARNING

- The key to feeling stronger and more self-confident is learning how to avoid becoming too upset.
- Other kids will notice the change and become friendlier.
- A trusted adult can be a great coach in learning new strategies.
- A simple, calm, and repeated response is often all that is needed to stand up to the taunting.
- Practicing with a "coach" will make the new response sound easy and natural.

A parent can offer important background help. Together you can come up with a plan that will work. However, no matter how much coaching you do, it is the child, tween, or teen who uses the strategy. They will feel like *they* made the situation better—because they did.

Kids who learn this new way to stand their ground, calmly but powerfully, can use this approach over and over again—right into adult life. Once you understand what is going on when someone attempts to make themselves bigger by making you smaller, and learn how to deal with it anytime and anywhere, life suddenly gets a whole lot better.

*My name is Sara. I'm sixteen. My story is about breaking out of a bad situation in which other kids have power over you and are having mean fun at your expense. Maybe hearing about my mistakes and how I worked things out can help you if this is happening to you. I certainly wish I knew when I started seventh grade what I know now. It would have saved me a whole lot of heartache.*

*Until I started seventh grade at Grover Middle School, just outside of Baltimore, I'd always liked school. I'd never been super popular or anything, but I'd never been the butt of everyone's jokes either. I was definitely not one of those kids you hear about who has a bright red target pasted on their backs.*

Amy and I have been best friends forever. Our moms too. They worked together at Macy's, until my mom was let go. They always had as much crazy fun as we did. When they got together, we got together. And that's pretty often, on account of my mom being single. She divorced my dad when I was two, and Amy's dad traveled a lot for work.

Amy and I talk about *everything* together—friends, clothes, school, parents, and even Mr. Olsted's weird haircuts. He was our seventh-grade homeroom teacher, and he's harmless. But I swear he must cut his own hair or something because it's always uneven in the back and up top, and sometimes you can get a glimpse of a bald spot here and there when he bends forward.

I know I said Amy and I could talk about anything but, to be honest, that all stopped suddenly in seventh grade. A few weeks into the school year, she started acting a little different toward me. Then everything kind of tumbled downhill.

I really didn't notice much of a change at first. Amy and I hung out a lot at recess, in between classes, and in the cafeteria. Sometimes Lisa and Marcie were there too. But when the new girl, Harriet, joined us, things started to get a bit weird.

Harriet had no trouble fitting in. Everyone wanted to hang out with her. She's cute and tall, funny and cool. And she has two older sisters, so she pretty much knows everything about boyfriends, clothes, makeup, and stuff. She looks good in just about everything: baby-doll tops, crop tops, tight outfits, baggy clothes. It just doesn't matter. I wished I looked half as good as she does on a bad day.

When Lisa, Marcie, and Harriet started hanging out together, everything changed overnight. They started to dress like her and talk like her and even roll their eyes the way she did whenever I said something that wasn't cool enough.

## A FICKLE FRIENDSHIP

The way they treated me hurt, but I could handle it. What really got to me is what happened with Amy. Whenever she and I were together, the others would come around and start talking to her as if I wasn't even there—about stuff I knew nothing about; about things they did with Amy. I'd just have to stand there, not knowing anything about what they were discussing and feel like a total loser. It was like I was invisible.

One day, four of them—Harriet, Lisa, Marcie, and Jessica, who I've never been friends with anyway—were together at the corner of John and Main Streets. It's not like I even wanted to hang out with them or anything. I wouldn't have even cared that much. Except that Amy was also with them.

I walked up to them, and Harriet totally ignored me and turned the corner. Everyone followed her like obedient ducklings. Amy hesitated a bit, lagging behind, but Harriet called out to her forcefully: "Come on, Amy."

So Amy turned the corner too. When I caught up to them, Harriet was waving her arms and talking excitedly. I kind of joined up with them, but Harriet rolled her eyes and turned away, and Jessica and Marcie gave me the cold shoulder too. Amy was caught in the middle, but Harriet insisted, asking her about some movie the five of them saw together on Saturday. I felt awful, totally excluded, and they all knew it. They were talking, on purpose, about a movie they knew quite well that I hadn't seen.

"Wasn't it awesome when she found that cave to hide in," Jessica said.

"Totally," Lisa said. "But it made me so nervous that something else was in there."

"Yeah, something really creepy!" Jessica added.

"OMG, Marcie. That's exactly what I was thinking. It's amazing that we do that all the time."

"Yeah," Marcie replied. "Isn't that crazy?"

"I think she was so brave to fight when all she had to do was hide and stay safe," said Amy. "I kept thinking, like, would I do that?"

"Yes, me too. But I think I would have if we had all been there together," Marcie said.

I just stood there, melting in place. I hadn't seen the movie or been invited to the party. They all knew that, of course. They just jabbered away, totally ignoring me.

Then they up and walked away. I couldn't believe anyone could be so cruel. *On purpose.* I started to follow them but with every step I took my legs got heavier, like I was wearing concrete boots. I felt stupid and ugly—unwanted.

Amy turned around for a split second and looked back at me. I could tell she felt a little weird about just abandoning me there on the sidewalk, but Harriet must have sensed it too. She linked arms with Amy and off they went.

That night I tossed and turned. I couldn't fall asleep. I kept picturing Amy looking back at me, her eyes big and uncertain. And the rest of the girls rolling theirs and shaking their heads like I was a lost cause, like it was no big deal. I resolved to try harder to fit in, to be cool like the rest of them. There had to be a way to get them *all* to like me.

## AMY IS BACK

The next Saturday, Amy and her mom came over. It was like night and day. Amy didn't mention Harriet or Jessica or any of what was going on at school. We just had a great time, like we always did when she came over. We went for a walk in the park and watched some kids playing soccer for a little while. We baked our favorite cookies—peanut butter with chunky chocolate chips—and did our homework together. And we talked about what we want to be when we grow up. Amy wants to be a nurse, and I want to be a social worker. We both want to help people.

When we finished our homework, we went downstairs and had dinner with our moms. They were laughing and drinking coffee.

"Hey, girls, how's the seventh grade treating you?" Amy's mom said.

"Fine, Mom," Amy replied.

"It's good," I added.

"I'm so glad to hear that," my mom chimed in. "I can't say middle school was the best of times for me."

"Me neither," Amy's mom nodded. "A lot of stuff can happen in those middle years."

"Well . . . nothing all that dramatic goes on at Grover, Mom," I said hurriedly.

"Yeah, it's no big deal," Amy added.

There was *no way* I was going to talk about how the girls made me feel—not in front of Amy's mom anyway. Besides, I felt so good about everything just then. Amy was back! We were besties again!

Our moms got to talking about adult stuff again, and we did the dishes, splashing each other with soapy water and snapping our tea towels. Then we went upstairs and watched a Harry Potter movie. Amy and her mom left pretty late. On Sunday night, as I snuggled under my duvet, I felt sure that things would be better the next day at school. I just knew it.

## IS THAT YOU, AMY?

Monday was a clear, warmish fall day, the kind I love best. The trees formed colorful, sun-dappled canopies along the streets I walked to school. It was the first day of auditions for the middle-school winter play and I was excited about going for one of the big parts. I was confident I'd do well enough to be seriously considered.

But the school day didn't start all that well. As I walked past Harriet, Jessica, and Lisa in the hallway, one of them whispered something about me and they all giggled and snickered. I couldn't make out what was said but it sounded like they were making fun of the way I was dressed. This was so unfair because Harriet's parents have tons of money and she could wear whatever she wanted, and she was always trading clothes with the others so they all had the best stuff.

That afternoon, a bunch of us were gathered outside the auditorium waiting for the bell so we could go in for auditions. Harriet, Marcie, Lisa, and Jessica stood in a circle talking and leafing through a magazine. A couple of times they looked up at me and burst into giggles. I saw Amy coming toward us down the hallway. She looked at me and slowed down. I thought she was going to stop and talk with me but just then Harriet came up.

"Hey, Amy, look at this," she said.

She pointed to a gorgeous skinny model in the *Elle* magazine they'd been leafing through.

"Look at this dress."

I craned my neck to try to get a better look.

"Sara! Why are you looking at this?" Harriet said in a loud, mocking tone. "Do you seriously think you would ever fit into a dress like that?" She gave the other girls a drawn-out look of exaggerated exasperation. "*I don't think so.*"

Everybody cracked up—not just Harriet and her "coven" but a bunch of the boys waiting to go in too.

I just stood there, frozen in place. The bell rang and everyone filed into the auditorium, including Amy. I couldn't believe she just left me there, totally crushed. I felt fat and ugly and unfit for any stage.

Just then Mrs. Crane, the gym teacher, walked by.

"Sara, are you okay?" she said. "What's the matter?"

"Someone is just being really mean to me," I managed to blubber through a teary haze.

Mrs. Crane put her arm around my shoulder. "Oh, Sara," she said. "I know. It can be really hard at your age. But you'll get through this. I did. And I was a lot like you. Very sensitive."

"I—I—." I tried to say something to her but I was too upset and embarrassed that she'd seen me like this to formulate a coherent sentence.

"It will work out," Mrs. Crane said soothingly. "It always does." She gave me a tender look, squeezed my shoulder, and then walked down the hall.

I was alone again. The hallway was dark and cold. I was broken up into a million bits. Nothing Mrs. Crane said helped. And I kept thinking, "Why didn't Amy stand up for me?"

It felt so weird. She'd pretended nothing happened and walked straight into the auditorium with the rest of them.

I realized there was no way I could go in there and audition. Not now. Not like this. I walked over to my locker, got my things, and headed home.

## MAKEOVER MESS

"Come on, Mom! Please? I'll clean my room. I'll rake the leaves and take out the trash for a month. And work with you on organizing the basement for an entire Saturday morning!"

Mom looked at me, exasperated. We were standing outside a store.

"I don't see why you need more tops. You have quite enough clothes already, what with our back-to-school spree."

"Please, Mom," I begged. "This one's only sixteen dollars. All the girls are wearing them, and I want to fit in better. All I ever wear is baggy sweaters and sweat tops."

"Okay, Sara," Mom relented, not sounding all that convinced.

We bought a really great dark-blue tank top. It felt a bit tight on me and different. But I felt good about it. I normally didn't wear those kinds of tops because I'm not that skinny. But I felt I looked too dumpy. I needed a new look. And I was excited to try something new.

I was walking down the hall to Mr. Olsted's homeroom class later that week. Harriet, Jessica, and Marcie pinned me down with their eyes. I felt like a tiny turtle hatchling, scurrying to safety in the sea as hungry seagulls threaten to pounce and peck.

Harriet and Marcie giggled as I walked past them. Then Lisa and Jessica gasped in tandem and pretended to fall back against their lockers and slide down to the floor in pained shock. Everyone cracked up.

I'd worn the new tank top for all of five minutes and I felt dead inside.

What an idiot I was to think that I could get away with wearing a tank top at school. I fought back tears as I opened my locker and pulled out my trusty burgundy wool sweater.

As I turned the corner and headed down the hall to class, I bumped into Harriet again. They'd decided to risk being late for class so they could launch another attack.

"Sara! Really. That sweater looks, like, a whole lot better now," Harriet said with mock sweetness. Then she shook her head dramatically. "What were you thinking, Sara?" She turned to the others and her eyes got really large.

Jessica and Lisa looked at her and then rolled their eyes in unison. Marcie just giggled as they walked off toward homeroom. I followed them into class, slunk over to my desk, and slipped into my desk chair.

The more I tried to be nice to Harriet and Marcie and the others, the worse they treated me. Nothing I did was good enough that fall. And everything I said was stupid or weird. Eventually things kinda just shut down. They stopped teasing me. They didn't talk to me at all, even to lure me into a prank or put-down. I became completely invisible.

## SOMETHING IS BREWING

I didn't really like it, but I realized that if I kept quiet, things were a lot less complicated. Weeks went by like this. I kept a low profile, praying that the stormy season would pass and all of this middle-school meanness would fade away.

When we got back from winter break, things seemed to take a turn for the better. I tested the waters, cautiously. I joined in on a conversation or two. I even sat one table over from Harriet's clique in the cafeteria a couple of times. And I tagged along a bit when they were clustered together in the hallways or at gym.

Until our second Monday back. Mrs. Clarke called on me to answer an algebra question she had written on the board in math class. As I opened my mouth to answer, I heard a strange sound, like a puppy's yelp.

Everyone cracked up. Mrs. Clarke got flustered and told us to settle down.

But she didn't try to figure out who the culprit was. Then in English class it happened again—"Woof, woof"—when I was asked by Miss Gambino to define *ironic*. This time Marcie and Lisa snickered. Someone muttered "Loser" under her breath. I spun around and caught Harriet giving Jessica a knowing smirk.

I had no idea what all this meant but each day it got worse. By Friday I couldn't say a word within earshot of Marcie, Jessica, or Lisa without them yelping or sticking out their tongues and making panting noises. What's worse, kids I didn't even know that well made little barking noises and cracked up as I walked by.

When I got home on Friday afternoon, I closed myself up in my room and cried. I was so exhausted and on edge that I fell asleep instantly. That night, Mom sensed something was wrong and asked me what it was. But I just shrugged. I didn't want to tell her what was happening. She had enough going on, and I didn't want to add my troubles to the pressure she felt taking care of us.

I never really went out anymore. I could tell my mom was worried that I wasn't "socializing" with kids my age enough on weekends. But there was no one to do stuff with. To be honest, I was quite happy to stay home. Nothing bad ever happened to me there. No one made fun of me or taunted or excluded me. I felt safe. I could be me and no one judged me or made me feel small or invisible.

Whenever Mom asked if things were okay at school, I'd quickly cut her off with "Of course, Mom!" or "Sure, everything's fine," and change the subject.

I was in my room doing some schoolwork on Saturday night when I got an email from Jessica. It was just about suppertime, but I was so surprised—these days she never spoke with me at school or emailed or texted me—that I decided to take a look before going downstairs. There was no message from her. It was simply a forwarded email. The subject line piqued my curiosity: "Remind You of Anyone?" I clicked it open and a screenshot of Harriet's Facebook page popped up.

There—front and center—was this image of a chubby little pug dog wearing a white knit sweater with the initials SJ printed on it, dutifully waddling after four elegant adult dogs: two poodles, a Doberman, and a Dalmatian. Beneath the picture there was a post from Harriet: "Remind you of anyone?" Followed by one from Jessica: "Did I hear someone say Sara Johnson?" There were a bunch of other likes, smiley faces, and comments from other kids in my grade. There was one near the bottom that read "woof, woof."

That's when it hit me: all the taunting, barking sounds, and tongue-wagging directed at me all week was because of *this* photo.

## HOW I GOT MY POWER BACK

I sat there on my bed, stunned. The tears poured out. I couldn't wrap my mind around what was happening to me. I'd always liked school before. I'd always pretty much gotten along with my classmates. Now I was the class *Facebook freak*. For an entire week everyone had known except me. People gossiped and mocked me because of this post, and all the while I was clueless. A complete idiot!

I racked my brain. I just couldn't figure out why Amy hated me. And Marcie and Lisa and Jessica. Why did Harriet hate me so, so much? What did I ever do to her? I'd never insulted her or told on her or gotten her into trouble or anything. I was just there.

She homed in and started picking on me from the start. Within a few months I'd become the class punch line. A total loser. Nothing I said mattered. Everything I wore was ridiculed. I was the fattest, ugliest, weirdest person in the entire world.

"Sara, what's wrong?" My mom had slipped into my room unnoticed.

"Oh, Mom." I hugged her tightly and started sobbing uncontrollably.

"Nobody likes me. I'm fat and ugly and—like a total loser."

"You are not," Mom said emphatically. "You are a smart, beautiful girl on her way to becoming a lovely young woman."

Mom looked at me reassuringly.

"Now tell me exactly what is going on, Sara."

"I will. But only if you promise not to go nuts. You have to swear you won't call the school or talk about this with *anyone*."

"Okay, Sara. Okay."

"Say it, Mom!"

"You have my word, Sara."

I pointed to my laptop.

"What is *this*?" Mom's voice was suddenly cold and hostile.

"Harriet's Facebook page."

"I thought I told you that you were too young to be on Facebook."

"It's not mine, Mom. I don't have a Facebook page. Honest. It's a screenshot of Harriet's page. Jessica forwarded it to me, and Amy knows about it."

Mom looked furious.

"Amy?" she said. "I thought you were best friends."

"Things haven't been that great since Harriet arrived," I confessed.

"Why didn't you tell me, love?"

"I didn't want to worry you."

"But this photo is horrible. It's downright cruel."

"Everyone at school has seen it and they're all making fun of me."

"Well, this is not right, honey," she said indignantly. "Those girls cannot do this. They can't just gang up on you and post hurtful stuff online for everyone to see. I'm going to call the school and each and every one of their moms and put a stop to this. These girls need to be disciplined."

"See, Mom. That's why I didn't want to tell you. I knew you'd go nuts and start calling everyone. It will only make things worse. I wouldn't have told you anything if you hadn't promised me you'd stay out of it. I've got to figure out a way to deal with this myself."

Mom suddenly got really quiet. I could tell she was taking in what I said and trying to stay calm even though she could barely contain herself.

"Look, Sara, what these girls are doing is not right. They are ganging up on you. And doing it in a nasty public way. I'll hold off for now. But we have to come up with a plan. You can't just let them step all over you like this or they will never stop."

"I know, Mom. I know."

Mom hugged me again and wiped the tears from my cheeks.

"Let's go for a walk in the park before dinner," she said.

At dinner I told my mom the whole story, starting at the beginning of the school year. It felt really good to let it all out. She listened carefully and did not interrupt once. I was so grateful she could just listen and, strangely, it gave me some hope. Isn't it weird that her not saying anything at all but just being there to listen was the thing that helped the most?

"Sara, I'm so glad you shared this with me. It couldn't have been an easy thing to do," she said when I was done. "Let's sleep on it and we'll work it all out tomorrow."

I could tell she was upset, but after telling her everything, I was so incredibly tired and grateful that she could see this. I guess it made me feel she understood.

The next morning I felt a bit better. Things seemed a bit clearer. Mom didn't say a word about our conversation. I brought it up as we were clearing our plates.

"What I don't get, Mom, is why they make fun of my body and how I dress? Why me?"

"That's a good question, Sara," Mom replied. "There are other kids who are a little larger, plump even. Not everyone in your class is skinny as a toothpick."

"I know, Mom."

"Well, do they get teased a lot?

"No." I said. "Not as much as I do anyway."

"Then it's not really about body shape."

"But it is!"

"I've been really thinking about this, Sara, and this just cannot be about your body shape," Mom insisted. "There are two or three girls in your class who are much heavier than you. Do *they* get teased?"

"Well, not really. No," I said, confused.

"Sara, I know this is hard. And I love you dearly. But you've got to understand that this is not about you or your body shape. It really isn't. It can't be."

"I guess I see your point, Mom. Maria and Anna don't get teased much. And they definitely aren't skinny, and they don't have cool clothes."

"I think I know what's going on, Sara. I think you are giving them an opportunity to have *mean fun* because of how you react. Couldn't it be because they enjoy getting a rise out of you? Does Anna react?"

"No, she totally doesn't," I said. "She just kinda blows them off. But it's not like I get angry and lash out at them. I just feel hurt."

"If they know they are getting to you, they'll just keep on doing it. We have to figure out a way for you to do what Anna does. Because it's clearly not just about cool clothing or body type."

"Thanks for listening and not making it worse, Mom. You're the best. I need to think about this because it kind of makes sense, but it's so different from what I thought was making them be so mean to me."

Mom and I went for another walk that evening before dinner.

"This may sound weird, Mom," I said as we stopped to admire our favorite oak tree. "But I'm kind of glad I saw that photo on Harriet's page."

"Why's that, honey?" Mom asked, looking puzzled.

"It made me realize that Harriet and Marcie and the rest of them—that's the way they see me."

"What do you mean?"

"To them I'm a pudgy little puppy just following them around."

"I see."

"It's like I've made them my master. I *make* them my boss. All I want is to be friendly, for them to like me. But by acting that way I'm making them my boss. I'm giving them power over my whole life."

"Sara," Mom said, beaming, "you are wise way beyond your years."

"I've got it, Mom. I know what I'm going to do. If they do those 'pug' things, if they call me 'pug' or make barking noises, I'll just say, 'Whatever. You can call me pug. You can call me that.'

"I'm not going to tell them it doesn't bother me because that's a lie, Mom, and they know it. And I'm not going to ignore them. I've tried that. It doesn't work. They can tell it bothers me, so they just keep coming at me until I break down.

"What I'm going to do—the only thing I can do that won't give them power over me—is just say, 'You can say that. I can't stop you. You can call me that.' And then I'll walk away."

"Sara, that's brilliant. You don't need to say anything else. Just that. That way you aren't giving them ammunition or riling them up. It's like a fire without the oxygen. Puff. It just goes out. If you don't let them see your reaction, there'll be nothing to fuel their attacks. If only I'd have figured all this out when I was in school—wow."

I ran the words I would use over and over in my head all weekend and, as strange as it sounds, I even practiced looking in the mirror and saying the words right out loud. I needed to hear myself saying them to see if it sounded okay. At first, when I did that, it sounded fake. I almost gave up. Then I had an idea. I remembered the plays I had been in at school and how when I first learned my part, the lines I had to say sounded fake. But the more I practiced them, the more it sounded like me, the more real. So I kept repeating what I planned to say to "the coven," and slowly it began to sound better and more relaxed.

## THE NEW "ME"

I slept well that night, but not because I wasn't afraid of what might happen the next day at school. Mondays were always hardest. And the Facebook thing would definitely still be on everyone's mind.

I just felt like I was more in charge, like there was hope. I wasn't going to be a shrinking violet and take whatever Harriet and her clan dished out.

Sure enough, it started that morning, right after homeroom.

"Hey, Sara. Nice sweater," said Lisa, standing in front of my locker.

"A bit snug, though, don't you think, Pugsy-Wugsy?" Lisa added.

And just like I practiced in the mirror, I turned squarely toward Lisa and said, "Whatever. You can say that if you like."

"Why? You think you can stop me?" Lisa fired back in a threatening tone.

I just shrugged my shoulders and said, "No, I can't stop you. Say it all you like. I gotta go. Bye."

I closed my locker—not too fast, not too slow. Then I turned and walked way.

I realized from the utter silence behind me that they were all stunned. It wasn't the reaction they were used to. Maybe I'd thrown them off their game. I even surprised myself with "I gotta go. Bye." It wasn't something I had planned. It just came out.

In math class they started in again. When I was called on, I heard a "woof, woof" coming from Harriet's direction. I just rolled my eyes, shrugged my shoulders, and proceeded to answer the question I was asked. Each time they made a noise, I shrugged slightly or rolled my eyes and got on with what I was doing.

This went on for days. Finally, Harriet, Marcie, Jessica, and Lisa cornered me on Friday afternoon. Amy was kind of standing off to the side.

"How's our little puppy dog today?" Harriet taunted.

I shrugged my shoulders. "You can call me that if you need to."

"Well, doesn't it bother you that you are ugly and fat and friend-less?"

"Yeah. It bothers me that you say that, Harriet. But I can't stop you. You can do it. Whatever."

I could see Harriet was annoyed. She was not getting the reaction she needed to keep things going, as Mom said. It was kind of like the wind had been sucked out of her taunting strategy.

"Why am I even wasting a precious few seconds on this loser?" she declared, and she stalked off. The others turned on their heels and followed her. But Amy took a bit longer. Our eyes locked. I saw a little twinkle in hers, like she got it, like she kind of knew what I was doing—and was glad. Something had begun to change, and I felt like I could breathe again.

The next week was similar. The girls tried to rattle me with doggy references or shoulder shrugs and eye rolls. It bothered me, of course.

A couple of times I hid in the bathroom and cried. It was so hard to hold it all in.

I told my mother what was happening—not every day but at least a couple of times each week. I felt more confident because I was not afraid she would tell the school and get people in trouble. I told her that things were going okay, improving even, but that I was a bit confused because Harriet and "the coven" were doing their mean stuff even more often. We talked it over and decided that maybe the fact that they were doing it more was a sign that things were actually working, that I was getting under their skin by taking their mean fun away from them. Later that night I pictured them doing it to me, and I could see that they were becoming sort of desperate. They even looked a bit weird to me when I visualized them doing it. I felt their power over me was fading away.

So I stuck to my script. If it was teasing words, I said things like, "Whatever. You can say that. I don't know why you need to, but I can't stop you." If it was an eye roll or a shrug, I responded by shrugging right back.

After another failed attempt to get me upset—this time by Marcie, and witnessed by Harriet, Jessica, and Amy—I found a note slipped into my locker:

*Way to go Sara. That was so cool.—Amy*

Later, in gym class, Amy gave me a big smile. Then to my surprise and relief, everything fell away over the next few weeks. The name-calling and doggie noises fizzled out. No one seemed to care about bugging me anymore.

It was Friday afternoon and I was feeling pretty good about things. I was standing by my locker sorting through the books in my bag when Amy came right up to me and started talking.

"Hi, Sara."

"Hi, Amy."

I felt kind of weird. It was the first time we'd talked to each other in school in months. There was the note and a bunch of times she'd looked over and caught my eye during the past two weeks but nothing like this.

"What are you up to tonight?" she asked.

"Just hanging out at home. My mom said she might take me shopping. Or for ice cream."

"Alright if I stop by?" she asked. I could tell she was super nervous, like she thought I might tell her to take a hike or get lost.

"Okay," I said, and I smiled.

Harriet came up to us, trailed by Jessica and Marcie as usual.

"Hey," she said in a normal voice. It's the first time she had included me in anything—in forever.

"Hi," I said.

"Did you see Mr. Olsted today?" she asked. "It looks like he's been at it again."

I nodded and decided to say something. "He's missing a big patch of hair next to his left ear."

"I'll say," Jessica said.

"Still, he's the coolest homeroom teacher," I said. "I'll take him over Miss Upshaw any day."

"Oh yeah," Harriet said. "She's so strict. You can't get away with anything. Like half her class gets detention every Friday!"

I am so happy now. Harriet has begun to be friendly to me—and I got Amy back. Of course I wish this whole thing with Amy and the others never happened. It was awful. But strangely, I'm kind of glad it did. Because I know—in my heart—that I have become a stronger person, that no one is ever going to have that kind of power over me again.

———————————

This story was about . . .

- Trying too hard to fit in
- Giving others too much power by overreacting

- Developing a clear, strong response to taunting
- Learning to stand your ground

Sara realized that her eagerness to fit in gave a group of girls who teased and excluded her too much control over her. By learning how best to confront her tormentors without overreacting and fighting back, she regained her confidence and reconnected with her best friend.

# 8

---

# A NEW GROUP,
# A NEW ME

## *Joey's Story*

It may not seem hurtful or damaging to be ignored or overlooked because it is a subtle, often undetectable form of exclusion. But children who are marginalized often feel invisible and alone. And they can be crippled by self-doubt and feelings of worthlessness when they internalize and accept their isolation.

While other kids might not be aggressive or outright mean to an excluded child, they are not likely to be friendly either. And it's hard to fight an invisible enemy.

But a simple strategy can thwart this damaging dynamic. In this story, Joey's father helps him realize that if you find one relationship door closed, you can look for others that may open and prove welcoming. It takes a shift in mindset to realize that though one group of teens may "ghost" or even belittle you, there are others who will *see* you and value you for who you are.

## POINTS OF UNDERSTANDING

- Look for the right friendship fit rather than accepting or forcing the wrong one.
- Accepting others who sideline you in order to avoid conflict is not a long-term solution.
- Disregarding someone is a subtle form of disrespecting them and needs to be seen for exactly what it is.
- Feeling unappreciated can be more damaging than most people realize.
- Having a parent or teacher who believes in you can be helpful and even critical to finding a new direction.

## POINTS OF HOPE AND LEARNING

- Your voice can be heard. You just have to find the right people who are open to hearing it.
- It takes courage to shift away from relationships that aren't working when you really *want* to be accepted.
- Being friendly to an overlooked person can make a bigger difference to them than we realize.
- You can find people who appreciate you in the most unexpected places.
- Seeking out new activities and people can be scary, especially when you are not feeling great about yourself, but it is well worth the risk.
- Once you've found people who value you, it's possible to confront those who put you down and challenge their hurtful behavior.

We should never underestimate the power of having just one person in our lives who values us. This is especially true for a child or teen who feels socially unappreciated and unseen. An adult can use this bond as a springboard to help a young person understand that others will like and appreciate them too. You can change everything for a child by helping them find just one other kid or group of kids with whom they can connect.

---

*My name is Joseph but everybody calls me Joey. I'm a big guy: 6'3".
Well . . . 6'2½", to be honest, but I always round up. And I'm only seventeen! I could totally have another growth spurt. I'm strong and pretty fast for a high-school senior. I'm a starter at power forward on my school's varsity basketball team. I guess that makes me a stereotype: the jock dude. It feels kinda funny to say that, though. Back when I was a twelve-year-old middle-schooler, I was scrawny. Not very solid at all. I got shoved around a lot, and it didn't take much to send me flying across the court. My teammates piled it on. To them I was "Fly Boy" and "Floppy Joe."*

*Don't get me wrong—I was athletic and scrappy and could throw down on the court. But our team was stacked, so I wasn't the go-to guy. I wasn't even a starter. But being on a team was crucial. I live in a small town in upstate New York where sports are sacred and basketball is pretty much the only thing that matters after football season ends and until baseball picks up in the spring. It's a vital passkey to social acceptance.*

*Middle school is all about survival, and survival depends on how cool you are. Being cool is all about who you know and hang out with. If you are on a team, you have a built-in buffer against bullying and all that craziness.*

It's just me and my dad. We live alone. My mom died when I was seven. Though my dad tries to be chill about it, I know how important it is for him to see me play the game he loves. Just imagine: he's never missed one of my basketball games, even though he holds down two jobs and does handyman work most weekends. When I graduate, I plan to work with him in construction. I want him to teach me how to build houses.

Anyway, playing ball, back in middle school, wasn't just about fitting in and keeping my dad happy. I loved everything about the game: going to practice, learning all the plays, working out, even running sprints at the end of practice when we were all dead tired.

## IF NO ONE SEES YOU, ARE YOU REALLY THERE?

The trouble was, off the court, things weren't going well at all. Jeff and Cedric, the team captains, didn't like me, and I couldn't figure out why. It's not like we got into it on the court or had some hard-core locker room throw-down. I kept my head down, practiced hard, and always avoided confrontations.

But the first half of the season had been all silence all the time from those two. And since they were our team leaders, everyone else followed suit and ignored me. That meant that I sat alone on the team bus, in the front near Coach C., and at the far end of the bench during games. The other guys on the team weren't mean or anything. It's just that no one went out of their way to be friendly.

That didn't help me in school much either. I'd thought that being an athlete would help me socially. But I guess Cedric and Jeff spread the word that I was weird or quiet. They certainly acted like I didn't exist and that got passed on. My isolation on the team quickly spread to the classroom and then schoolwide.

At first I was okay being alone. I studied, read a lot, and hung out with my dad on school nights and weekends. Dad is a really good carpenter. He builds and renovates houses. But he also makes stuff. I like to work with him in his workshop in the garage. He has every kind of tool you can imagine—for everything from heavy-duty framing and custom finishing to his favorite pastime, furniture making. When I was younger, he helped me build a tree house and a skateboard ramp in our backyard. Sometimes, on weekends or holidays, he'd ask me to help him build a desk, coffee table, or dining room set he'd been commissioned to make.

"Hold on there, Joey," Dad said one Saturday afternoon during seventh-grade winter holiday break. "You're putting way too much mustard into it."

I was hand-sanding a slab of cherrywood for a tabletop he was making.

"Sorry, Dad," I hadn't noticed how hard I'd been grinding away at it.

"You okay?"

"Yeah."

"Focus is the key to quality work and good results, Joey."

"I know, I know. I just zoned out there for a bit."

"Looks more like you're taking out your lifelong frustrations on an innocent piece of cherrywood. Be gentle with it. That stuff's gotten real expensive."

"Sorry, Dad."

"What's really going on, Joey?"

"I dunno."

"Is it something to do with the team?"

"How did you know?"

"I noticed you don't talk much during the shoot-arounds before games. And I never see you hanging out with your teammates."

"They're not the friendliest crew, Dad. Cedric and Jeff kinda run the show and I'm Fly Boy and Floppy Joe to them. And they never pass the ball to me in practice unless I'm the only option and Coach C. is watching."

"They sound like jerks, Joey," Dad said. "What about the rest of your teammates?"

"They're okay," I sighed. "But they do as the captains do. Follow the leader, I guess. But it's not just that, Dad. I'm not that good at making new friends. I just don't fit in well with other kids. It doesn't come easy for me."

Dad put down his hammer and wiped his forehead with his handkerchief. "Look, Joey, I love that you're on the school team. And you know I'm not a take-the-easy-way-out kind of guy. You aren't either. You fight hard for every minute of playing time you get on a very competitive team, and when you're in there, you go all out. But I want to be clear with you about one thing: If things get bad, you don't need to put up with it. We'll find another team or even switch you to a different sport, if you decide you've had enough."

"Thanks, Dad."

We worked silently for a while.

"Dad?"

"Yup."

"I don't want to quit the team. I'd just like the guys to treat me better. Like—normal."

"Okay, Joey. Let's figure this out together."

Dad suggested we find a way to better integrate me into the team.

"I can talk to your coach," he said. "I can tell him that Cedric and Jeffrey mistreat you. But that just makes them out to be the bad guys. Whether Coach C. pulls them aside for a quiet talk or punishes them outright, they'll figure you sold them out and hate on you worse than before."

"That would really suck," I said.

"Your mom had a pretty good handle on this kind of thing, you know," Dad said.

He stared at his tool belt for a few seconds.

"I miss her so much, Dad."

"Me too."

"She told me that her college softball team was loaded with talented, hypercompetitive players. Kind of like the kids on your team. But they all got along great. Everyone treated one another like family, and the older players were supportive of the younger ones even though everyone competed for the same spots in the starting lineup."

"How is that even possible?" I asked.

"Her coach placed a great deal of emphasis on team-building exercises," Dad said.

"What are those?"

"Before spring training, the entire team would go on a weeklong trip to get to know one another better. One year they went canoeing, another hiking. Mom's senior year they white-water rafted down the Delaware River."

"That sounds awesome."

"The coach divided the team into mini groups that cooked together and slept in the same tent. Each group was made up of veterans, rookies, and everything in between. She also divided them up so any cliques or best friends from previous years were separated out. One year your mom was put on a team with a really tough new girl who didn't seem to get along with anybody. On the second night of the trip, your mom discovered a spider in their six-person tent. Everyone yelled and screamed and jumped around, waving their flashlights wildly. When they'd all escaped and figured out how to remove the spider, they laughed and cried together and became best friends for the entire season."

"I don't know if that would ever happen on my team, Dad," I said. "Cedric and Jeff are pretty hard core. And everyone else does whatever they do."

"Don't you think it's worth a try, though?"

"I guess so. If they softened up a bit, everyone could chill out and work together more."

"Exactly, Joey. Let's give it a go."

## A SHOT WORTH TAKING

Dad talked to Coach C. and two other team parents and arranged for us to host a team dinner that Saturday night. It was cold out, but Dad fired up the barbeque, which he positioned on the back porch just outside the door to the garden. Everyone showed up—except for Cedric and Jeff. Their excuses seemed valid enough to Coach C., who let them off the hook. But I knew they were bogus. They just didn't want to have anything to do with something I'd helped set up.

Carlos, Kevin, and Jacob, the other three regular starters, came. That was a good sign. We all sat in the living room playing Xbox and watching Duke beat Michigan State 73–71, with an incredible buzzer-beating three-point shot. I kept on my winter coat because I was outside flipping the burgers and rotating chicken legs.

Everyone seemed to have a good time. As Carlos was leaving, he said, "Yo, Joey, yo' pops is straight up," which was, in Carlos-speak, high praise.

"See you, Monday, Floppy," Jacob smirked. But I could tell he meant it in a good way.

I felt a lot better after that dinner, and I thanked my dad. My teammates had enjoyed themselves, my dad was a hit, and I was confident that things would turn around. Everyone—except Cedric and Jeff—had been guests in my home. They'd hung out, eaten our burgers, laughed at my dad's jokes. At least now they knew I wasn't some weirdo freak who had been raised by wolves in some broken-down backwoods shack. They all thought Dad was cool. So maybe I was too, by association.

I got to my locker late on Monday afternoon. Everyone else was already in the gym warming up at our pre-practice shoot-around. I put on my jersey and felt around for my sneakers. Weird—they weren't in my locker where I always kept them. And they weren't in my duffel bag either. I started to panic. Coach C. was strict about lateness—a zero-tolerance policy.

After searching frantically for several minutes, I spotted one of my high-tops peeking out from the top of a garbage can outside the shower area. I rushed over, removed the trash top, and rummaged through sticky papers, cans, and bottles. Nothing. I stood on a bench and scanned the tops of all the lockers. Nothing. My other sneaker was gone.

I wanted to rush into the gym and grab Cedric by the neck and shake him. I wanted to tell Coach C. what his star captains had done—not just with my sneakers but every day since I'd joined the team; how they ignored me all the time, hardly ever passed the ball to me, excluded me from informal team get-togethers, iced me out so much that no one else on the team talked to me in fear of retaliation. But I knew I couldn't. If I confronted Cedric or Jeff physically, I'd just get suspended, or worse, kicked off the team. If I told Coach C. about how they were treating me, I'd get them into trouble and then become even more isolated—if such a thing were possible, because I was already pretty much invisible. And anyway, half the things they'd done to me all season were so subtle or sneaky that I couldn't really prove them.

I decided to take my lumps, and I told Coach C. I'd left one of my sneakers at home. He shook his head and said, "Okay, Joey, but you know the rules. A practice missed means a game not played."

"I know, Coach. I'm sorry," I replied. It wasn't too harsh a sentence given that I averaged no more than four minutes of playing time per game anyway. But I hated looking unreliable to Coach C., especially when it wasn't even my fault.

## CHANGE NEVER COMES EASY

I watched practice from the stands that afternoon and felt worse than ever. No one on the team so much as glanced over at me—not even to smirk or gloat. Operation Floppy Joe had been an unqualified success. And they'd moved on. Any points I'd earned by hosting a team dinner the previous Friday had been erased. I was back to square one. I didn't exist.

Coach C. took to heart my dad's suggestion about holding more team-building social events. Before the end of the season, we had two more gatherings: a sports movie night, hosted by Jeff's parents (we watched *Hoosiers*, an inspiring old-timey movie about an underdog Indiana high-school basketball team); and a team bowling night. Both were fun for everyone except me. Because, again, hardly anyone talked to me. With two weeks left in the season, I was ready to quit. I only hung on after talking it over with my dad.

"I'm proud of you, Joey," he said. "I see how those two guys behave around you. And I don't know if I could have taken it as long as you did, or handled it as well. But you have just two weeks left. I suggest you finish. And if things don't get better for you with them at school, don't try out next year. But a lot can change in a year, so I'd wait until the fall to decide. I'll support whatever you choose 100 percent."

After basketball season ended, I decided not to sign up for any spring sports. Why bother? Why put myself through more isolation torture? Jeff and Cedric were the most popular kids in school. If they didn't like you, no one else dared make an effort to get to know you. It was too risky. I couldn't really blame them. They were scared that if they tried to befriend me, they'd suffer a similar fate.

So I just kept to myself. I hit the books hard, went straight home every day after school, read a lot of sci-fi books, and got the best grades I could. I also prayed Dad would get a job in a galaxy far, far away, so we'd be forced to move to a completely different solar system, light-years away from anyone who knew Cedric, Jeff, and all their mini wannabes.

That summer we did move, not intergalactically, though—and only temporarily. Dad got an offer to work for three months on a crew building a fancy summer cottage 150 miles northeast of us, in Massachusetts.

"We'll rent a little cabin by a lake, Joey," he said excitedly. "I saw one a half mile from the town. We can go canoeing and kayaking on my days off, and fish straight off our dock. You'll love it."

I didn't need any convincing. I was just happy to spend the summer somewhere else, anywhere no one knew me as Floppy Joe or Fly Boy. A place where I wasn't the silent kid who you steered clear of.

## STAGING A COMEBACK

"Check this out," Dad said, handing me a colorful flyer he'd picked up in town. "Says here there's auditions for a summer festival play. Some kind of casting call."

"Come on, Dad. You know that (a) I know nothing about acting, and (b) I don't know a single person around here anyway."

"Says here it's a youth theater program," he continued. "Perfect opportunity for you to meet kids your age. Don't worry about the acting. Theater isn't only about who's on stage. There are all kinds of other things you can do: lighting, set design. Kid like you, handy with a hammer, could be a huge asset to a troupe putting on a summer production in a short time span."

"Why do I feel like there's something you're not telling me, Dad," I said.

"Okay, Joey, I give up. You always see right through my ploys anyway. I spoke to a lady—a Mrs. Sharon. She's the director of the program. She says they desperately need help, and she's eager to meet you. Tomorrow afternoon at the community center. You can take your bike. I'll stop by and pick you up in the evening when I've wrapped things up at the job site. And we can chow down on burgers and milkshakes at the diner on Main Street."

"Chow down, Dad?" I grimaced. "Nobody says 'chow down'—ever!"

We laughed.

I didn't let on but I was secretly glad Dad had found this for me. Hanging out alone at the cottage all day was getting old, even if Dad checked in on me by phone every couple of hours.

I was also nervous. What if nobody liked me?

The first week went pretty well, though I kept mostly to myself. Then one afternoon, while I was framing a set wall, a voice startled me: "When you're done here, I could use your help at home. In my backyard. I'm thinking of expanding the east wing of my tree house. Putting in a bay window maybe."

I looked up. Looming over me was a pretty, auburn-haired girl.

"Huh?"

She pointed to my tool belt.

"You look like you know your way around a job site!"

"Oh." My shoulders relaxed. "I get it."

She smiled.

"I'm Suzanna."

"Joey."

I stood up and realized she was a few inches taller than me.

"I can tell you know what you're doing."

"Thank you. Mrs. Sharon asked me to build a bunch of wall partitions so cast members can enter and exit the stage from different angles."

"See this?" She bent down a bit and pointed to a spot near the top of her head.

"What?" I asked. She spread her hair farther. I spotted a jagged little scar.

"Battle wound from last year's production of *Little Shop of Horrors.*"

"What happened?"

"A partition fell on me while I was kneeling down—pouring my heart out—during my first-ever solo. I coulda killed Oscar. He was in charge of set design."

"That's horrible," I cried. "I'll make sure these are 100 percent safe. I promise."

"Thank you!" Suzanna beamed. "You're my carpenter-prince!"

She disappeared behind the curtains. A few seconds later, a perfectly pitched, angelic voice filled the auditorium accompanied by a piano. "Wow," I thought to myself. "What just happened?" I finished banging nails into the frame of the partition I was building and tacked on two sheets of half-inch plywood. And added extra nails, just to be triple safe. The last thing I wanted was for one of those sheets to pop out. Or anything else to come loose, which could endanger my new friend.

"What's going on?" Dad said grinning when he picked me up that night after rehearsals.

"What do you mean, Dad?"

"You look different."

"I dunno."

I did know. I'd been working as lead set designer for two weeks and met twenty middle- and high-school-aged kids who were actors, musicians, or stagehands in the youth program's production of the musical *Into the Woods*. Everyone was friendly. And the older, more outgoing kids didn't try to lord it over everyone else. But I'd mostly kept to myself, like I always did.

I was polite with everyone, but I didn't go around initiating conversations—until I met Suzanna. That one brief talk with her was the longest one I'd had with someone my age in more than a year. And I didn't think about it or plan it in my head. It just happened. What my dad had picked up on was how happy I was.

"Can we stop for a milkshake at the diner, Dad?"

"Sure!"

At first I felt elated, sitting at the counter. A popular, beautiful, kind girl had taken the time to speak to me, had noticed me. Then it hit me, all at once, like a flash flood.

I got up, muttered something to my dad, and hurried to the bathroom where I hid for the next ten minutes, trying to stop the tears, waiting for my chest to stop heaving. Talking with Suzanna, even for those few seconds, made me suddenly aware of how starved I was for any kind of connection with someone my age.

I guess that's all it took for me to realize the damage people can do to someone when they ignore them, turn away from them, devalue them. I'd become invisible to almost everyone at school. I had tried to shrug it off, to bury the sense of rejection, to turn away from the pain I felt at being ghosted by everyone over and over again, no matter how hard I tried to make them stop.

I'd worked as hard as everyone else on the team—harder even— hoping that Cedric, Jeff, and the others would praise me, appreciate me, accept me. But that hadn't worked. Nothing had worked. No matter what I did, I couldn't get them to see me as a good person. As any kind of person actually. I was invisible.

People talk a lot about the taunting and bullying that happens in school, about how bad that kind of mistreatment can be for kids. But until that night at the diner, when my dad wondered out loud what had changed for me—why I looked different—I had never realized the negative impact being ignored, excluded, avoided, or full-on ghosted could have on a person.

The worst thing Jeff and Cedric had done to me physically was hide my sneakers. No big deal. I'd missed one practice, so what. But the other subtler stuff? Day in and day out? Not passing the ball to me. Ignoring me when I asked questions (until I stopped asking, and later, stopped talking at all). Turning their backs to me. Acting like I wasn't there.

But my teammates didn't just ghost me in the locker room. They did it online too. If I posted a photograph or made a comment on our team chats, total silence; no one ever responded. When anyone else shared a photo or made a comment, they got at least five or six replies, like "No way!" "That's fire, dude," or "True dat!"

I wasn't making this up. You could actually see it right there on the screen. Weirdly, I felt better. There was no denying what was being done to me. I wasn't making any of this up. But it had also made me feel much worse. It had chipped away at every ounce of confidence I'd built up over the years until I was numb.

I showed up at school every day. I practiced. I played. But I never said a word to anyone. Seldom answered a question in class. By the middle of basketball season, I was mute even in classes that neither Jeff and Cedric took. My withdrawal was almost complete. It had become more than a habit. It had become who I was.

Until that night. Until Suzanna.

## NEW SEASON, NEW DAY

On opening night, I peeked out at the audience and saw my dad in the front row—at the far left—sitting right next to Mrs. Sharon, who held the prompt book and looked anxiously at the stage. She had nothing to worry about, though. The cast was fantastic. Suzanna sang beautifully. So did everyone else.

At the end of the performance, the cast bowed several times. Mrs. Sharon thanked everyone, including the stagehands, and she singled me out for the stage design. My dad caught my eye and gave me a thumbs-up.

At the cast party, after our third and final performance, Suzanna came up to me.

"You free tomorrow?"

"Uh, yeah. Why?"

"To keep your promise?"

I looked puzzled.

"You swore you'd take me fishing on Panther Pond. You forgotten already?"

"Nope. I just thought you might be too busy."

"Too busy? It's all I've been thinking about for the past week. You promised you'd teach me how to clean and fillet all the fish I catch. And fry them up with me—on an open fire too."

I laughed.

"I'll be by your place early."

Suzanna and I hung out for the rest of the summer in a group of six theater-camp kids who all got along great. We hung out in town, biked around, watched movies together, and went on a few hikes. When Dad and I headed home, I was sorry to leave our quaint summer cottage, but also happy. I'd made so many cool new friends.

I kept in touch with Suzanna throughout the fall.

"How's school?" Suzanna texted me my first week back.

"Okay," I replied.

"Just okay?"

"Kids here aren't like you guys," I wrote. "They're not that nice."

"Sorry to hear that!" she responded. "Call if you wanna talk!"

Not much changed at school that fall. No one spoke to me much, and I kept to myself. But that didn't really matter to me anymore. Because I had Suzanna and the rest of my theater-group friends, I felt totally different. I now knew that somewhere in the world there was a bunch of kids who saw me—who *actually liked* me. And things didn't always have to be the way they were at school.

Suzanna and I talked on the phone at least once a week and texted each other a lot more. The entire summer crew stayed in touch in a theater-camp chat group we'd started. We posted wacky photos of ourselves and cracked endless jokes to one another. And best of all, no one ever ghosted me. I fit right in.

In late November I tried out for the basketball team. Dad was really happy. And I was determined to give it another try. When we got our uniforms, I took a selfie and sent it to Suzanna.

"Luv it! I c u put on some muscle! You taller than me now?"

"I guess so," I texted back.

"Looks like you grew two inches, three even!"

She was right. I'd had a little growth spurt. And I'd filled out and gotten stronger too. It wouldn't be as easy to push me around on the court anymore.

Cedric and Jeff were no different, but I was. I felt stronger, more confident.

"What's up with you, Joey?" Dad asked one Friday evening. "You seem preoccupied."

"Everything's fine, Dad," I said. "Just got all this stuff goin' round and round in my head about being there for the team. In the summer I was there for the production. We all worked great as a team. I just wish I knew how to speak to my teammates at school about how we should be like that too. We should come together. Work together. It would make us so much better."

"Well, do it then!" he exclaimed. "Don't just turn those ideas around in your head. Treat it like a dress rehearsal for a play. Practice exactly what you want to say until it's fully formed—until you know it by heart."

I called Suzanna that very night and told her about Cedric and Jeff, what my dad suggested, and what I wanted to say to my team. When I was done, I heard this weird noise on the other end of the call.

"What's that?" I asked.

"Slow clapping, all the way from Massachusetts, Joey! You should totally do that. And you can practice what you want to say to them with me on the phone if you want."

"I do," I exclaimed. "I'll call you tomorrow!"

We spoke several times over the weekend. And I'm so glad we did. Because on Monday, before practice, I got into an argument with Cedric after he told me I was hopeless at basketball.

"Dude! You really think you can be a part of this team?" Cedric said. "You rode the bench all last year."

I nodded. "Can't argue with you there. I sat on the bench all year. I worked really hard to get minutes. You and Jeff get all kinds of playing time—way more than me. That's totally true."

"You got that right, Floppy Joe!" Jeff chimed in.

"You guys are more athletic. And more skilled. But I pitch in any way I can. I'm a team player. I try to boost the team. When you refuse to pass to me or you put me down, you aren't really just pulling me down. You're pulling down the entire team.

"You can do it. I can't stop you. But you guys are captains. Why would you do something that's bad for your own team?"

"If it's all so bad, why don't you just quit?" Jeff asked.

"If I walked away from this team right now, you would just start doing it to someone else," I replied. "So I'm going to stay right here and do whatever I can, because I care about this team."

Cedric and Jeff tried to play it cool, but I could see that they were stunned. Neither of them had expected that I'd stand up for myself. Because I never had before. And they couldn't really argue with my logic because they both knew I was right.

No one else in that locker room said a word but I could almost hear what they were thinking. After Cedric, Jeff, and the rest of my teammates had filed out, Carlos stopped in front of my locker.

"You're right, bro," he said, extending his arm. "That's some bull." We fist-bumped. Then he slipped past me. I realized the six words Carlos had just strung together were the most I'd heard come out of his mouth at one time—ever.

The moment I stepped onto the court I felt different. Hey! This was a new year, a new season, and a new me. I had friends—my theater friends. I had a girlfriend even—sort of. If Cedric and Jeff didn't like me, so what.

We stretched, ran sprints, then drilled for about an hour. Then Coach C. divided us up into two teams. As we moved the ball down the court, I broke free in the corner. Cedric called for the ball at the top of the key, but Carlos, spotting me open, faked a pass to Cedric, then hurled the ball to me instead. I quick-released a three-pointer. It sailed toward the basket and hit the front of the rim. I raced to the basket and grabbed the rebound. Then I bounced a pass to Carlos, who was cutting toward the basket. Easy layup.

"Nice play, Joey. Way to follow up your shot," Coach C. shouted across the gym. "Keep it up, boys. Keep it up!"

As we raced back down the court to set up on defense, the other team called a timeout. I turned toward the bench. Kevin looked over and nodded. "Great play," Jacob said. Cedric glared at me and started to say something, but Carlos cut him off.

"Why don't you just chill, bro," he said pointedly. "New season, new day."

When Carlos jogged past me a few seconds later, he called out. "I got you, bro."

I smiled. "I got me too, bro," I thought to myself. "I got me too."

---

This story was about . . .

- Being ignored, excluded, and feeling invisible
- Finding the right friendship fit rather than forcing the wrong one
- Seeking friends who value you for who you are

Joey was excluded to the point that he felt invisible in school and on his basketball team. Then he learned that it's pointless to knock on a locked door. He tried a different door and found new friends who valued him for who he was—and that's when everything changed.

# 9

---

# IT'S LIFE THAT'S BULLYING ME

## *Sophie's Story*

The fast-paced, high-pressure, too-much-too-soon lifestyle that many kids lead is overwhelming them. Their nervous systems are almost constantly in the amber to red zones, seldom calming down to green. Stressed kids tend to take things personally. When their nervous systems are overtaxed, they become hypervigilant. They don't just sit in classrooms or playgrounds; they scan them for possible threats. And they often overreact and end up attracting unwanted and unkind attention.

It's important to understand that the same is true for kids who bully and try to control others socially. Such children and teens are also overwhelmed by the unrealistic demands that daily life can place on them. The main difference between the teaser and the targeted child, tween or teen, is that the former's default reaction is to attempt to hyper-control social situations. When their life pace becomes overwhelming, they grasp for whatever they can control, including other kids—especially ones who react openly and therefore can be more easily manipulated.

The more stress we put on our kids, the more likely they will become enmeshed in social problems and controversy. The opposite is also true. A child who is more at ease and relaxed is far more likely to shrug off put-downs or exclusion. They may even laugh them off, which can be disarming to the teasers and draw other kids toward them because of the natural resiliency they demonstrate.

This story explores both social polarities by walking us through Sophie's slow journey to understanding why she is so stressed and reactive, and what she can do to change it.

## POINTS OF UNDERSTANDING

- Even though everyone is doing way too much, it is not healthy.
- Living at a crazy life pace can make you really vulnerable to teasing.
- No matter how good anti-bullying strategies are, they don't work that well if you are stressed and oversensitive.
- There is no point trying to *live up* to other people's expectations or *keep up* with siblings or classmates if it leaves you exhausted and unhappy.

## POINTS OF HOPE AND LEARNING

- You can stand up to bullying very effectively when you are coming from a calm, centered place.
- Dialing back the pace of life is not as hard as it may seem.
- Doing less but doing it better is far more satisfying.
- It's not unreasonable for a child to want to have a childhood.

It takes courage to support a child, tween, or teen who needs to step off the rapidly revolving treadmill of unspoken expectations. While it is understandable that parents worry that their children will be "left behind" if they are not running hard with the pack, it's much more important for their emotional health that we shift our thinking from an obsession with "winning" the unnamed race that promises outer success to helping our kids be the best they can be. When they meet life at the proper pace, they can develop the foundations they need to become confident, resilient, and socially well integrated.

---

*My name is Sophie. I'm eighteen and I just graduated high school. I live with my mom, dad, and sister just outside of Boston. My story is about how trying to keep up with the crazy pace of my life when I was in elementary school caused me so much stress that I became really sensitive and vulnerable. I started overreacting to everything and became a teasing target. At first I thought it was just me. But when I looked around, I saw that a lot of other kids were over-whelmed, trying to keep up with everything—just like me.*

*The fact that everyone is living stressfully may seem normal, but that doesn't make it right. There's nothing healthy about being crushed by stress. I hope reading this story helps you realize that feeling pressured all the time is not okay. We all need to dial back the stress and be calmer and happier. We're kids. We've got a right to have a childhood. We shouldn't be treated like mini executives being trained to run big companies when we aren't even high-schoolers yet!*

I loved everything I did when I was a fourth, fifth, and sixth grader. I took piano lessons once a week, played on a great travel soccer team that practiced three times a week, and played in games and tournaments on weekends all year round. But I also had a ton of homework I could barely keep up with. Looking back on it now—even after going through high school—I can't believe so many teachers in elementary school piled that much work on us *so early.* Don't they realize that we have lives outside of schoolwork? That both being socially active and having time to ourselves are just as important to our personal growth?

Anyway, up until the end of third grade, things went smoothly for me. I was a good student, I played lots of sports, and I was pretty popular at school. My best friend in the whole world was my big sister Amanda. We got along great, even though she was three years older. We shared a bedroom, played board games with our friends a lot, and went to the same summer camp. She never excluded me from her activities and friendships. She let me hang out with her when her friends came over. We all had so much fun together.

But that all changed when I entered fourth grade and Amanda moved to Riverton Middle School across town to start seventh grade. We'd been so close for so long. Suddenly we were headed in completely different directions. Now that she was in another school, I never ran into her during the day in hallways, at recess, or during lunch.

I joined a travel soccer team that year, and Amanda swam for her school team, so we didn't see each other after school much either. Then a few weeks into the new school year, Amanda's swim coach—impressed by her work ethic and trial times—convinced my dad that she should join an elite swim team he co-coached that trained six days a week and had four mandatory early-morning workouts. That meant that four days a week, when I woke up to get ready for school, she and my dad were already gone. He'd drive her to 5:30 a.m. practices and then to school, and head straight to work. The first few times it was nice to have Mom all to myself at breakfast. But pretty soon I started feeling sad because Amanda and I had always laughed a lot and acted so goofy together, and now I almost never saw her anymore.

Things changed a lot for our family over the next two years. Mom and Dad—who had both been college athletes—were really pumped up about Amanda's development as a competitive swimmer and my dedication to soccer. And because our schedules rarely corresponded, Dad often spent weekends traveling to swim meets with

Amanda, while Mom drove me to practices and weekend games. Our vacations were often split up in a similar way: Dad took Amanda to swim camp or out-of-state meets, and Mom took me to Columbus Day or Memorial Day tournaments.

At home there was never any time for us to just hang out together. It was almost like we weren't really a family anymore. Amanda was always doing swim stuff, and Dad worked in his home office every night to catch up on what he missed when he was driving Amanda around. Mom had a little more time because she was a high-school teacher, but she often had a pile of papers to grade in the evenings. And because of soccer, she became less my mom and more my team manager and chauffeur. We got to talk a bit when we drove to and from practice, if I wasn't so tired that I fell asleep. But what I missed most were all the things Amanda and I used to do with Mom, such as bake cookies and cook dinner.

When I was younger, I'd spend hours in the kitchen helping Mom cook. But there was no time anymore. I'd just sit there, at the kitchen table, buried in homework assignments, while she put meals together as quickly as possible. Then she and I would eat right there in the kitchen while we worked and leave Dad's and Amanda's dinners in the pot so that they could have them when they got home from Amanda's afternoon practices or school activities.

I really missed the days when the four of us ate together because that had been when everyone relaxed and we all connected over what was going on in our daily lives. Now we often ate at different times because everyone was so *on the go*. Sunday-night dinner was the one meal we sat down at as a foursome, and that only happened if we were all back in time from away games or competitions.

As Amanda got older her attitude toward me changed too. It wasn't just that she wasn't around that much anymore. She basically just didn't want to hang out with me. I don't know when exactly it happened, but somehow my big sister—and best friend in the whole wide world—became my chief rival. At least that's the way I felt.

Everywhere I looked, I was reminded about how great Amanda was. She was a straight A student throughout middle and high school. She was beautiful and popular and won races so often that Dad bought a wall-to-ceiling wooden trophy case that he mounted in the hallway next to the living room to house all her swimming awards. I worked hard at soccer and did well at school but I could never measure up to her academically or athletically. I was a good athlete and one of my travel team's best defenders, but I was nowhere close to becoming the star athlete Amanda was. She was one of the top swimmers in her age group in the entire state!

I had one or two good friends at school, but Amanda was a middle-school starlet. She was on student council at Riverton and co-chaired the dance committee. She had loads of followers and friends on multiple social media accounts. When she was home, she was always on her phone texting and messaging with her girlfriends and all the guys who liked her.

When I was little, being around Amanda had always made me feel happy. Now I felt small and sometimes even invisible. She was so bubbly and energetic. She never really sat down or sat still—like a ballerina who never stopped spinning. The only thing that kept her from being perfect was the fact that she chewed her nails and talked really fast.

The older Amanda got, the deeper she disappeared into her expanding social world. I felt as though I barely existed to her. Whenever I asked her if she wanted to hang out with me, she was curt—or downright mean. But I kept trying because, once in a while, when I caught her in the right mood, I could get her to play a board game with me or just goof around and laugh.

We never went anywhere together as we did when we were younger. I sensed that she was embarrassed to be seen with me, and that felt awful. All she wanted to do was chat with her friends on her phone. When she wasn't doing that, she'd walk around with her earbuds on and get annoyed if I spoke to her. If I walked into her room, she'd snap at me: "What?" she'd say, and glare at me. When I couldn't think of anything to say, she'd get exasperated and say, "You're so annoying, Sophie!"

"Well, sorrrrry!" I'd reply, and stomp out, biting my lip, and sit back down at the kitchen table and disappear into my homework.

"What's wrong, sweetie?" Mom said one evening after I'd had another argument with Amanda.

"Nothing, Mom," I answered. "It's just—Amanda never wants to do anything with me anymore."

"She growing up, isn't she?" Mom reasoned. "And she's very busy with school and everything else."

"She's not that much older, Mom. And she's not around often, but when she is, she's on her phone all the time. She is so addicted."

"All kids are constantly on their phones at her age these days, Sophie. It's pretty normal."

"Well, if that's normal, Mom, I don't know," I said. "It doesn't seem right to me."

## YOU CAN'T DO IT ALL

At school I wasn't a total loner. I had two steady friends: Jennifer and Sammy. But we never got to hang out and goof around after school because each of us had activities we had to get to. Jennifer played the flute in an intraschool orchestra, and she studied jazz dance. Sammy was following her sister Dora's path, hoping to become a lacrosse prospect. Dora was a scholarship athlete, playing for a nationally ranked college lacrosse team. The three of us had sleepovers, but not very often because it was always so complicated trying to schedule them around our games, tournaments, practices, and performances.

Fifth grade was chaotic but I got through it. And I was really looking forward to summer vacation, to relaxing. But it didn't work out that way at all. As soon as one sports camp ended, another began. At the end of the summer—when I was hoping for a week or two of total downtime—I got stuck rush-writing three book reports on books from my summer reading list. I also kept up with the piano—even when I was away at camps—because I liked playing and because Mom, who was an accomplished musician herself, didn't want me to miss out on becoming a proficient player.

Sixth grade was no different. Right from the start, everything closed in on me. I had a piano recital at the end of October to prepare for, travel soccer was in full swing, and though I didn't think it could ever be possible, we were assigned more homework than ever before!

My parents were thrilled about Amanda's summer swim-meet successes: she got promoted to an even more competitive elite program. I was happy for her too. But to be honest, I was also a little jealous because Dad got so worked up about her. He had been a top swimmer in high school, and he was excited that she was following in his footsteps.

I felt weird about it all because I had the sense I'd have to match or surpass her success if I wanted my parents to notice me anymore. What was even more weird is I didn't really want to do more of what I was doing anyway. It was already way too much. But it seemed like that was the only way I could make them proud of me. I was also upset because any hope I'd had of getting my sister (and best friend) back was clearly over. There was no room for me in her life anymore. She was just way too busy being spectacular at everything.

Things got more complicated for me at school too. Back in fifth grade, our homeroom teacher, Miss Tawny, had been really involved. We played games with her at recess, and she wasn't just interested in our schoolwork and test results. She kept an eye on our social lives. Once, when Sammy and I had a mega fight, she noticed we weren't talking to each other and intervened and made us both feel better. We patched things up immediately. She always knew when to step in to smooth things out if fights broke out or rivalries got too heated.

Our sixth-grade homeroom teacher was totally different. Mrs.

Brown hardly spent any time with us, except when she had to. She didn't try to get to know us well, so a lot of stuff happened that she didn't notice. Boys fought. Girls got on each other's nerves. Cliques formed, and some kids even got teased, though nothing really nasty happened.

In the first two months of sixth grade, I started feeling miserable on many levels. For one thing, life just seemed way too intense. There was always a test to prepare for or a practice to dash off to. And it seemed like we had a tournament every weekend that fall. I felt like a hamster bumbling along on an exercise wheel. The faster life got— and the harder I tried to keep up with everything—the more sensitive and reactive I got when things didn't go exactly right. And I don't think it was just me. Everyone seemed on edge. But clearly some kids dealt with it better than others.

Mornings were especially hard because I was so tired. Mom insisted we have a good sit-down breakfast, but I couldn't even think about food. I just wanted to crawl back into bed. And it made me grumpy. I'm pretty quiet, and I almost never argue with my parents. But one morning I just snapped. Dad and Amanda were already up and gone to her morning swim practice.

"Good morning. Come sit down, love," Mom said. "Do you want raspberry jam on your toast?"

"Sure," I muttered.

"Well, someone seems a wee bit grouchy this morning!"

"Mom!"

"How are things going at school, Sophie?" Mom asked. "Are you getting all your homework done?"

"What do you mean by that?"

"Nothing, dear. I was just making conversation."

"Why do you have to check up on me all the time, Mom?" I cried out. "Don't you see how hard I'm working?

"I was just—"

"You're always interrogating me," I interrupted, as I stood up. "Don't you trust me?"

Tears streamed down my cheeks as I dashed out of the kitchen.

"Just leave me alone!" I cried as I grabbed my schoolbag and headed out the door.

I didn't stop shaking until I was a few blocks away. I was shell-shocked by my reaction. Why had I freaked out on Mom like that? She'd asked me about school a million times before and I'd never gotten upset. What was wrong with me?

To get to some weekend soccer tournaments, Mom and I had to leave home early on a Friday night. And we wouldn't get back until late on Sunday afternoon. I'd do homework on the drives to and from the hotel we stayed at and on the way to games. I loved playing soccer, and our coaches constantly reminded us that having fun was our team's top priority—way more important than winning, they'd say. But that's not at all how they acted come game time. That's when they'd get all intense and shouty on the sidelines.

"Slide, Tina," they'd yell. "Get her, Sarah! Take her down," they'd scream. "Come on, girls, be aggressive!" Some dads yelled at the refs when they disagreed with calls. And every so often they'd get into snarly arguments with a dad or two from the opposing teams, particularly when they thought one of the other team's players had committed a nasty, unnecessary foul.

In one game, a girl we were playing against, who was really good, got yelled at so much by her own dad that she finally screamed back, "Leave me the hell alone!" She walked off the field, crying, right then and there in the middle of the game! We all felt really bad about that, and my teammate Sarah actually went over to her and gave her a hug at halftime. My dad never acted that way at my games. Maybe that's because he hardly ever got a chance to watch me play in a competitive tournament. He was always with Amanda at swim meets in totally different parts of the state, or driving her to weekend practices.

## THE COOL GIRL

On the last day of October, Miranda joined our sixth-grade class. She was tall, pretty, and, well, just really funny—though her jokes could sometimes be cutting and sarcastic. With a single comment or eye roll Miranda could make anyone feel like the center of the world or an insignificant beetle that deserved to be crushed by a giant boot heel. Jennifer and Sammy laughed at her zingers. They never took anything too seriously.

Sometimes I'd have to change in the locker room before I left school for travel soccer practice. The first time Miranda saw me doing that, she said, just loud enough for everyone present to overhear, "Here comes our hero, Little Miss World Cup Soccer."

Everyone laughed and moved on. But I didn't. I felt hurt. And nervous. Everyone liked Miranda, but she'd barely been at school for a week. And I'd been there forever. Why had no one stood up for me?

"Why did Miranda talk to me that way?" I asked Jennifer the next day. "Do you know what's going on?"

"I don't know, Sophie," she replied. "It was no biggie. Just ignore her."

But I couldn't. Something about Miranda put me on edge. And pretty soon it felt like she was making fun of everything I did, not just sports. She joked about my drawings, my clothes. She'd roll her eyes whenever I said something. I knew I wasn't handling her teasing well. I was taking everything she said or did way too personally. She was like that with everyone, but I was letting her get under my skin. Sammy and Jennifer told me so over and over, but I couldn't help myself. I got upset and reacted every time she said something I thought was off-color.

Finally, after weeks of holding back, I decided I had to confront her. It was during recess. I was chasing Sammy and tripped over a tree root.

"That's pretty klutzy for a star athlete, Sophie!" Miranda teased.

"You have no right to talk to me like that," I shot back, picking myself up off the ground.

"Oh, you are such a darling little thing," she replied. "Isn't she?"

A few girls chuckled. Others smiled.

"Why are you being so mean to me?" I said.

"You're overreacting a bit, don't you think?"

"I am not!"

"Yes, you are! Right, girls?"

No one agreed with her. No one defended me either.

"Before you came, everything around here was fine, Miranda," I said.

"Well, I'm here now, Sophie. So get used to it."

The next day in class, Miranda bumped into me as I was drawing a line at my desk. I flew into a rage.

"Why'd you do that?"

"Why'd you do that?" she repeated mockingly.

It was no big deal, really, but I just snapped.

"Would you just stop it!" I yelled, standing up. "You ruined my work."

"Sophie? Sit down, please," Mrs. Brown said. "What's wrong?"

"Yeah," Miranda called out. "That's what everyone is wondering."

"Miranda hit me," I responded. "On purpose."

"No way. It was a total accident, Mrs. Brown!"

"Sophie! I saw no such thing," Mrs. Brown said.

"Did anyone else see Miranda hit Sophie?"

No one said a word.

"Okay. See me after class, Sophie," Mrs. Brown said. "Everyone, take out your math books, please."

That afternoon, Mrs. Brown suggested I was overreacting. I didn't see it that way at all. But I also didn't see any point in trying to convince her otherwise. To avoid any more blowups, I steered clear of Miranda—and pretty much everyone else at school, to be honest—for the next month. I just wanted to get the fall term over with, to get to Christmas break.

Jennifer asked me once at recess if everything was okay. I smiled and reassured her that I was fine. But I wasn't. I was tired all the time. I fell asleep often on our drives to and from soccer practice. At home I stopped hanging out in the kitchen with Mom when Dad and Amanda were at swim training. I'd retreat to my room instead.

"Honey, are you okay?" Mom asked on a rare Saturday afternoon when she and I and Amanda were at home together, sitting in the living room.

"Great, Mom! Everything's fine," I replied, trying to act cheerful.

"Are you sure?" Amanda asked. "You look kinda pale."

"Really, I'm fine," I insisted. "Just a little tired. But I'm really looking forward to Christmas at Nana's."

Mom and Amanda exchanged glances. They weren't buying my bravado act, or at least Amanda wasn't. For several years now, we'd shared a secret dread of the obligatory annual holiday visit to our grandmother's. Nana was so old-fashioned. She liked to sit and chat, sipping away at a piping hot mug of chamomile tea, and bake cookies and cakes every day. When we were little, we'd loved it.

But after three or four days of talking, baking, and nightly turns at Go Fish, Monopoly, or Risk, we plotted our escape. The worst part of it—for Amanda, at least—was that there was no internet service at Nana's. She refused to have it installed. And her TV—with all of four channels available and a fuzzy picture—was basically useless. Nana also had a steadfast no-cell-phone-use policy. Being cut off from friends and virtual entertainment was more than a teenage girl could handle. We usually had fun for the first day or two and then died a thousand deaths by boredom.

As I walked up the stairs to my room, I overheard Amanda say, "Mom, I don't think Sophie's doing all that well." She was right. I was not myself. I'd become quiet and withdrawn. I had almost no appetite, and my stomach felt like it was tied up in knots. Mrs. Brown had called my mom to inform her that several teachers were concerned about me not handing in assignments on time, something I'd never done before.

I tried to look on the bright side. My piano recital had gone well and soccer practices were done for the holiday break. With no end-of-year tournament coming up, I figured I could rest and recover from all the fall stress.

## DIALING THINGS BACK

Nana lives in a quaint, winterized three-bedroom cottage just twenty minutes west of Augusta, in the heart of Maine. As we turned the final bend of the gravel road that led into her driveway, I spied the dark-blue expanse of Maranacook Lake and instantly felt better.

The next three days were a dream. Mom and I teamed up with Nana and Amanda and whipped up three different pies for Christmas dinner. And I stayed up extra late on Christmas Eve helping Nana make and decorate two sheets of gingerbread cookies. Because cell-phone service was so sketchy in the area, and the TV so fuzzy, Amanda couldn't disappear into a device or veg out in front of a screen. So she joined me, Mom, Nana, and even Dad, who took part after he finished chopping wood for the crackling fire we were nursing. We played Uno and Monopoly, and Dad performed a half-dozen card tricks he'd learned as an aspiring teenaged magician. Who knew? Way to go, Dad! He even secretly taught me one while the others were wrapping presents, and I totally fooled Mom and Amanda when I performed it for them.

We were supposed to stay for three nights, but when it came time to leave, I just couldn't. I begged Mom to let me stay with Nana for the rest of the week. Dad and Amanda were adamant about getting back to Boston because Amanda had a two-day swim meet on December 29 and 30.

"Please, please, *please* let me stay, Mom," I pleaded. "I promise to be on my best behavior and help Nana clean and everything. I just feel so much more relaxed here with her."

After a private talk with Nana, Mom and Dad agreed to let me stay on for five more days. To be honest, I was kind of glad that Amanda was leaving. We'd had a great time for the first two days. (I felt like I'd gotten my sister and best friend back!) But early on the third day, Amanda figured out that if she bundled up and walked out to the end of Nana's neighbor's dock—and positioned herself just so—all her texts, emails, and DMs poured in. Cell service in that one spot, perched right above the frigid water in a tiny three-foot pocket of space, was just good enough for her to send and receive messages, watch short videos, and make brief, shaky calls to her friends.

For the rest of the day Amanda shuttled back and forth, drinking hot chocolate or herbal tea during her indoor intervals to warm up, and she ignored me completely.

Nana and I hugged Mom, Dad, and Amanda and they hopped into our minivan. When everyone was gone, Nana turned to me.

"Now I have you all to myself!" she exclaimed, wrapping me up in a soft, cushy hug.

"I'm so happy to be here with you, Nana," I replied.

"You sure you won't get too bored hanging out with an ancient like me?"

"You're not ancient, Nana. You're awesome."

"Well, I feel the same way about you, my dearest Sophie," Nana replied as we walked back into her cozy home.

For the next four days we baked, cooked, played cards, and went for long nature walks. And I did not feel bored once, not even for a second. In fact, I felt a lot better on the whole. My stomach pains vanished. The sore throat I'd been nursing when I arrived disappeared. And I slept like a log until nine or ten each morning and woke up full of energy and enthusiasm.

But on the night before Mom was scheduled to pick me up, all that changed. I woke up at 5:00 a.m. in a cold sweat. When I got my bearings, I realized Nana was by my side.

"Are you okay, Sophie?" she asked worriedly.

I tried to respond but I couldn't make a sound.

"That's okay, love," she said. "You don't have to tell me a thing."

My shoulders started to shake uncontrollably as tears poured down my cheeks.

"I-I do-don't know wh-why I'm crying, Na-na," was all I could manage.

I just cried and cried and cried.

"I'm so glad you came to stay with me, Sophie," Nana said after I'd settled down a bit. She took me into the living room, sat me down on the sofa, and covered me in a warm, puffy duvet.

"I'm going to make us some chamomile tea, my love," she said, and she shuffled off into the kitchen.

By the time Nana returned bearing two gigantic loon mugs brimming with piping hot tea, I'd calmed down quite a bit.

"I don't know what it is, Nana," I confided. "I just haven't felt all that well since the beginning of sixth grade."

She smiled.

"You did look a bit worn out when you arrived," she said.

I nodded.

"You look so much better now, though," she added, patting my hand.

"I feel a lot better too, Nana," I replied.

"There's something about being here with you, on the lake, and baking and cooking and *just being* that makes me feel so much more *me*."

Nana and I talked for an entire hour. I told her about school, piano, and soccer. About tests, essays, and prepping for my piano recital. And how Amanda was never around and most days I ate alone or just with Mom. I even told Nana about my issues with Miranda and

Mrs. Brown. And I confessed to feeling like I didn't fit into the sixth-grade social scene at all. I went a bit overboard perhaps, but Nana was so easy to talk to. I poured my heart out, and she just listened. She didn't interrupt me once the way Mom always did. Mom would offer assurances and advice or hollow compliments meant to make me feel better. Nana just sat there. She really heard me.

Then we hugged and cleared our mugs into the kitchen, where we fried up a half-dozen apple-maple sausages, scrambled five eggs, and sat down to a breakfast feast that included giant slices of whole wheat toast covered with locally churned butter and wild blueberry jam.

"Nana," I said in between eager mouthfuls.

"Yes, Sophie," she said, laughing good-naturedly at my piggishness.

"I had the scariest, weirdest dream ever last night."

"Is that why you woke up so suddenly?" she asked.

"I think so."

Nana sensed my hesitation, because she did not probe any further. Instead, she disappeared into a small crawl space on the side of the wall halfway up the stairs to her bedroom and came back down with several dusty photo albums and a shoebox.

"I'd like to show you some old photos and tell you a bit about your grandpa and your mom when she was little."

We looked through grainy black-and-white photos of Grandpa building the house, and posing in Europe with his World War II army unit. There were also pics of him and Nana sledding down Badger Hill with Mom and Uncle Timmy, and skating on a completely frozen Maranacook Lake when Mom was my age.

"Your mother was a happy, outdoorsy little girl," Nana said. "She loved singing and playing the piano. And jumping and running and skating. When she was a girl, things were a whole lot different from how they are now. She didn't play on teams that traveled to a different town every weekend. And she most certainly didn't spend her summers in camps that trained her to be better at everything. For one thing, we couldn't afford that. But more importantly, all she and your

Uncle Timmy had to do was walk right out that door into the woods or jump in the lake when they were hot. They swam, fished, skated and skied, hiked and climbed right here with a dozen or so friends who lived around the lake or in town."

"I kinda wish I'd lived back in those days, Nana," I whispered. "Things get too pressured for me sometimes."

"Well, we have to play the hand that's dealt to us, Sophie," Nana replied. "But that by no means justifies overloading your plate in life. Overscheduling is very much like overeating. Both can cause fatigue and indigestion. And your body and mind seem to be sending you a clear message."

Nana was right. Being overscheduled and overwhelmed all the time had worn me down. And even if it looked to Sammy and Jennifer, my teammates, or my piano teacher that I was fine and in control, I'd actually been struggling to get through each and every day. I felt so much better now, hundreds of miles away from my crazy life.

I looked at Nana. She was so wise and kind. I felt like I could tell her anything.

"Can I tell you about the dream I had last night?" I asked.

"You can tell me anything you want, dear," she said.

My dream was equal parts weird and scary, and it didn't make a whole lot of sense. We were driving to a soccer tournament in Connecticut. Only it wasn't me and Mom, as it always was. Oddly enough, Dad was driving me. We were listening to the Beatles—Dad's favorite band from what he calls his "salad days"—and singing along. He was happy and relaxed, not stressed about work or anything.

Then suddenly everything got blurry and shaky. A car swerved in front of us and Dad stepped on the brakes as he turned hard to the left. I heard the tires screeching and felt us getting smashed from behind. Our van spun over an embankment, into a ravine. I remember feeling like a pair of jeans spinning around in a washing machine. We kept flipping over until finally everything was still.

The next thing I remember is lying in a bed covered by a stiff white sheet, hearing machines beeping and muffled voices. I looked to my left and saw Dad lying in the bed beside me. He was covered in bandages but I could make out a grin and then a toothy smile.

"Hiyya, Sophie," he said.

"Hi, Dad," I whispered. "What happened?"

My body ached from my head to my toes.

"We were in a car accident."

"Oh," I replied.

"The doctor says we should be discharged in about a week."

"Dad?" I said.

"Yes, Sophie."

"Promise you'll stay right here next to me, no matter what."

"I'm not going anywhere!"

I don't remember much else about the dream except that Mom and Amanda never visited us, which was beyond weird. Dad and I talked and laughed for what seemed like forever. As we got better, we took short walks together, hobbling up and down the hospital halls on our crutches. Someone (I don't have a clue who) gave us a pack of cards and we played Go Fish and endless games of War. Dad even taught me four new card tricks. I don't remember much more of the dream except that everything got hazy and then suddenly Dad was back in his hospital bed hooked up to a machine and an IV drip, and he wasn't doing well at all. That's when I woke up, terrified.

All Nana said when I finished was, "Wow, Sophie, that was quite a dream." She hugged me, and we sat there quietly for a few minutes. Then she stood up.

"Why don't we get bundled up and go for a walk along the ridge," she said.

And off we went.

I learned later that Nana and Mom had talked about me for hours when she came to pick me up. Grandma pointed out things to my mom with the kind of honesty only a mother can impart directly to her daughter. They agreed that things had gotten too intense for me and that they'd never had to cope with anything like what I was being asked to deal with when they were my age.

"I think things will get better for you at school when you go back, Sophie," Nana said as she kissed me goodbye. "When you're really tired and overworked, you get grumpy and you just want to be left alone. And it gets harder to let things slide or to laugh them off. Now you're rested and strong. Things will look a lot different, I promise."

My eyes filled with tears. "Thank you for everything, Nana," I said. "You're the best grandma in the whole wide world."

## THE POWER OF LESS

Nana was right. When I returned to school in January, I felt different—so much more relaxed and confident. Sammy and Jennifer noticed too.

"Did you cut your hair?" Sammy asked before homeroom on our first day back.

"No," I said.

"You look different, though," Jennifer said.

"Whaddaya mean?" I asked.

"I dunno," she replied. "You look good."

"Yeah," Sammy added. "Really pretty!"

"Did you guys go to some spa resort thingy or something?" Jennifer said. "You look so refreshed!"

"No. I stayed with my grandma. We had such a great time together."

"What'd you guys do?" Sammy asked.

"Nothing," I said.

"Nothing?"

"Yeah, nothing. It was great!"

I felt like everything had shifted, and it really had. Mom and I had a long talk about what I wanted to do that spring. We decided that plunging back into the fast-paced, overcommitted, stressful daily routine that had consumed me the last few years wouldn't be the best thing for me.

I didn't want to give up soccer altogether but I needed to cut back a bit. Mom spoke to my coaches and they agreed I could skip one of our weekly practices for the rest of the season. And she told me that she and Dad wanted me to take next summer off too. That way I'd have a three-month break from organized sports.

Mom also spoke to my subject teachers at school and they arranged to cut back on the amount of nightly homework they assigned me. They set me up on something called time-based study. That meant I should study each subject for a certain amount of time and then stop, even if I hadn't completely finished the work. That way I wouldn't spend hours and hours on one subject and fall totally behind on everything else. And I wouldn't stay up late trying to fit everything in. They knew I'd act honorably about the work I did because I'd always been a trustworthy student.

For the first time in forever I had more downtime at home because I'd signed up for fewer activities. My stomachaches disappeared. I stopped getting nagging head colds, and I slept much more soundly. Amanda was nicer to me, and Dad switched with Mom sometimes, so he could spend one-on-one time with me. He even drove me to a tournament and saw me score my first and only goal of the season.

At school, things got better socially too. Oddly enough, I realized Miranda wasn't all that bad. In fact, she could be really funny in her own quirky, unique way. When I thought back to the barbs and zingers that stung me so deeply, I wondered how much being exhausted and on edge had played into my reactions to her comments. Like the Little Miss World Cup line—that was kind of funny when I thought it over. For one thing, I sorta deserved it because I had gotten in the habit of bragging a bit about my soccer exploits and how good our team was. Maybe Miranda had felt a little intimidated herself, because she didn't look that comfortable playing any sport. What's more, nothing she'd said had been all that nasty or that big a deal.

She was definitely not some out-of-control bully. If I'd ignored her comments or just laughed at them and played along, they would have meant nothing to anyone.

Back in the fall I had definitely felt like a victim. Life had been moving too fast for me, and I guess that's why I became so hurt and reactive when I thought Miranda was picking on me. But spending time with Grandma, away from everyone and everything, helped me see it all in a different light. I'd blamed others, but in fact it was my hectic life that had been bullying me.

I promised myself never to let that happen again.

---

This story was about . . .

- Doing too much and feeling overwhelmed
- Trying too hard to live up to everyone's expectations
- Giving yourself permission to dial things back
- Becoming centered, calm, and connected to family and friends

Sophie found the modern pace of life overwhelming. When she dialed things back, she discovered that she stopped overreacting, felt calmer, and connected better with her friends.

# 10

## THE SHY KID'S GIFT OF INNER STRENGTH

### *Destiny's Story*

Introverted kids often feel like they are standing on the *out*side looking *in* at the complex social relationships they see each day. And it certainly often looks like the world is set up for outgoing, confident people, not quiet, inward-looking ones. In this story we see how Destiny struggles with the tension between feeling safe within her own low-key but isolated life and her longing to be noticed and accepted.

What many people don't realize is how rich and deep a quieter kid's inner life can be. Such inner strength can be a real asset. This story demonstrates a simple way to tap into this power and help a child or teen find their place in the social life that swirls around them.

### POINTS OF UNDERSTANDING

- Just because a child or teen is reserved does not mean they can't be an integral part of a group.

- Still waters run deep. Don't underestimate what a reserved person notices.
- Finding a way to enter the busy and changeable flow of social life is not easy.
- The challenge is learning to translate what you see into what you can do to become a part of things.

## POINTS OF HOPE AND LEARNING

- An inner whisper can become a clear, guiding call. You just need to tune in and channel that voice.
- Inside talk has amazing power, which quiet people can connect to much more easily than bold and assertive kids.
- There are ways to calm anxieties in social situations.
- Confidence to get involved does not just come naturally, but it can be learned.
- There are people who can perceive the inner beauty of quieter individuals.
- Find friends who possess the equilibrium to look more deeply.

Working discreetly with an introverted child or teen to help them navigate the social world can be rewarding. Parents or educators need to find their own inner still point so that their enthusiasm is balanced by gentle encouragement. Above all else, remember that being quiet, thoughtful, and restrained is not a deficit but a gift waiting to be unwrapped.

------

*Hi. My name is Destiny. I'm nineteen and a sophomore in college. I'm majoring in psychology because I'm fascinated by how people behave and what motivates them to act the way they do. Things are going pretty well for me. I've met a lot of great people at school and made several really close friends. But if you knew me when I was younger, you'd be shocked at how well I've adapted to college life.*

When I was little, I was a total loner. It's not that I was antisocial or anything. I was just too afraid to talk to other people, so I had no friends at all. I was always on the outside looking in, which made me feel sad and left out. Right up to the middle of seventh grade, I never once had anybody over or went over to someone else's house to hang out.

When I was nine, I realized how different I was. Back then I was enrolled in a big elementary school in Orlando, Florida. There were lots of kids to make friends with and all kinds of after-school activities to do. But I was too timid to join in; and I rarely spoke, so no one ever paid much attention to me.

Once, at the beginning of fifth grade, I struck up enough courage to follow a group of girls around who always seemed to have a lot of fun playing together. I felt embarrassed trailing after them like an eager little sister, but I wanted so badly to be included. I'd purposely sit near them at lunch and watch them play at recess, wishing they'd ask me to join in. But they never did. They just ignored me. I guess I was invisible to them.

Looking back, I don't think they were trying to be mean on purpose. I probably just made them feel super uncomfortable because I was so awkward and desperate. So they just did what came easiest. They acted like I wasn't there.

After hanging back in the shadows for a few weeks, I willed myself to do something to try to fit in. I asked my mom to take me to the mall on Saturday and buy me a pair of ultra-skinny lean-fit leggings—the kind all the girls were wearing. I figured if I wore what they wore, maybe I'd blend in better.

The next Tuesday, before math class, Anabelle, a girl I barely knew, stopped me in the hallway.

"Destiny," she said.

"Yes?" I replied, trying to conceal my shock. How did she even know my name?

"That's way, way too tight on you, girl!" she said, an impish grin spreading across her face. Several girls who were standing beside her cracked up.

"Yeah, like, as if everything you wear fits you perfect and looks so great on you, big girl!" I snapped back almost instantly.

Everyone was stunned, including me.

"It speaks!" a girl named Allison called out after what felt like forever. Everyone laughed.

"Oooh, Destiny! A little touchy, aren't we?" Anabelle added.

Everyone shook their heads as if I'd committed some sort of violent crime.

"Did you hear her?" said a girl named Erica. "She's so mean."

"Yeah, sooo sarcastic," said another.

"Downright nasty," Allison declared, as she spun on her heels. "Let's go, girls."

Alone in the bathroom, as I gripped the sink to steady myself, I realized my hands were trembling. I couldn't believe what had just happened. Who was that? Was it even me? An angry voice had sprung out from somewhere deep inside of me. I knew why I'd reacted. What Anabelle said had cut deep. I wasn't fat but I was a good deal bigger than most of the other girls in the class. Momma said I was an early bloomer. Anabelle's comment really hurt, but the voice from inside me was way worse. It scared me. Where did it come from?

I realized right away that I'd overreacted, and I promised myself I would never speak out like that again. That morning I withdrew into my shell—and stayed there for years—until eighth grade, when I finally figured a few things out with the help of one of Momma's friends.

Momma and I were super close. She and my dad got divorced when

I was five and soon after that he moved out West, so I hardly ever saw him. But Momma was always there for me. We watched movies together, went shopping, even played dress-up—and charades when her adult friends were over for dinner. We did everything together.

Everyone says middle school is the worst. But seventh grade wasn't all that bad for me. It was no different from grade school, really. I didn't become a target or someone's punching bag. No one teased or bullied me. I just didn't factor into people's lives at all.

I was the same awkward, quiet girl I'd been in fifth and sixth grades. I'd grown taller, and I wasn't bad-looking, I guess. And I'd filled out a lot, so I was no longer a knock-kneed little girl. But I was still super shy and quiet.

Everyone around me at school was so amped up. They all liked to hug and kiss and fall all over one another when they met up. That kind of behavior didn't come naturally for me. In fact, it made me feel even more uncomfortable. So I steered clear of after-school clubs and other activities. And I wasn't into sports at all. I'd just go home when school was out and do my homework right away. When Momma got home, we'd cook dinner together and then watch a show, if neither of us had any work to do.

I could tell Momma worried about me, and she occasionally straight up asked me if I'd made any friends. But I'd always say, "Momma, you're my bestie. You are all I need." And she'd smile and hug me and drop the issue.

But when I went into eighth grade, Momma started asking me more regularly if I'd met anyone I liked at school and if I wanted to have a friend over or host a party to get to know other kids better. She was clearly worried about me. And Momma was certainly not known for her subtlety. One night, as we were washing the dishes after dinner, she launched in.

"When I was sixteen, your grandma taught me a song I'll never forget, about a teenager who felt invisible. Just like I did back then and I believe you do now, baby girl."

"Momma," I said, "that's gotta be like a hundred million years ago."

"Do I look like a dinosaur to you, young lady?" she shot back.

"No, ma'am." .

"People don't change all that much, and the song is still quite relevant today," she said.

We looked it up on *Wikipedia*. "At Seventeen" was written by Janis Ian in 1975. Then we listened to it together on YouTube. The song really moved me. A few of the lyrics stood out, like the couplet "I learned the truth at seventeen / That love was meant for beauty queens." In other words, while the cool kids experienced love and social affirmation, kids like me were totally ghosted.

The way I interpreted the song, the "pretty" or popular girls, who were confident and easygoing, had lots of friends and boyfriends and plenty of fun. They got the most out of school social life. Whereas people like me and the song's narrator "disappeared" or got "disincluded." I didn't have a "ravaged" face like the narrator, as the song goes on to say, but I definitely lacked "social grace" and "remained at home."

"I get it, Momma," I said. "I really do. But I don't really know what to do about it."

"Well, baby girl," Momma said, "I think you oughta try to get out there more."

"Okay, Momma," I said. "I'll try."

But I didn't. In fact, things only got worse over the next month. For the first two weeks of eighth grade, I'd kept to myself. That was how I liked it—safe. But with Momma pressuring me, I decided to make an effort. One day at recess I walked over to a group of kids and stood there. They were all talking excitedly about some party they'd been to and totally ignored me. At one point a girl walked straight toward me and looked me in the eye. I smiled and said hi. But she just looked right through me. Then she walked past me toward the water fountain. I felt like such a nothing.

I know now that it's not uncommon for kids to become quieter and turn inward when they enter eighth grade. But I was much more extreme. I had always kept to myself. But now I started to retreat from the few healthy relationships I had developed over the years—with my grandma, my aunts, and most importantly with Momma. I became a porcupine—quills extended—ready to pierce anyone who drew near. I couldn't relate to anyone. I had no self-confidence or self-worth. Pretty soon everything Momma said or did to try to make me feel better became unbearably irritating.

When I look back on those days, I realize Momma must have felt incredibly lonely too. We had always been so close. I was her only child, and I no longer did anything with her. I stopped cleaning my room and avoided all the chores we used to do together. I now spent most of my time in my room listening to dark music and feeling sad and alienated. I withdrew into a dark mental cave. Every time I tried to open up to her—I just couldn't find the words. I was too deep at the back of the cave.

I could sense that Momma was getting more and more worried.

One Friday night, while I was sitting on the couch watching a show, Momma tried to snuggle up to me like we always had.

"How's school going, baby girl?"

I winced and pulled away abruptly.

"Huh—okay. Why do you ask?" I said.

"Have you made any new friends?" she pressed.

"No. I don't like anyone there," I said. "And I really wish you'd stop hassling me about that. Cuz I don't care—anyway."

Momma was shocked. I'd never talked to her like that before—ever. After a near unbearable silence, she started to say something. But she held back for some reason. I could tell she was disappointed and hurt, but I didn't care. I felt so angry. I stomped off to my room and slammed the door behind me. Then I cried and cried.

Momma stopped pressing me about my nonexistent social life. But one day, a few weeks later, she opened my bedroom door and called out.

"Destiny, I want you to meet my friend Carole Johnson. She's the varsity girls' track coach at Kennedy High." Kennedy High School was where my mom taught math.

"Why?" I asked defiantly.

"She'll be over for dinner on Thursday," she replied.

## ON THE RIGHT TRACK

Mrs. Johnson was tall, beautiful, and athletic. She towered over me and Momma. She also had a dazzling smile and kind eyes. I'd looked her up online. She was a former nationally ranked four-hundred-meter hurdling champion. A two-time North Carolina State All-American track star.

"Your mom tells me you've had a bit of a rough time fitting in at New County Middle School."

"Yes, ma'am."

"My middle-school days were no fun either," she confided. "I didn't have any friends, Destiny, and I felt really alone. Also, I had a really bad skin condition in eighth and ninth grades. My face would break out often. That made me really self-conscious. I tried to make myself invisible, and I didn't feel I was worthy of anyone's attention or love."

"When did things turn around for you, Carole?" Momma asked.

"Well, if I hadn't tried out for soccer in tenth grade, I don't know if I would have ever made any friends in high school at all. I didn't connect with any of the other girls on the soccer team. I always felt really uncomfortable in groups. And the whole locker room thing was a nightmare for a shy, self-conscious kid like me—everyone laughing and talking and carrying on, and me tucked away in a corner getting dressed as quickly as I could and dashing out the door.

"One day during soccer practice I saw a man standing on the far sideline. Every time I looked over, he was staring straight at me. I felt flattered because no one ever noticed me. I had begun to believe I was invisible. But I also felt a little weird too.

"After practice the man approached me.

"'Hi. You're Carole, right?'

"'Yes.'

"'Coach Karl. I'm the track coach here.'

"'Hi, Coach.'

"'I've been watching you, Carole. You have great acceleration. Have you ever thought of running track?'

"'No. I—'

"'Would you like to try out?'

"'Okay.'"

"After I joined the track team, things really started to shift for me. The girls I trained with on the team were a lot like me: quiet, serious, competitive, focused. We got along well because we were so different from the other high-school girls. None of us liked contact sports. We were basically a group of misfits. All loner types. Growing up, I'd always felt physically awkward. I didn't like all the touching and hugging and high-fiving that went on at school. I just didn't like people getting all up in my space.

"But as I trained at track, I got better and better, and I gained a lot of body confidence. Coach Karl worked with me a lot. 'You have great speed, Carole,' he told me, 'but you're a slow starter. We have to work on your explosiveness off the block.'

"We worked on strength and conditioning, and I learned a lot about technique. But the lynchpin for me was when he taught me how to tap into my imagination. You see, I had a really vivid imagination. I was good at picturing things and drawing them. He told me to use that ability to visualize what I wanted to do and then to talk myself through doing it step by step. He called it 'inside talk.' Whenever I started to feel a surge of self-doubt, he said, I could talk myself into a feeling of strength."

"I wish I could do that," I said.

"Well, you can, Destiny," Mrs. Johnson replied. "It just takes a little time, focus, and practice. For me, the change happened within three or four months," she continued. "Coach Karl had confidence in me, and he taught me how to develop it inside me. I learned to talk myself into a state of strength and poise. Once I was able to do that, I got better and better until I could pretty much explode off the block.

"I won in the four-hundred-meter hurdle for my age category at our third meet that spring. As a team, we all bonded, and we performed really well in all competitions. We ended up winning the state championship in my senior year. But more importantly, those girls quickly became my best friends. They made high school not just survivable but bearable, and sometimes even fun."

Momma got up and went into the kitchen.

"I kinda feel the same way you did," I confided. "I want to have friends but I also just like to keep to myself."

"Your mom tells me you are super well-organized and conscientious," Mrs. Johnson said, as we shifted from the living room and sat down at the dinner table.

"I guess so," I mumbled.

"We have an opening for a coach's assistant right now, and I could use some help making sure things run smoothly on the team."

"But I don't run," I replied. "I don't play any sports at all."

"That's okay," she said. "You'd be in charge of practice schedules and equipment and be my righthand gal at practices and meets. And you'd even get to travel with us on the team bus to away meets too."

It sounded fun and exciting, but a bit scary too. Mrs. Johnson had this way of making you feel okay about yourself, that you were needed and could be useful. I'd felt instantly at ease with her, which almost never happened to me. "But what about the girls on her team?" I thought. "They were high-school athletes—popular, successful alpha females. How would they treat a mousy girl like me? Would they accept me? Be mean or bossy? Or worse, just ignore me like everyone else did?"

I just wasn't sure.

"Why don't you think about it over the weekend, Destiny," she said. "Talk it over with your mom," she added, sensing my hesitation.

"Okay."

"Just to be clear: it's a volunteer position, but you do get a Kennedy High track suit and sneakers, which you can keep when the season is over."

"Thank you, Mrs. Johnson."

"Good, Destiny. Let me know early next week. And you can call me Coach Carole."

Momma didn't say a word either way. She left it entirely up to me. In the end, that's probably why I decided to give it a try, because she let me be—and because I really, really liked Coach Carole.

## MY FIRST PRACTICE

Coach Carole moved into the middle of the circle that formed around her.

"Okay, girls," she called out, "let's get started."

Everyone got quiet and lay down on the grass. I had headed out onto the track to space out the hurdles, and I turned to see what was going on.

"Hey, Destiny," Coach said. "Come and join us. This is how we start every practice. You might as well get used to it since you are a part of the team now."

I walked over and lay down. But my mind kept turning, thinking. I wondered how weird I must look just lying there.

"Okay, everyone. Deep breath in, long breath out. Feel your shoulders melt into the ground."

I tried to do what she said, but I felt kind of awkward, so I opened my eyes and looked about. Everyone else was lying still, eyes closed, totally focused. I wondered why it was so hard for me to simply relax like they did. I closed my eyes again and took a deep breath. As I breathed in and settled down, I could feel my body sinking into the ground. My shoulders softened and my back and hips melted into the grass. I could feel my heels and feet softening, too, and getting heavier.

"Okay, guys. Now visualize all the people who tell you that you can't do something. Let's hear those voices."

"You got no time to be doing this, girl!" someone called out.

"Why are you even' tryin' that? You're not that good," said another.

"We just don't see you anymore! Why you spending so much time with the track team?" says a third.

"Good. Good," Coach Carole said. "Now what are your inside voices saying, girls?"

"Maybe they're right!"

"What if it's true?"

"I can't do this. It's too hard."

"I'm not good enough."

"Good," Coach said. "All right, everyone. You can't change what comes at you in life," she called out.

"But you can change what you do with it!" everyone replied in unison.

"What do you say to all this self-doubt, girls? What are your inside words? Say them loud. Say them bold."

Everyone was sitting up now and clapping. I got up too.

"I can do this. I'm okay," one girl said.

"Push through it, girl," said another.

"I can beat this," exclaimed a third.

We all stood up, laughing, calling out and high-fiving each other. It was so energizing.

"They're not right."

"I am good enough."

"I'm strong."

"I can do anything."

"I'm me and that's okay."

A couple of days later, at practice, I overheard some of the sprinters talking about movie night.

"Can you make it?" one was asking.

"Definitely!" the other two replied.

A little later I asked Chiara, a kind, quiet junior who ran the five thousand, what movie night was.

"Everyone goes over to Coach's house and we make dinner and watch a movie together," she said. "We get to blow off some steam and just relax and hang out together."

On Friday, as I was putting all the equipment away, the two senior captains came up to me.

"Hey, Destiny."

"Hi, guys," I responded shyly.

"You about ready?"

"For what?" I asked.

"Movie night, girl!"

"Oh, I didn't know I was invited to that."

"You're our assistant coach, aren't you?"

"Yes."

"That makes you an integral part of the team, Dee. See you at Coach's at 7:30. Don't be late!"

I smiled and nodded. But inside I felt awesome. I was one of them. That's what they'd said.

After I'd been working as Coach Carole's assistant for a month, I felt different. I wasn't as scared or insecure at school. After all, the girls on the team liked me and talked to me. And they were high-schoolers!

## PASSING THE BATON

It's not like my nervousness at school disappeared, but my social anxiety didn't overwhelm me like before. And if I started to feel bad—like I sometimes did at lunch when everyone was talking and laughing in groups and I had no one to sit with—I applied the technique we used at practice and it totally calmed me down. I'd take three deep belly breaths and then repeat to myself several times, "I am here. I am enough," and I felt a whole lot better.

It even worked for public speaking, which I'd always hated. When I had to recite a monologue in English class, I panicked—like I always did. But before my turn, I did the breathing and inside talk. I did it twice. And I felt so much better that I presented my monologue, from start to finish, without stopping once or messing up a single line.

A few days later at recess, I walked toward the swing set where a few girls were gathered. When I realized all the swings were taken, I started to turn away.

"Hi, Destiny!"

It was Tianna, a friendly, animated girl who I barely knew and had never spoken to.

"Hello," I answered hesitantly.

"You want my swing? I'm done," she said.

"Thank you!"

She smiled and passed it to me.

"See ya later."

For anyone else, this brief exchange would have meant nothing. For me it was huge. A first. An affirmation. Someone in my class acknowledging my existence and being kind to me.

A week later I spotted Tianna talking heatedly with three other girls by the playground fence.

"That's not true at all, Allison," Tianna cried out. "We always do it your way. I'm so done with this." She stalked off, leaving her three friends staring after her and shaking their heads.

When I turned the corner, I found Tianna sitting on a bench, her shoulders still shaking. I sat beside her but said nothing. After a minute of silence, she let out a loud sigh.

"I just don't get it," she said. "I've got things to say too."

"Isn't that so annoying?" I said.

"Yeah, it's more than just annoying," Tianna replied. "It happens every time. And Allison always has to get her way. We always have to do what she wants."

"She's the super-bossy type, isn't she?" I said.

"Does it even matter what I say?" Tianna added. "They don't even listen and—and I end up shouting. And why do I even do that? It's embarrassing."

"Well, you shout because they're not listening," I said. "I get that."

I really wanted to help Tianna. She was the only kid who actually acknowledged me in school. If it weren't for her, I'd be totally invisible. "Should I risk it?" I wondered. "Should I tell her what I'd learned from Coach Carole about 'inside talk'? Would she think I was a total freak? What if—"

"It's just not working," Tianna said, interrupting my inner monologue. I decided to go all in.

"You know—uh . . . so my mom is friends with Coach Johnson, the track coach at Kennedy High, and I'm an assistant coach."

"Really? That's cool," Tianna said.

"She taught all the girls on the team this thing she calls 'inside talk.'"

"What's that?"

"We take three breaths deep down into our bellies," I said. "That helps us relax. Then we take whatever's bugging us and talk to it."

"No way," Tianna said, breaking into laughter. "You talk to it?"

"Yeah. You label your fears. Say them out loud. Then you kinda have a pep talk with yourself. Some of the girls shout out, 'I'm me, and that's okay,' or 'I can do anything.'"

"Does it work for you?" she asked.

"It kinda does, actually. I used to be super shy. Now I just don't feel that way as much."

"I wondered what was going on with you," she said. "You seem different lately. Is that what you've been doing?"

"Yeah," I said. "I mean, sometimes I forget. But it's been helping me more and more. I just don't feel sad as much anymore, or as left out."

"Cool. What would I say to myself?"

"Well, don't forget the first thing you've gotta do is the breathing right down into your belly. I know that sounds kinda strange, but you do it. And then once you are a little more relaxed, you could say something to the part of you that gets so mad."

"Well, what would I say?" Tianna asked.

"Maybe you could try 'Not now. Later. I'm not doing this now. Later, when I've calmed down.' And that's when you respond to Chloe or whoever. That's when you make your point, when you aren't caught up in the emotion of it."

"How do you even know all of this, Destiny?"

"Some of the girls on the track team argued a lot," I told her. "Coach Carole taught us that breathing deep when you are upset and talking to yourself can help you put the brakes on all of that emotional stuff. You delay saying what you want until later, when you can say it properly, without getting mad."

On Friday afternoon, as I walked out of school, I spotted Tianna talking to Allison and the others on the front steps. As I walked past, she broke away from them to join me.

"Oh my god, Destiny," she said, almost out of breath. "You are not going to believe this. I tried your 'inside talk' thing at lunch. I just breathed deeply and told myself, 'Not now. Later,' over and over. Even though Allison tried to map out our entire weekend, I didn't say a word."

I smiled and nodded. Tianna kept talking.

"So just now I said to everyone, 'Why do we have to go to the mall all day again tomorrow? We always do that. Let's go down to Beaver Park instead.' And they actually listened to me, Destiny. Even Chloe! Then Nancy suggested we go to the mall for a little while in the morning and then to Beaver Park and then to Eliza's place after that to make brownies with her mom. And we all agreed, because Eliza's mom makes the best brownies ever."

"I told you it works," I said. "It worked for me."

"But this has never, ever happened before. And, like, I didn't even come up with the idea of going to Eliza's place. But it was my idea not to go to the mall all day, because that gets so boring. This all happened because of the inside talk, Destiny. If I had said that at lunch when I was mad, no one would have listened to me. It totally, totally works."

"I'm so glad for you."

"I gotta go, Destiny," she said, as she gave me a quick hug and jumped on her bus. I smiled and waved and then got on mine. I was glad that the inner-talk exercise had worked so well for Tianna. It was certainly working for me. I didn't feel that lonely anymore, and having someone like Tianna to touch base with throughout the day really helped.

On Monday I was walking through the cafeteria, from my table in the back, when I heard my name called out. "Destiny! Destiny!" Tianna waved me over. She was sitting with her friends.

"Hey, how are you?"

"Good," I said, setting my tray down on the edge of the table for a second.

"That's a really cool badge you got on your backpack, girl!" Tianna said.

"Thanks. I got it when I went on a march with my mom," I replied.

"You went to a rally with your mom?" Eliza said.

"Yeah. We do that sometimes. She's pretty passionate about causes, like gun violence and women's rights."

"That's so cool," Allison added. "I went on a march with my mom once and got a T-shirt."

"They gave us T-shirts too," I said. "With the same design as the badge."

"Sweet!" Allison said. "You wear yours tomorrow and I'll wear mine."

"Okay," I said. "I will."

Just then the bell rang and everyone went to class.

As I got up, I began to realize how many things were changing for me. Discovering inside talk has allowed me to be less shy and yet still myself—no longer worried about being too quiet. Because I have friends who like me just the way I am. I'm me, and that's okay.

---

This story was about . . .

- Being okay about being a quiet person
- Realizing that your inner voice has power
- Learning to let your inner beauty shine
- Finding your place in the outside world with quiet confidence

Destiny overcame her shyness and developed self-confidence when she learned to listen more carefully to her inner voice.

# 11

---

# STOP PUSHING
# ME AROUND

## *Michael's Story*

Physically bullied kids often get told things like "Ignore it" or "Just walk away." This is not exactly *bad* advice, but it is most certainly incomplete. First, if they try either of these strategies and are unable to disguise their frustration or fear, bullies will sense weakness and respond by following their target or escalating their taunts. Second, by the time parents learn what's going on and make such suggestions, many kids have already tried one or both these tactics unsuccessfully, in which case the adult giving such advice loses all credibility.

In this powerful, unsettling story, Michael tries both. He also tries a third common suggestion: "Fight back." The nostalgic image of kids duking it out, and later shaking hands and patting each other on the back, comes to mind. But that rarely happens. More typically, the targeted kids get beaten up or, if they are lucky enough to overpower their tormentor(s), they become the targets of other, bigger kids who want to challenge the unlikely victors. What's more, bullied kids who fight back are also often the ones who end up getting into trouble for fighting, even if they were just trying to fend off their aggressors.

## POINTS OF UNDERSTANDING

- Almost all physical bullying is triggered by strong reaction to verbal taunting.
- Being picked on physically can be scary and embarrassing, and leave you feeling isolated and ill-tempered, even with your own family.
- Interfering with your property is just one more way that kids who bully try to control you.
- Fighting back often leads to more and more aggression.
- It's often the child who retaliates who is "caught" and gets into trouble.
- It's not *if* you walk away but *how* you walk away that counts.

## POINTS OF HOPE AND LEARNING

- There are specific ways you can de-escalate a situation that is moving toward physical violence.
- You are not alone in being subjected to cruel and aggressive behavior.
- There are ways you can deflect taunts and hostile action from others.
- There is really no need to defend your *space*. It is yours and it moves with you.
- If you walk away calmly and with confidence, the kids bullying you will often lose interest in following you.

It's important to support a child who is the target of physical aggression because they are likely feeling hopeless and scared. But often the advice given to kids faced with physical bullying sounds out of touch to them, and when followed, makes things worse.

However, if we provide the right kind of support—based on the reality they face on a day-to-day basis—and the proper social tools, they can learn to stand strong and de-escalate a situation where bullying has become physical. What's more, they will gain confidence and their social life can start to improve.

———————

*My name is Michael. I'm nineteen. I live in Pittsburgh, Pennsylvania, where I work in my dad's landscaping business and attend community college. I am studying biology because I want to major in ethology, which is the study of animal behavior. Observing how animals interact has taught me a lot about how people behave. It's helped me understand what happened to me in grade school, which I'd like to share with all of you elementary- and middle-schoolers out there. I hope you can learn from what happened to me and avoid becoming targets of taunting, teasing, and physical bullying.*

*People say the middle-school years can be really hard for kids. But that's not always the case. I did okay in sixth, seventh, and eighth grades. My problems actually started earlier—at the beginning of fifth grade, when I'd just turned ten. I didn't know anyone that well. And early on I got into trouble with some boys in my class, who taunted and bullied me regularly.*

It's hard for me to pinpoint exactly when things went wrong that fall. But what sticks out in my mind is a windy Tuesday in early October when a bunch of us were playing soccer at recess, out in the park near school. That's when I had my first serious run-in with five kids I nicknamed the Wolf Pack. There was Big Jacob, the silver-backed alpha wolf, and then Ezra, Arlo, Damian, and Quinn, who were smaller and less intimidating but could be just as fierce and nasty.

I was tall, skinny, and a bit awkward back then, but I wasn't a weakling or a nerd. I was friendly and clever, and a bit hot-tempered too. I liked to play sports, and I was a pretty good dribbler. In the middle of our game, I faked out two kids and sprinted toward the goal. Then suddenly, when I was about to score, I went down, tackled really hard from behind.

"You didn't even go for the ball," I yelled as I got up. "Why'd you do that?"

"Come on! I barely touched you," Damian said. "Stop being such a baby."

"That's a total lie," I shot back, taking a step toward him.

"What's up?" said Jacob, stepping between us. He was the biggest kid in fifth grade. In fact, he was bigger than almost all the sixth graders too.

"I'm done," I said. "I'm not playing anymore."

As I hobbled off toward the school building, I heard a strange animal sound: it was one I would come to know well in the months that followed. I guess you could characterize it as half snarl, half laugh—the kind of sound a wolf might make as it eyes its cornered prey before the pounce. I shudder when I recall that sound, even though it's been nine years since I heard it last.

Later that day I got into trouble with Ezra and Arlo, the two other members of the Wolf Pack who had played in the soccer game at recess. We were at gym, doing basketball drills. Coach Taveras instructed us to form two lines to shoot layups.

Ezra stood in front of me. As I awaited my turn, he lurched back into me, sending me stumbling backward into Arlo.

"Hey, what's your problem?" Arlo cried, shoving me forward straight into Ezra.

"Yo, dude!" Ezra cried, as I crashed into him. "Why'd you do that?"

"What's going on, boys?" Coach Taveras called out from center court.

"I dunno, Coach T.," Arlo said. "Michael's acting like a total spaz. He just shoved me for no reason!"

"And me too!" Ezra claimed.

"Michael," Coach Taveras said, "why don't you take a br—"

"But I—"

"Take a two-minute break, Michael. Now!"

It was clear from Coach T.'s tone that it would be utterly useless to try to convince him of the truth—that my teammates had staged this fake "shoving" incident and that I was 100 percent innocent.

Those two encounters with the Wolf Pack—at recess and gym—were not my first. They'd teased and pestered me before. They preyed on several kids in our class to one extent or another in the first few weeks of school. But that day, things with Jacob, Damian, Ezra, Quinn, and Arlo definitely took a turn for the worse—and then just kept snowballing from there.

## EASY PREY

Over the next few months, I spent many a night lying in bed, going over in microscopic detail what the Wolf Pack had done to me that day and wondering, "Why are they doing this to me?" But nothing became any clearer. I couldn't figure out why they kept pushing, shoving, and insulting me. It made no sense, and it wasn't fair. I'd done nothing to provoke this kind of treatment.

Pretty soon there wasn't a single place in school where I felt safe. The Wolf Pack got to me everywhere: in bathrooms and hallways, at recess and during lunch. And they never hunted alone. There were always two or more of them when they attacked. A shove here, a trip there. One time I opened my math textbook and found dozens of gum-glued pages. And they snuck stuff straight out of my book bag. Like my sneakers: they disappeared one day before gym, which I had to miss, and then reappeared later in the day on the locker room floor twisted up and knotted together. It was endless.

One Friday night, when I was at my wit's end, I explained everything that was happening at school to my cousin Tommy, who slept over at my house whenever my uncle and aunt went away for the weekend. We got along really well. Tommy was three years older than me and really cool. I knew whatever I told him would stay between us. He listened carefully as I described what was going on.

"The key is to ignore them," Tommy said. "If you do that, they'll lose interest and move on to something or someone else. The next time they come at you, ignore them. And if they keep bugging you, just walk away. If you're not there, they can't do anything to you."

I decided to test out that strategy the next time the Wolf Pack came after me. Walking away seemed like sound advice. Until now, I'd always gotten all worked up when they did stuff to me and lashed out. But that clearly didn't work. They just fed off my anger and things escalated. Maybe Tommy was right.

On Monday, Quinn pushed me as I passed him in the hallway. He bounced me up against some lockers, but I didn't say a word. I acted like nothing had happened and just walked away, like Tommy suggested. But I was really anxious, and Quinn and the others must have smelled my fear because they didn't let it go at that. Jacob, Arlo, and Quinn trailed behind me and, when I ducked into a nearby bathroom, they followed me in. Jacob grabbed me and shoved me toward one of the stalls. As I stumbled forward, I tripped. I was on my knees now. The stall door swung open. Then I felt pressure on the back of my neck. It was Jacob's forearm. He locked my arms behind my back and shoved my head closer and closer to the toilet bowl.

"You thirsty?" he snarled.

Quinn and Arlo snickered.

"Cut it out, man," I pleaded.

"It ain't Evian or Poland Springs," he said, pushing until my mouth was barely an inch from the toilet water. "But it'll quench your thirst."

Just then the door swung open and five sixth graders piled in.

"Yo! Chill, chill," one of them called out.

"Yeah, get outta here—all of you," said another.

"Aight, dude," Jacob replied casually, as if all he'd been doing was washing his hands. "Catch you guys later, man."

## ROCK BOTTOM

I learned that day that how you leave really matters. If you walk away confident, things may work out in your favor. But if you are just trying to escape, they'll sense it and come after you. Bullies can smell your fear. And when they do, they'll stalk you. Because there's nothing they enjoy more than a hunt.

A few days after the bathroom attack, the Wolf Pack was nipping at my heels again. Arlo pushed me in the hallway. And though I tried to play it cool, Ezra opened up my book bag and dumped out all my stuff.

"Stop it!" I yelled.

"Stop it," Arlo mocked as he grabbed my Spanish workbook and flipped it to Jacob, who immediately tossed it to Ezra.

"Give it back!"

"Come and get it," Ezra goaded.

I rushed him to grab it, but he crouched down and slid it right past me along the hallway floor. Damian scooped it up.

"He shoots. He scores!" he called out, as it sank into a garbage can a few feet behind him. The bell rang, and in an instant they were gone. I walked over to the trash can and fished out my now grimy, wet workbook. Then I walked over to a Teachers Only bathroom, entered, locked the door behind me, and cried.

Life at school was lousy, and things at home weren't all that great either. I was grumpy and distracted. Mom noticed and started asking questions. She claimed I'd started bossing my little sister and brother, Jemma and Ty, around a lot. Jem must have told on me. Ty wouldn't. I know that much.

"What's going on, Mikey?" Mom asked. "Why are you such a grouch?"

"What do you mean, Mom?" I replied.

"Why did you take Jemma's jacket? She says she can't find it anywhere."

"Well, maybe she could leave me alone—stop following me around and coming into my room uninvited—"

"Mikey, you can't be mean to your sister. That's just not how we treat one another in this family."

"Mom," I yelled, "why are you picking on me?" I ran out of the kitchen and up the stairs to my room and slammed the door.

I called Tommy that night and told him how bad things had gotten at school; how I'd tried to ignore Jacob and the others—and walk away—but they'd come after me anyway.

"I wish I could show up at your school," Tommy said. "Even just for one day. I'd sort out all those morons good, and they'd never come at you again, Mikey!"

"Thanks, Tommy. I appreciate that. Sometimes I think I should just go tell Mom and Dad what's going on."

"No, dude! You don't want to do that. They'll just go nuts. Call the school. Set up meetings with everyone's parents. There'll be hella trouble and you'll end up the most hated kid in school."

"I know, I know," I said. "I just wish I knew what to do, Tommy."

"At this point, I think you gotta fight back, Mikey. You gotta stand up to them."

"You think so?" I asked.

"Ignoring them didn't work," he said. "Walking away didn't either. If you fight back, maybe they'll see that you can't be pushed around that easily and just leave you alone. Kids like them like to bully kids they don't think will do anything about it. If you fight back hard, they may just cut their losses and move on to an easier target."

"How do I do that?" I asked.

"I don't know. Just fight, dude. Just fight!"

The whole idea made my stomach hurt. I didn't even know how to throw a punch!

I got a chance to stand up for myself sooner than I'd thought. On Monday after lunch, as Damian and Ezra walked past me in the main hallway, Damian knocked into me hard with his right shoulder.

Instead of confronting him or pretending it didn't happen, I squared up and shoved him into the wall.

"Whoa. What's up?" he said.

"Try that again, I dare you," I replied.

He stepped toward me menacingly. I grabbed his left arm and pushed him again—hard. Then I lost my balance and fell into him.

"Hey! What's going on there?" Miss Jensen, the third-grade teacher, called out.

"Nothing, ma'am," I said, covering for all of us. "I just bumped into Damian by accident."

"Okay. Well . . . you kids get to your next class right now," she said.

"Sorry about that, Damian," I said, looking him right in the eye.

"No worries," he replied.

As we walked away, I overheard Ezra saying, "Dude, Michael's got a little spunk in him."

"Nothin' we can't stamp out," Damian replied.

"Oh, you know it, D.," Ezra said, high-fiving him. "It's on now, dude. It's totally on!"

What I'd just heard—two members of the Wolf Pack threatening revenge—should have made me nervous, but it didn't. I was too excited about what had just happened. I'd stood up for myself, big time. I fought back. The look on Damian's face as he fell backward and onto the floor underneath me, stayed with me for the rest of the school day: shock mixed with fear. I'd sent the Wolf Pack a clear message: "You can come after me, but it ain't gonna be easy. Michael isn't gonna roll over anymore. Push me, you'll get it back—twice as hard."

## WHAT GOES AROUND COMES AROUND

Later that day, as school let out, I looked around nervously. My excitement had abated. I'd had time to consider the consequences of my actions—and the odds, which were not at all in my favor. After all, there was only one me, and they were five—including Jacob, who could be counted twice because he was so much bigger than the rest of us. So really it was six on one!

But when I got outside there was no sign of the Wolf Pack. It was safe to leave. "Maybe Tommy was right," I thought. "Maybe standing up to them and fighting back really worked." I smiled to myself as I walked through the school gates and down the street.

"Hey, loser!" Arlo called out.

"You fight like a girl," Ezra hissed.

The two of them had suddenly popped out from behind a parked school bus. Ezra shoved me in the chest as Arlo circled behind me. I stumbled backward, then steadied myself. Arlo grabbed my book bag and tugged at it. I tried to shake it free, but he held firm.

I wasn't scared at all. Just mad. Fighting mad! I let my bag slip off my right shoulder, catching Arlo off guard. For a split second he let go. I swung it around as fast as I could, and—*thwack*—the bag slammed into Ezra's head, full speed. Ezra crumpled to the pavement.

I was stunned.

So were they.

"You okay, Ezra?" Arlo said, standing over him.

"I think so," he replied in a shaky voice.

I looked up. A second school bus was pulling out. I spotted Jacob and Damian through a window at the back of the bus, their faces pressed up against the glass. Jacob pointed at me, then drew his finger across his throat and scowled. Damian laughed. I gulped as my heart dropped to my boots.

Ezra and Arlo didn't say a word. They just walked away. They hadn't seen their pack mates but I certainly had. And no matter how hard I tried that night, I couldn't erase the image of Jacob from my mind.

After dinner that night, Dad went out to a meeting. Mom and Jemma hunkered down in the kitchen to work on a beaver drawing for her third-grade animal presentation and Ty wandered around aimlessly, as he often did. He ended up in my room playing with my LEGO.

"What are you doing here?" I said when I entered my room.

"Playing," Ty replied.

"Did I say you could come into my room?"

"You always let me."

"Didn't give you permission."

He looked puzzled. Little Ty was my guy. I loved playing with him. I took care of him. He was my baby bro.

"Get out!" I screamed.

"I don't wanna go. I'm doing LEGO."

I walked up to him and grabbed him by the shirt.

"Stop it, Mikey," he cried. "You're hurting me."

I don't know what came over me. I've always been so protective of my little brother, but I had so much anger inside me. I dragged him out of my room and shoved him. Then I shut my door and locked it. I could hear him crying outside my door for a minute or two. Then there was silence.

A few minutes later there was a knock on my door.

"Michael," Mom said, "we need to talk! Open this door."

"I don't want to talk."

"Why did you kick Ty out of your room?"

"It's my room."

"I don't understand what's going on with you, young man, but I'm not going to stand for this. Your father and I are going to have to talk about this."

Mom was angry, and I knew Dad would not be happy either. But there wasn't much I could do. All I could think about was what Jacob and the rest of the Wolf Pack would do to me at school the next day. I replayed the day's events over and over in my head. How I'd pushed back when provoked in the hallway and then fought back after school. I'd done exactly what my cousin Tommy told me to do. At the time, it had felt great. But now my stomach was churning and my mouth was dry. I barely slept that night.

In the morning, my mom appeared at my bedside.

"Are you okay, Mikey? It's almost time to go."

"I don't feel that great."

Mom felt my forehead. "You don't have a fever, dear."

"Can I stay home, though?"

"Honey, you have a math test today, remember? You can't miss that. Look—if you don't feel well when you are at school, call me and I'll pick you up if I can. But I don't want you to miss your test."

"Okay, Mom," I said, conceding defeat. I couldn't bring myself to tell her why I didn't want to go. It would trigger way too many questions.

When I walked into school I felt a weird vibe everywhere. Everyone seemed to be staring at me. As I passed the main staircase I saw Jacob, surrounded by his boys. He pointed to me, then bent over and whispered something to Quinn and Damian, who got up and lumbered toward me.

"Jacob wants to see you out back behind the portables," Quinn said.

"At lunchtime," Damian added.

"What for?" I asked.

"You better be there," Quinn replied.

"Otherwise we'll come get you," Damian said. "Remember, there's nowhere you can hide that we won't find you, tough guy."

The lunch bell rang. I got up slowly from my desk and placed my completed math test face down on Miss Hemshaw's desk. As I walked to the door, a thousand thoughts hit me at once: "Should I run to the bathroom and hide? Or find some nook in the basement? Should I go to the nurse's office? Or call my mom and ask her to pick me up?" It's not like I could ask any of my classmates to help me. All the other kids in fifth grade had backed off. No one dared hang out with me in case the Wolf Pack turned on them.

But none of my escape routes worked out, because as soon as I exited the classroom I spotted two wolves to the right and two to the left. Quinn and Ezra with a guttural growl; Arlo and Damian with that familiar smiling snarl.

"Okay," Arlo said, "let's go."

I felt powerless. I did what I was told. As we walked slowly down the whole length of the corridor, I felt everyone's eyes on me. Everyone watching. It was like I was in a trance. Everything was happening in slow motion. It was the longest walk of my life.

I was almost blinded by sunlight when the doors swung open before me. Across the broken black tarmac we went, predators and prey. When we turned the corner behind the portables, I saw a chain-link fence at the back of the school grounds that I'd never seen before. I noticed it now because it meant there was nowhere to run.

Jacob was there, his sweater already off, his sleeves rolled up. And he was surrounded. I wondered, "How is it possible there are so many kids here?" Classmates. Kids I didn't even know from other grades. They formed a circle. I got pushed into the middle.

Jacob shoved me hard and I fell to the ground. I looked up at his snarling face. Arlo offered me a hand. I stood up. Down I went again. All I could see when I looked up was Jacob's grinning teeth. I realized I had to do something, so this time when I got up I charged at the Wolf Boss and headbutted him clean in the stomach. We both fell down and rolled apart. When we got up, we looked at each other. I started to put up my fists as he moved in on me. He wasn't laughing or grinning anymore. He was laser focused. Ready for the kill.

Jacob cocked his right hand, but as I flinched and prepared for impact, his left fist, which I never saw coming, smashed into my stomach so hard it lifted me off my feet. He hit me so hard he knocked every ounce of air out of my lungs. I went down gasping, flapping around like a fish on a deck. And all I could hear was laughter.

All the kids who had gathered around us were gawking at me with a mixture of pity and disgust on their faces. I must have looked pathetic because I had no clue about how to fight. I guess the hardest thing was realizing that it wasn't just the Wolf Pack who was enjoying watching me suffer. As they came into focus, I recognized the faces of more and more of my classmates and I realized everyone had enjoyed the show. And now they were all walking away, as I lay there alone, staring at that chain-link fence.

When Mom picked me up after school, I nodded and got in and sat there silently.

"How was your day? Did the math test go okay?"

"Yeah, it did. I'm fine."

I think my mom knew something was up, but she didn't say anything.

Halfway home my mom got a call. I couldn't tell who it was at first, but I figured it must be from the school. It had to be serious because she pulled over into a parking lot, unplugged her cell phone from its charger, and got out of the car.

All I could hear was "Yes. I see. Okay. Thank you, Miss Hemshaw. Yes, I'll do that."

I braced myself. But when she got back into the car all she did was look me over once. It was obvious she wanted to say something, but with Jemma and Ty in the back, she didn't say a word.

When we pulled into our driveway, Mom turned to Jemma. "Jem, can you take Ty into the kitchen for me? I'll be right in to prepare you guys your snacks."

"K, Mom!" Jemma said cheerily.

Then Mom turned to me.

"Mikey, that was your teacher. She told me things haven't been going so well with you of late."

"What do you mean?"

"Well, you've been late on several assignments. You've fallen behind in math, English, and history. And she says there was an incident at school yesterday, in the hallway."

A wave of relief swept over me. Miss Hemshaw didn't know about the real fight with Jacob.

"It wasn't that big of a deal, Mom."

"What do you mean? She says you got into a fight. That you shoved one classmate and punched another!"

"I didn't punch anyone, Mom. That's a total lie. It wasn't that bad!"

"Do you know what I think? I think something is going on at school that you're not telling me about, Michael Hendriks."

"Nothing's going on, Mom!"

"How can you say that to me, Mikey? You've been moping around the house for weeks. You're grumpy and mean to Jemma all the time. You hurt your little brother yesterday, for goodness knows why. And now this?"

The evidence against me was irrefutable. But I just couldn't bring myself to tell her what was going on. I stared at her. Silent.

"This is not like you at all, Mikey," she said. I could tell she was getting really upset.

"Tell me. What's going on at school? Are you being bullied?"

"No, Mom!" I replied, biting my lip, as I opened the passenger door and made my escape.

"Mikey! Come back here," she yelled. "We're not done talking."

But I was already through the front door.

Mom gave Jemma and Ty their snacks and then called me down into the kitchen.

"Mom, can't you just leave me alone? I don't want to talk anymore."

"Miss Hemshaw mentioned the camping trip, Mikey. That's coming up in a few weeks."

"I'm not going," I declared.

"What are you talking about? It's a class trip, honey. Your entire class is going."

"Well, I'm not," I said, fighting back tears. I didn't want my mom to see me cry. That would just trigger more questions and make things ten times worse.

"Can I go now?" I called out, already halfway up the stairs. She couldn't see my face.

"Yes, Mikey. We'll talk about this more later with your father."

"We can talk all you want, Mom, but I'm not going on any damned camping trip."

"Mikey!"

I ran up the stairs and locked myself in my room. About a minute later I heard a knock on my door.

"Mikey? Are you okay?"

I didn't respond. After about a minute I heard her heading back downstairs.

## GOTTA STAND YOUR GROUND

I felt horrible. I never cursed in front of my mom. In fact, I'd hardly ever been rude to her like that. But I was so angry and scared. And my ribs were really sore from Jacob's punch. My heart raced. Eight days in the woods with the Wolf Pack? No way I'd survive that!

I knew my mom meant well, and she had every reason to be worried. But there was no way I could let her know how upset I was. She would just dig and dig and find everything out and then get furious and contact everybody. She'd make things way worse for me. I couldn't bring myself to tell her anything about what was going on at school.

I convinced my mom to let me stay home on Thursday. I told her my throat hurt, and she didn't put up much of a fuss. On Friday I was back at school. To my surprise, no one said anything. I kept to myself and slid into homeroom and sat at my desk. Everyone was milling about, chatting, and getting their books out.

I looked around nervously and spotted Ezra. He walked to the back of the classroom where we stored our stuff and turned and smirked at Jacob and Quinn as he started to take my classmate Kylie's backpack off its hook. But they didn't look up and notice what he was doing. Kylie did, though. She looked right at him and rolled her eyes, and turned around and pulled her books out of her desk and readied herself for class. That stopped Ezra in his tracks. He didn't seem to know how to react to Kylie's disinterest. He pushed her backpack up against the wall, slid it back onto its hook, and retreated sheepishly to his desk. Kids were getting their materials together and settling down. Watching all of this, I realized Kylie knew something about how to deal with the pack that I needed to figure out.

When the bell rang, I walked with her to our next class, in the library.

"I saw what Ezra did with your bag," I said.

"What do you mean?"

"When class was starting," I reminded her.

"Oh, yeah. That," she laughed.

"How did you get him to stop so quickly?"

"Oh, they're just idiots."

"Do they bother you a lot?" I asked.

"They've just been messing with my stuff a little. And sometimes they bump me when they walk by my desk."

"Yeah, me too."

"But I don't really pay much attention to it," she continued. "It started when we got back to school. I used to hang out with Megan— she's my best friend—but she moved away, so I don't have anyone I hang out with. I've been kinda on my own. That's probably why they started in on me. They're just so dumb."

"I know," I said. "They bug me all the time too."

"They did it five or six times in the first few weeks. But every time they try to get to me, I just say 'Whatever.' And now it's only Ezra, and he's just trying to get their attention. But like—whatever. No one thinks it's all that funny. No one really cares. I definitely don't."

As I listened to Kylie, I realized I'd been approaching everything with these guys the wrong way. Her approach—her whole attitude— was amazing because she was so comfortable with herself, comfortable sitting in her own space. Nothing they did could really faze her.

Later, Ezra tried to get to her again. We were getting our lunches out of our backpacks, and everyone was talking at once. Ezra pushed Kylie and laughed. Kylie looked straight in his eyes and, like a princess in some fairy tale, said, "Ezra! If you really want to stand in this space, here, I grant it to you."

And with a graceful flourish she withdrew a few feet away. He just stood there, tongue-tied. Everyone around us smiled. A few kids even chuckled. Ezra changed right before my eyes. He no longer looked like a vicious member of the bloodthirsty Wolf Pack that had been hounding me for the past few weeks. He was now just a kid in my class, standing there alone, not knowing what to do, looking embarrassed and confused.

"Ezra, I need to get my lunch now," Kylie added. "You may leave." And he slunk away without saying a word. Everyone else grabbed their lunches and sat back down. But I stood there stunned. Ezra was a wolf. And without pushing him back or putting up any kind of fight or even raising her voice, she'd just stood her ground and forced him to retreat, tail between his legs. Kylie walked over to her bag, pulled out her lunch, and sat down at her desk.

"That was so cool," I said to her when I'd sat back down at my desk.

"Yeah, pretty good, right?" she replied, smiling. "I think he's done. It doesn't look like Ezra's having much fun bugging me anymore."

She took a big bite out of her egg salad sandwich and chewed thoughtfully.

"I know you've been having a lot of trouble with those guys," she said. "You've just gotta stand your own ground. And if they try to take it, give it to them and walk away. Because when you walk away, you, like, just take your ground with you. You see? You don't have to fight them for every inch, like rabid dogs do."

"Yeah, you're right," I said, laughing nervously. "It's kinda funny you say 'dogs' because I call them the Wolf Pack."

"Exactly! Don't fight over who gets to stand there like an angry wolf. Just stand wherever you want to. Because wherever you are, that's your space, not theirs. That's what I think anyway. They don't own it and they don't own you. Unless you try to fight them for it. If you do that, they are going to win because there's five of them and only one of you. And they are mean. If you fight them, they will win every time. Why would you fight over something that's yours any-way?"

"I don't know why I've been doing that," I said. "But it hasn't worked."

"I know," she replied. "It's been bad, right?"

"Yeah. I tried ignoring them. I tried walking away. Then I tried fighting back."

"Yeah," Kylie said, looking right into my eyes. "That was really bad. Jacob is so big, and he can be so mean."

## BENDING ISN'T BOWING

The next day the whole class had a free drawing project outside. Kids were scattered about in ones or twos on the playing field. I went over and sat on a bench near Kylie, and I watched as she drew a tree. It was really good, and I told her so.

"Yeah, I've always loved trees," she said. "I can see them from my bedroom window at home. I just lie there and watch them some-times. When I was little, I used to try to dance just like them. And I would put on shows for my family. Weird, right?"

We were quiet for a little while as she drew leaves and branches. Then she said, "You know, they can teach you a lot, trees. It's hard to explain, but when the wind blows, the leaves kind of feel it and move. But they don't, um, hold on to the wind. They just let it blow through them. The branches bend but move right back into place."

She switched to drawing the trunk and then the roots, "Now this part is strong because they go down a really long way into the earth and spread out." She put down her pencil for a moment. "That's what I think of when those kids try to be mean to me," she said cheer-fully. "They kinda create a storm, but if you grab and hold on to the horrible stuff they say and do, it will break your—well, your branches, if you know what I mean."

I was beginning to understand. "The tree is kind of blown around but it doesn't fight back, right? It just lets the storm move on through."

"Something like that," she replied, smiling.

Something big was happening inside my head, like when you finally understand a math rule and a whole page of problems that was too hard suddenly becomes easier. When the teacher called us inside, I felt I'd learned a lot even though I'd barely gotten any drawing done.

When I got home that day, I decided to go look at some trees. I biked over to a park where it was a bit wilder and more natural. As I rode around, I came to a big tree that had been partly blown over. The trees around it had prevented it from falling down completely.

The big roots were sticking out above ground. If what Kylie said was true, then why was this tree damaged and broken? Was that going to happen to me? Then I saw that the leaves were still green, and there were new shoots growing out of where the roots were still in the earth. I felt so happy. It was clear that the tree would grow again!

That night, as I lay in bed, I wondered what Kylie would say. Probably something like, "You see, even if the storm is a big one, the other trees caught the tree's fall, just like a friend or your family will catch you if you let them. And just think, if it hadn't fallen over, new trees wouldn't be growing there."

I kept thinking about what Kylie said and did and what I had noticed in the park. Even now I'm amazed at how Kylie, at such a young age, figured out all that stuff—how what you see in nature can help you deal with bullies. I remember waking up the next morning and thinking to myself, "Yes. That's exactly what I'm gonna do!"

Uncle Joe, Aunt Helen, Tommy, and his sister Jenny came over that weekend for a cookout. While Jenny was racing around with my brother and sister, I sat by the pool and talked with Tommy.

"Yeah, this girl at school, her name is Kylie," I said. "She is so cool. Those dudes tried to hassle her and she totally shut them down."

"Sweet," Tommy said.

"What are you guys talking about?" Dad asked. He'd been standing at the grill, turning the burgers over and we realized he'd overheard our entire conversation. Tommy looked at me and I nodded.

"Well, it's like this, Uncle Joe," he said slowly. "Mikey has been having a really hard time at school with these—bullies, I guess. And we've been talking a bit about how to deal with it. But it sounds like Mikey has a really good idea how to work it all out."

"Mikey," Dad said, stiffening up a bit, "is this why you told us you don't want to go on the school camping trip next week?"

"Uh, yeah. I guess," I confessed.

"What have they been doing exactly?"

"Well, it's a couple of guys, and they've been pushing and shoving and I guess there was kind of a fight. And that didn't really work out. But I totally know what will work now, Dad. Honestly, I really do."

It was amazing. My dad didn't react like I thought he would. He didn't get all mad and rant about calling the school principal. He just said, "I got into a fight or two at school when I was your age. Or a little older, maybe. It didn't really make things any better for me either. Are you okay?"

"Yeah. It was just one punch. And I'm fine."

"What do you think is going to work?"

"Well," I said. "There's this girl at school named Kylie. And what she does is—she says you own your own ground and you don't have to fight over it. She learned it from watching trees: how they let storms kinda blow through them, and stuff like that."

I told him about how she handled Ezra.

"That's a pretty clever girl," Dad said.

"Yeah," Tommy said. "A whole lot smarter than me! My advice sucked!"

We all laughed.

"Well, it sounds like you may have this situation under control, Mikey," Dad said. "Who wants cheese on their burger?"

## TAMING THE PACK

Later that night, when I was in bed, Dad came into my room.

"I think you are being really brave, Mikey. You've been through a lot. I want you to know you can always talk to me and your mom about this stuff."

"I know, Dad," I said. "I just didn't know what to do, and it was all really embarrassing."

"Okay, Mikey. I get that. But let's just go over what you are going to do a little more. Because kids like that—they're gonna keep coming back at you. They just will."

"Okay, Dad."

I told my dad the whole story, from the beginning. How things had started simply enough: an insult here, a shove there, someone hiding my jacket on me. The Wolf Pack playing keep-away with my stuff whenever they wanted to amuse themselves at my expense. How I tried what Tommy suggested and that just made things worse.

"Two things keep happening over and over again, Dad. If I push back when teachers are around, I get blamed and get into trouble. They act all justified and innocent, and laugh behind the teachers' backs. If there aren't any teachers around and I fight back, the group gangs up on me and two or three of them steal my stuff or throw me down hard and try to punch me."

"I see," Dad said.

Then I told him about everything that led up to the big standoff with Jacob, and how I lost that fight.

"I wish I'd stood up to him better, Dad. I wish I'd just knocked him out!"

"I get how you feel, Mikey. But winning a fight doesn't really solve all that much. I got into a lot of trouble back when I was at school. I got into a lot of fights. They always started first with insults, then taunts. The kids who targeted me—it was like they wanted to control me or own me. They'd say something and see if it bothered me. And if it did, they'd come at me harder. Maybe a nastier comment about my mom or a little shove in the hallway. Things would escalate from there."

"Dad! That's exactly what happened to me! I got really angry and reacted and they just got worse and worse."

"Well, I figured I'd just fight one of them and put a stop to the whole thing," Dad said. "Boy, was I wrong!"

"Really, what happened?"

"The opposite. I fought the kid who was bugging me the most. He was supposed to be the toughest kid in the class. We met after school. And I won—I punched him and hit him in the stomach and he fell down and the fight was over."

"But that's great, Dad! Everyone else stopped messing with you after that, didn't they?"

"No. That's what I'd hoped, but instead things got worse. Some people call it the Billy-the-Kid principle. Basically, once I'd beaten that kid up, another kid said he wanted to fight me. And then another. Everyone wanted to challenge me because suddenly they considered me to be the top gun. The toughest kid."

"Wow, I hadn't thought of that," I said.

"So I ended up getting into a bunch of fights. Other kids wanted to test themselves out against me. Instead of ending my problems, that first fight created a bunch of new ones. New enemies. Until a couple of weeks later, a kid who was two years older than me knocked me out."

"That's so crazy, Dad."

"Basically, when kids are trying to push you around and you fight back physically, you can get caught up in a cycle of violence, where bigger, meaner kids want to challenge you. And you can't beat up everyone, so that's when kids sometimes join a gang to protect themselves."

"Really?"

"Yes. I guess what I'm trying to say is things will get worse, and fighting back physically often doesn't work out very well. That's why I like your friend Kylie's approach a whole lot better."

"Yeah, she's pretty cool, Dad. I like the way she handled those guys."

Dad and I talked about everything that night—for hours. We went over what Kylie did and what I should do the next time one of the Wolf Pack bumped me, stole something, or tried to intimidate me in any other way. I felt so much better because I had Tommy and now my dad behind me. And my mom. Because I knew Dad would tell Mom everything as soon as I fell asleep. And at school there was Kylie. It wasn't like she was my best friend, but I definitely wasn't totally alone anymore.

Sure enough, the next day, in the main hallway, Ezra elbowed me in the ribs as he walked by. Then when I was at my cubby at the back of classroom, Quinn shoved me as I reached up to hang up my jacket. Just then I spotted Kylie looking over.

"Hey, Quinn," I said, turning around. "You really wanna stand here? So . . . okay, be my guest."

My voice was calm and steady. I could hardly believe they were my words coming out of my mouth. Quinn couldn't either. He stared at me, stunned, as I turned and walked over to my desk.

At recess three periods later, I walked by Jacob, Ezra, Damian, Arlo, and Quinn. They were playing soccer.

"Hey, tough guy, why don't you join us?" Ezra called out.

"No, that's okay. Thanks, guys," I replied.

"Ahh, come on," Damian said. "We'll play clean. Promise!"

While Ezra and Damian distracted me, Arlo snuck up from behind and snatched my hat off my head. It was my favorite baseball cap—the one Tommy had given me, the one he'd worn last year when he played on the county travel baseball team. The five of them now started tossing it to one another tauntingly.

"Hey," I yelled, as I lunged toward Arlo, who had just caught a pass from Damian. They'd done this to me so often—taken my pencil case, my lunch bag, or whatever else they could grab, and played keep-away with it while I chased after them, getting angrier and angrier, and they laughed and kept it just out of reach.

But in that split second a thought flashed into my mind: "What would Kylie do right now?" As my hat landed in Quinn's hands, I turned to him and said, "Hey, Quinn. You can have it if you want. That hat won't look that good on you, but you can keep it. Really." I turned and walked away.

When I passed by that same spot later that day, I found my hat on the ground right where they'd been talking. I picked it up and went back to class.

The next day at school, Jacob walked up to me, two members of his pack in tow: Quinn and Ezra.

"Hey, tough guy," Jacob said flatly. Gone were the snarling smile and threatening tone.

"Hey," I said.

He nodded. I nodded back, and he walked past me. Quinn and Ezra followed him, silent.

When Miss Hemshaw read out tent assignments that morning, two kids I liked, Cedric and Jose, were part of my five-person camping unit. When I turned and looked at them, they were high-fiving each other. Twenty minutes later, as we lined up to go out to recess, I heard Cedric and Jose behind me.

"Yo, tentmate!" Cedric said to me.

"Hey, man," I replied.

"It's gonna be an awesome trip, Mikey," he said.

"Yeah. We asked to be with you, dude!" Jose added.

"Cool."

"You guys wanna come over to my place Friday?" Cedric asked. "So we can work on our food and equipment lists for the trip?"

"Definitely," I replied.

I felt good. Really good. This was the first time anyone in my class—other than fearless Kylie—had reached out to connect with me since the beginning of the school year! I couldn't blame them either. With the Wolf Pack coming after me almost daily, I'd become radioactive. The other kids instinctively kept their distance. I guess they needed to protect themselves. Now that I wasn't the Wolf Pack's primary target, the smell of danger around me had washed away.

When I look back on my experience in fifth grade that fall, I realize that things were not that black and white. I wasn't just an innocent bullying victim. I was fueling the problem. Because as the taunting and teasing built up, I got more anxious. And the more nervous I was, the more reactive I got. And the more I reacted and lashed out, the more fun the Wolf Pack had goading me and watching me suffer. They escalated their attacks because they relished the control they had over me.

What I also figured out was that I needed to be comfortable being in my own space, and understand that wherever I went, my space went with me. That I owned the space around me and no one could take it from me. I didn't have to fight for it. It was mine.

Luckily I had the support of my dad, my cousin Tommy, and Kylie, my supercool classmate. Between the three of them, they helped me figure out how to handle myself and navigate my way out of the entire mess.

I had a great time on that camping trip with my new friends Cedric and Jose. And Kylie too. And now that I wasn't so alone and so reactive, the Wolf Pack's attacks tapered off. They basically lost interest in me and let me be. I never became friends with Jacob, Arlo, or any of the others. But we were okay around one another—and that was just fine by me.

---

This story was about . . .

- Why advice like "Ignore them" or "Just walk away" doesn't work
- How fighting back can make things worse

- Learning to stand firm when provoked without becoming angry or hostile
- Respecting yourself and making new friends

When Michael got physically bullied, he tried to ignore, walk away from, and fight back against his tormentors. But things went from bad to worse. When he learned from a classmate how to stand firm without getting anxious or becoming hostile, he became confident and secure in his own space.

# 12

---

# RUMORS AND
# WHISPERS

## *Elena's Story*

To have rumors spread about you is not only painful but also complicated and confusing. In this story, Elena worries about who is gossiping about her, what they are saying, and why they are doing it. Is it just a few mean kids or has it gotten much bigger? Concern can quickly grow into full-blown anxiety as you wonder if every person you meet has heard what is being said about you—even when you are not sure what that is.

In today's online world, this kind of fear has become much more intense. A rumor can be posted and shared so quickly and broadly that what was previously a relatively contained social issue explodes far and wide. When we factor in that online postings cannot be easily taken down, we are confronted with the fact that a simple lie or taunt can quickly grow into a long-lasting toxic situation.

Even if the children or teens who spread the hurtful rumors are confronted, it is hard to hold them accountable. They often hide behind excuses such as "I was just repeating what *everyone* is saying." A concerned adult, faced with this kind response, is left with two main options: let the kids know that it is "not okay" and they should stop, or normalize their behavior by accepting that "it's just a part of growing up." The latter response can further empower the teasers, who then realize they will most likely not be held responsible. Meanwhile the targeted child suffers as they become more and more marginalized. In Elena's case, there is an added vulnerability, because she is from a minority family that is struggling financially.

## POINTS OF UNDERSTANDING

- Just because rumors are quiet doesn't mean they don't hurt as much as any other form of bullying.
- While rumor-spreading is covert, even cowardly, it is always about gaining control and power over someone.
- Cyberbullying is particularly cruel and "effective" in slandering and spreading malicious rumors.
- The resulting embarrassment and anxiety can cause a child to experience severe self-doubt and withdrawal into loneliness. In extreme cases, it can even lead to suicidal thoughts.

## POINTS OF HOPE AND LEARNING

- You do not have to let yourself be questioned by other kids or feel the need to desperately defend yourself.
- You can deflect attempts at cross-examination while projecting confidence—without inflaming a situation.
- You can't stop what's being said about you in person or online, but you absolutely can control how you respond to it.
- There are ways to stand strong and call out the rumor spreaders.

It's hard for schools to catch kids spreading rumors and saying nasty things about others behind their backs. That's why it's critical to coach and support children and teens to develop ways to stand up to such comments and taunts. When children learn how to overcome hurtful rumors and cornering questions, they become empowered to move through life with new confidence—and are likely to attract new friends in the process.

---

*My name is Elena. I'm nineteen. I'm in my first year of college. I study 24/7 because I want to become a lawyer just like my cousin Lucía. She is smart and tough; she never lets anyone or anything intimidate her. That's how I want to be.*

*When I was twelve years old, I got into a pretty ugly situation at school. Just thinking back to those first few months of sixth grade makes me shudder. Some girls in my class spread a bunch of nasty rumors about me. Things got so bad that at one point I wanted to drop out of school. I stuck it out because of the two most important women in my life: Mami (my mom) and Lucía. And though it was really painful at the time, I wouldn't trade what I went through back then for anything in the world. Because everything that went down helped shape who I am today: a confident, determined young woman who doesn't get pushed around by anyone.*

*I hope that hearing my story helps you protect yourself from malicious gossip, rumors, and bullying. Kids can be crazy mean. But if you learn how to respond—how not to react—you can stay in charge, instead of letting other people control and manipulate you.*

I live in Los Angeles with Mami, who's a nurse; three younger brothers; and my uncle, aunt, and their family. Things can get kinda crazy at my house. It's not that big a place, and there are a lot of us packed in. (I share a bedroom with my three brothers.) Plus, there's always family or friends staying with us on their way north or heading back south to Mexico. (I'm a proud first-generation Mexican American.) Everyone loves one another. We all pitch in and take care of each other. Because family is everything, right? Mami works long hours at the hospital, so I help with my brothers a lot. When Mami's not around, I can always count on my aunt or uncle for grown-up support.

Sixth grade started out okay for me. It's not like I knew a lot of people. I wasn't an outgoing, popular kid, but I wasn't mousy shy either. It definitely helped that I met up on day one with Kayla, who I knew from fifth grade. We weren't besties or anything, but we were friendly and talked to each other between classes and at lunch too.

I had connected with Kayla earlier that summer to work together on a food drive. Kayla and her mom picked me up and took us to a homeless center downtown, where we distributed canned beans and rice I'd collected in my neighborhood. We stayed for three hours and served a lot of desperate people. Afterward, Kayla's mom took us roller skating.

I was so embarrassed when I saw Kayla's shiny white skates. Mine were worn-out hand-me-downs from cousin Lucía. When Kayla's mom saw me wobbling by on my trashy pair, she was so sweet. "Honey, those skates might just be a little too tight on you," she said. "Let's rent you better-fitting ones." And set me up with much nicer ones from the rink, and she paid for them too. Kayla and I had so much fun that day that we promised each other we'd be good friends in sixth grade and have each other's backs if things got gnarly.

## WHEN RUMORS CATCH FIRE

Anyway, things *were* okay, mostly. Kayla and I hung out a bit, and sometimes a cute boy named Jason and his best friend, Miguel, joined us at lunch. They were both pretty funny and low-key. Then one Monday, two weeks after school started, everything changed. When

I walked into school, I felt a weird vibe, like everyone was gawking at me and talking about me as I passed by. At first I figured I was just being silly and hypersensitive. Then at lunch, an entire table of girls burst out giggling right when I walked by.

When I glanced back at them, they stopped suddenly. But they stared back at me wide-eyed, as goofy grins spread across their faces. Something was up. I could tell. I ran into one of them later in the hallway, before social studies. Her name was Megan, a girl Kayla was friendly with. Megan wasn't all that cool, but she hung around Shana, Carmen, and Brittany, who was the prettiest, most popular girl in sixth grade.

"So . . . what's with you and Jason?" Megan blurted out.

"What do you mean?" I replied, clueless.

"You know," she said, grinning.

"No, I don't!"

"Everyone saw you two at the party."

My heart sunk into my toes.

"What are you talking about?"

"Last Saturday at Denise's party. Like three different people saw you kissing Jason back behind the kitchen."

"What? That's crazy. I don't even know Jason, really."

"That's totally *not* what I heard."

Megan started walking away.

"Wait, Megan! What party?"

She shrugged her shoulders and headed toward the main hallway.

"I didn't go to *any* party," I said. "Who's saying this?"

"Everyone," she called back over her shoulder.

"That's a total lie, Megan," I insisted.

"Whatever," she shot back. "None of my business. You do what you do. It's just—everyone says you did."

She disappeared through the swinging doors.

I was so upset I started shaking. I hadn't been to any party. I didn't even know Denise—or Megan, really, for that matter. She was in my science class but we'd never even spoken before.

I kept to myself for the next few days. No one talked to me anyway—not even Kayla. She seemed upset with me, though I had no idea why. After a few days, the Jason make-out rumor fizzled out, which was good. I figured people either didn't really care anymore or they'd realized it was a lie and the whole thing was over with.

I was so wrong.

The next Monday at recess, I spotted Kayla in the playground talking animatedly with Megan, who showed her something on her phone.

"Send me that," I overheard Kayla tell her.

Seconds later, Kayla's phone buzzed. She stared at the screen for what seemed like forever. Then she scanned the playground until she spotted me.

"Oh my g—!" she said, covering her gaping mouth.

All afternoon I wondered and worried. Finally, when school let out, I spotted Kayla leaning up against the playground fence.

"Kayla, can I talk to you for a sec?" I asked. She was standing by the swings, looking at her cell phone.

"Huh, I—," she stuttered. "I don't know."

She looked over at Megan, Shana, Carmen, and Brittany, who were crowded around a bench about ten feet away. I caught Shana nodding her approval to Kayla, who turned toward me.

"What's up?" she said, as if there was nothing strange going on.

"You tell me," I replied. "Everyone is giving me weird looks—like last week when they spread that total lie about me and Jason. Only this time it's worse."

She shrugged.

"Kayla," I pleaded. "Please tell me what's going on. You're the only person I know and trust."

"I don't know what to say, Elena," she replied.

"Did I do something to annoy you?"

"Maybe you should just try to be a little *less* friendly with everyone."

"What does *that* mean?" I asked. "I hardly know anyone here. You're pretty much the only person I ever talk to."

"Check *this* out, guys!" Shana called out, loud enough for everyone around her to hear. She and Megan and Brittany were clustered together, like vultures picking something (or someone) apart. Shana covered her mouth with her hand in mock shock. Then three heads swiveled toward us in unison. They stared right at me! Shana, a total drama-queen type, shook her head in disbelief.

"No way," she said.

"That's just so wrong," Carmen added.

"I guess you never really know," Megan mused. "You think you have someone pegged and then they do something totally out of character. Like this!"

I walked up to them.

"What are you all talking about?" I said, my voice cracking.

"You, my dear," Brittany smiled back smugly.

"You've certainly had *another* busy weekend!" Megan exclaimed gleefully.

"What do you mean?"

"One boy not enough, Elena?" The question came from Shana, who I'd never spoken to before *in my life*!

"What are you guys going on about?" I stammered, close to tears.

"*This!*" Megan held up her phone triumphantly. The photo on her screen was of a boy and a girl making out.

"What's that?" I cried.

"Ha. *Nice try*, Little Miss *Inocente*."

"What do you mean?" I looked at the screen again, more closely.

The boy in the photo was our classmate Miguel. He was locked in a kiss with a brown-haired girl who looked, well, a whole lot like me—although her face couldn't really be made out clearly. The photo was too grainy.

"Well?" Shana prompted.

"Well, what?"

"Last week, Jason," she replied, exasperated. "Now Miguel? What is your deal, girlfriend? Why are you going after all the boys in the class— *at the same time*? People have boyfriends, you know. Or boys they like. And feelings too. You can't just prowl around kissing every guy."

"But I didn't—"

"That's you and Miguel at Tommy's party."

"That's not possible," I cried. "I wasn't at Tommy's house. I don't even know where he lives!"

"So what you're saying is I'm lying," Megan replied. "That *the photo* is lying?"

"That's not me!" I insisted. "I don't like Miguel. Or Jason. I barely know them. And I haven't been to any freakin' party."

"Look at her," Shana said knowingly. "This *chica's* face is turnin' chili-pepper red."

"But I—uh—" I stammered. My mind went blank.

"The telltale sign of a guilty conscience!" Kayla said.

"Tongue-tied with guilt, I'd say," Megan added gleefully.

"What? You guys are crazy!" I fired back. "I swear, Megan. I don't like Miguel. Or Jason. And I haven't been to anyone's party, ever. I'm not allowed."

"Not allowed?" Brittany asked, her eyebrows arching.

"I wasn't at that party," I insisted. "That's not even my top or dress in the photo."

I figured I had them there.

"She's got a point," Brittany conceded.

"Yeah," Kayla added. "That outfit is way too cool for Elena."

I looked at her, shocked. Why was Kayla so against me all of a sudden?

"Too expensive-looking, right?" Megan said.

"Not the ratty thrift-shop specials Elena usually scrapes together, huh?" Shana smirked.

This cut deep. I did my best to mix up my wardrobe and come up with a cool look. My mom barely had any disposable income. And I couldn't work because, well, first of all, I was too young. And second, I was always stuck at home watching my brothers and cousins for Mami and Tía Clara. I was crying now. But they just kept picking away.

"She could have borrowed that ensemble, though" Shana posited.

"Yeah, you're right," Kayla conceded.

"From one of the twenty relatives packed into that slummy half-way house she lives in," Megan added.

"Mamma mia!" Brittany said in the sweetest tone you could imagine. "Aren't you all the kindest. Shouldn't we give Elena the benefit of the doubt? Whatever happened to 'innocent *until* proven guilty,' anyway?"

"Photos don't lie, though, do they?" Megan asked, her voice wavering a little.

"No, they definitely do not," Shana interjected. "You're worse than a slimy politician, Elena, with all your little lies and denials."

Brittany yawned and looked down at her fingernails.

"Enough of all this silliness, girls," she proclaimed. "We're gonna be late for volleyball practice." And just like that, she turned away. The others followed obediently.

Except Megan, who hung back for half a second and whispered, "Don't think you're gonna get away with this," and then quickly caught up with her new crew.

As I walked to the bus, I trembled all over. Why had they made up all this stuff about me? Why were they picking me apart like coyotes feasting on a fresh kill? In two weeks they'd turned me into a weak, worthless, blubbery blob.

## THE ULTIMATE BETRAYAL

What hurt the most was that Kayla had acted like nothing weird was going on and all of them were right and I was terrible. And now they were all going off together to have a great time playing after-school volleyball, and I couldn't play even if I wanted to.

I couldn't hang around after school for even a minute. I had to head straight home to cover for Tía Clara, who was watching my three brothers for Mami, so that Mami could squeeze in double shifts on weekdays. The second I got home, Tía Clara would head out to her evening job. Then I'd watch my *hermanitos* and Tía Clara's two daughters until Tío Leo got home. He'd cook dinner for all of us and we'd eat. Mami would get home just in time to hug everyone and tuck them in, so I could settle down to my homework. We worked seamlessly, like a team. But there certainly wasn't any time for after-school activities—ever.

A few days later, I gathered enough courage to confront Kayla.

"Why are you being so mean to me?" I asked. "And why are you guys spreading rumors about me and Miguel? I thought you were my friend."

"I thought you were *my friend*. Then you go around kissing Jason, even though you told me you thought he was gross."

"But I didn't kiss Jason. I swear." I said.

"Everybody says you did."

"They're lying."

"What about yesterday? I saw him standing by your desk in art class. You guys were talking like you were going steady or something."

"No we weren't!"

"But I saw you!"

"That's just because I'm a really good drawer, and he was looking at my drawing."

"Oh, right. You're a really good drawer, are you?"

"But I am!"

"Whatever. To be honest, I never liked you that much anyway," she said angrily. "I didn't even want to come over to your house this summer. My mom forced me to. She said I had to be nice to you because you're *disadvantaged*. You were just a charity friend."

I felt a sharp, stabbing pain in my stomach. What she said was so hurtful. And why was she being so weird about Jason?

Just then Megan and Shana walked by.

"Why're you hanging out with this loser, Kayla?" Megan asked.

"I'm not," Kayla said. "She's following *me* around."

"Whatever," Shana said, rolling her eyes.

Megan turned to me.

"How's the fund going?" she asked pointedly.

"What fund?" I said.

Megan shot Kayla a quizzical look.

"You haven't told her?" Megan said.

"No," Kayla replied.

"What are you guys talking about?" I asked.

"Nothing important," Shana said. "Let's go, girls."

That night I found out exactly what they all meant. Tío Leo served *caldo de pollo* for dinner. And after three games of Go Fish and twenty minutes chasing my brothers and cousins around the house in my witch hat and cape, I finally got them to settle down for the night.

The house was suddenly quiet. Mami and Tía Clara were still at work, and Tío Leo went to visit a neighbor down the street. I sat down at his laptop to work on a poem for English class. I typed in his password—ELSANTO12. Tía Clara, Mami, and I were the only ones who knew it because none of the other kids were allowed to touch Tío Leo's computer—ever. El Santo was the nickname of Tío Leo's all-time favorite *lucha libre* fighter. And Tío Leo was a mega fan. He'd subjected the whole family to countless hours of watching Mexican pro wrestlers prancing around on TV in freaky face masks and colored tights, beating on each other. My little brothers loved imitating them. They'd jump around, tackling and fake stomping each other all over the couch and living room floor.

When I'd finished writing the poem, I checked my email. I had one new message. It contained a single link and was otherwise blank. When I clicked on the link a colorful page popped up.

I stared at it for what felt like forever, taking everything in. Then I guess my heart stopped—literally. Because when I woke up, I was lying on the kitchen floor. The laptop was still open on the counter. I logged off quickly, fighting back a wave of tears. Then I slipped into the bathroom, locked the door, and sat on the edge of the bathtub and cried until I almost passed out from exhaustion. When I heard the front door opening, I quickly slipped into bed before Tío Leo or anyone else could see me.

When I woke up the next morning, my head felt like a bag of bricks. I couldn't move. Tía Clara was the first to come in and ask me what was wrong. I didn't respond.

I just closed my eyes.

Then Mami appeared.

"*¿Que pasa, mi hija?*" she said softly. "You okay?"

I shook my head. She felt my forehead.

"Well, at least you don't have a fever."

I stared up at her.

"You want some breakfast?"

"Not hungry."

She must have figured it was serious because I wasn't the type to lounge around in bed, and I absolutely never missed school. She knew something was wrong, but she decided not to pry.

"I'm going to call the school, *mi hija*," she said. "You stay home and get better, okay?"

I nodded, relieved. And I sank further under my blanket.

I slept most of the morning. When I woke up, I lay in bed feeling weak and nauseous until about an hour before my brothers and cousins were supposed to get home from school. When I went into the kitchen to pour myself a glass of milk, I spotted Tío Leo's laptop across the counter. I willed myself to stay away from it. But the more I tried, the more I was drawn to it.

There were three new messages waiting in my inbox—all from the same anonymous sender from the night before. I opened the most recent one and clicked on the link. The number $137.45 popped up in bold red in the middle of the page. I logged out, slammed the laptop shut, and buried myself back in bed.

When the kids arrived, I got out of bed for a few minutes to square them away with snacks. But mostly I let them do whatever they wanted to that afternoon. I had no energy to organize card games or discipline them for being too rowdy when they wrestled. I left the bedroom door open and crawled back into bed. Every little while one of them would race in, jump on my bed, and bounce around—or give me a hug or kiss—and then dash back into the living room.

When Tío Leo got home from work, he appeared in the doorway.

"Everything okay, Elena?" he asked, looking more than a bit worried.

"*Sí*, Tío," I replied.

"Can I get you something to eat?"

"*No gracias*, Tío. I'm not really hungry."

I had lost my appetite completely.

"Okay. You rest," he said. "I'll get these *loquitos* something to eat and keep them out of your hair. Feel better, *pequeña*."

I thanked him and closed my eyes.

## THE INTERROGATION

I stayed in my room the rest of the evening and did not go to school the next day either. But when Mami got back from her first shift, she called my cousin Lucía and asked her to come over and hang out with me that evening. She was really worried. I hadn't eaten in two days— and I am a total foodie freak.

Mami clearly didn't want to leave me alone in the state I was in. She waited until Lucía arrived to speak with her, even though that made her a half hour late for work. I overheard Tío Leo promise to keep my brothers and cousins busy in the living room so Lucía and I could have a little privacy in the bedroom.

When Lucía came into the room and sat down on the bed next to me, I burst into tears. We hugged for five minutes without saying a word to each other.

"Oh, Elena, what's wrong, baby?" she whispered finally, brushing sticky strands of hair away from my face.

I was silent.

"You don't have to tell me unless you really want to," she said.

"I—I just," I blubbered. "I thought she was my friend."

"¿*Quien, mi linda*? Who?"

"Kayla."

"What did she do?"

The entire story poured out of me in an emotional avalanche. I told her about the friendship promise Kayla and I had made to each other at the roller-skating rink a few weeks before school started. About Beautiful Brittany, who ruled the sixth grade with her two near-perfect ladies-in-waiting, Carmen and Shana. And about how mean Megan had been to me from day one, even though I'd never done a thing to her. And worse, how Kayla had suddenly flipped on me after Megan accused me of kissing a boy named Jason. And now the two of them had been accepted into Brittany's clique and all five of them had ganged up on me.

"Wow," Lucía interrupted at one point. "It's like nothing has changed since I was in school. There's always a girl who acts all queenie and sweet while she and her besties lord it over everyone else. And you know what? Those types of girls usually aren't even all that bad. It's the ones who want to hang out with the Brittanys and Shanas—the wannabes who crave acceptance from the popular girls. They are the worst. They'd do anything to get in good with the quee-nie types. This Megan girl you mentioned, she sounds like a sneaky little social climber."

"I never really liked or trusted Megan," I said. "But when Kayla turned on me, that made me feel *awful*, like I have nobody."

"Why do you think she did that?"

"I'm not 100 percent sure," I said. "But I think it had to do with Jason. She's convinced I kissed him at a party that I wasn't even at."

"It's always about a boy, isn't it?" Lucía said, shaking her head. "Do you think Kayla liked him and thought you were making a move on him?"

"Yeah," I said, seeing everything much more clearly now.

"And this Megan, I'd bet she's the one who started all of this by making up the rumor about you and Jason."

"Wow! Yeah," I said. "That makes total sense, Lucía."

"I've seen this all before, Elena," she said. "I know how painful it can be, and I'm sorry you are going through this."

"After the whole Jason thing blew over, I thought everything would go back to normal. But a week later, the entire class started treating me like a freak again."

I told Lucía about the fake photo of Miguel kissing "me" at another party I had not attended and how someone had texted the photo to the entire class.

"I see," she said.

"I swore to everyone it wasn't me. I even told them I'd never been kissed by a boy—any boy. Then some of them starting making fun of me for being a clueless girl who'd never been kissed."

"When kids make up rumors like that, Elena, no response is going to work. The more you defend yourself, the worse they get. They just want to get a strong reaction from you. They want you to get all worked up. Then they use anything that you say against you. It's like what happens in a courtroom. I'm learning all about this in college. When lawyers cross-examine a witness in court, they come at them from every direction. They try to rile them up. And when the witness gets upset, they seize on their reactions and trip them up verbally and get them to say things that will make everyone believe whatever the lawyer wants the jury to believe about the case. In your situation, those girls are putting you on the witness stand. Do you get what I'm saying?"

"I think so," I said.

"In a courtroom there is a judge who sits up on a raised platform. And beside the judge is a box where a person sits in a chair and is asked a bunch of questions. It's called 'being examined.' You sit up there and everyone in the courtroom is looking at you, and you have no one with you. You are on your own. And a person who doesn't care about you—the lawyer—is trying to make you sound guilty. That person asks you questions and forces you to defend yourself. The person sitting there is sometime even called 'the defendant.' The same is true when cops stop people who aren't doing anything wrong. If that person gets nervous, argues, or tries to defend themselves rather than staying calm, the police take control of the situation and start asking more and more questions."

"But I didn't do anything wrong!" I said. "Everything they said about me was made up."

"That's often the way it is. But when you are on the witness stand or being questioned by cops, you have to prove it. When your class-mates accused you of stuff you didn't do, you felt like you had to de-fend yourself and prove that they were wrong."

"Yes, that's exactly how I felt," I said.

"Well, you don't. You don't have to prove anything. This is school, *querida*, not a courtroom or police station. And you definitely shouldn't even be on that witness stand or in that interrogation room. Do not let them put you there."

"What do you mean?" I asked.

"When they blame you or accuse you of something, like kissing a boy like Jason or Miguel, they are trying to get you to react. If you don't get upset, if you keep your cool, then they can't put you on trial or question you."

"I see," I nodded. It was all beginning to make sense.

Lucía and I talked about a bunch of different things I could say. We did this thing called role-playing, which is like rehearsing your lines for a play until you get them right. Lucía was the Mean Girl and

I was the Defendant. Finally, we came up with what seemed like the perfect solution.

"If someone like Megan said something like, 'You kissed Jason at that party,' instead of denying it, you turn the whole thing around by asking the question, 'Why do you need to say that, Megan?' And if she says, 'I dunno,' all you say is 'Neither do I.'

"And if she said 'Because it's true,' you simply reply, 'You can say it if you like. It's not true, but that's up to you.'"

"Okay," I said.

"But the most important thing, *mi linda*: don't get drawn into any arguments."

We decided I would try that out the next time someone started a rumor about me or said something false.

"It's not always that easy to keep your cool," Lucía warned me. "That takes practice. And you have to realize you can't stop them from saying things, no matter how much it hurts."

"But I want to stop them!" I said.

"No, you can't, Elena. You can't stop them from saying things. But you can change the way you react to what they say. If you don't react, or you don't show them how upset it makes you, you cut their attack off at the knees. They can't interrogate you, so don't let anyone do it. Okay?"

"Okay," I whispered.

"Now you know something big, *mi linda*," she said. "Fire can't burn without fuel. When you don't react, when you convince them you're totally cool either way, when you say 'Whatever,' you pour buckets of water all over that firewood. When you don't let them see you react, you suck all the oxygen out of the situation. With no fuel, that nastiness? Those rumors? They fizzle right out."

I nodded, feeling a little bit stronger already.

"I'm going to call you every night," she added, "for the next four days and we are going to practice this until you feel really confident. Okay?"

"Okay," I said.

"And when you are back at school and they start in on you, you just picture me right beside you. And you stick to the script."

I nodded and put my arms around Lucía and squeezed her as hard as I could.

"I wish I'd spoken with you about this sooner," I said, feeling a whole lot better.

"Well, now you have," she said. "And we have a game plan. Why don't we get something to eat now?"

We went into the kitchen and had some of Tío Leo's leftover *arroz con pollo*. I ate a bowlful. Then I had another one. My appetite was back!

After dinner, Lucía and I continued our conversation.

"Then Jason comes up to me and asks me why I'm spreading rumors about us making out!"

"He did?"

"Can you believe it?" I said laughing. "I was so embarrassed."

I was feeling so much better.

"Listen, Elena. None of what's been going on with you at school is cool. But there's got to be something you aren't telling me, because I can tell that you are deeply hurt. Rumors can be nasty, but I know how tough you are, girl. There's something more to this, isn't there?"

I nodded slowly.

"But you have to promise you won't tell anyone, Lucía," I pleaded.

"*¡Lo juro!*" she said, making the sign of the cross with her right hand and kissing her fingertips.

"Not even Mami!"

"I swear I won't tell a soul, Elena, on *Abuelita*'s grave."

I got up and walked out into the kitchen, motioning for Lucía to follow me. When we were at the counter, standing in front of Tío Leo's laptop, I flicked it open. The screen lit up and I typed ELSANTO12 into the password field. When my email account popped up, I saw I had fifteen new messages. I opened up the most recent one and clicked on the familiar link.

A big, bright photograph of me appeared, standing in front of our house, grinning. Across the top of the screen in thick, bright green letters were the words "Help Elena's Family Replace Their Leaking Roof and Buy Her New Clothes." On the righthand side was a mustard-yellow "Donate Now" tab. Above it were the words "You've Raised $213.91 of $15,000." On the right side in italics was a message for prospective funders:

> Hi. My name is Elena. Our roof leaks. When it rains, the water drips down in my room, even when I'm asleep. I also don't own any new clothes. My wardrobe is made up of hand-me-downs and thrift-shop buys. Please help us buy a new roof. No amount is too small. Thank you for your support.

Lucía stared at the page, speechless.

"A GoFundMe page," she muttered. "Unbelievable! Wait a sec. How did they even get this shot of you in front of the house?"

"That's the worst part," I replied. "Kayla's mom took that photo in July when they stopped by to pick me up to go downtown to help in the homeless center's soup kitchen."

"That's *sooo* nasty."

"I know," I said, tearing up. "I don't think I can ever go back to school and face everybody."

"Oh yes you can! And you will, girl," she said, standing up. "I'll help you every step of the way, Elena. You'll show them!"

"You don't think I should show this to Mami, do you?"

"Let's hold off on that for now. Mami would march right up to the principal of your school and demand that every one of those girls be suspended."

"You're so right," I said.

"And then you'd be public enemy number one. All the popular girls would hate you, and everyone would call you a snitch. Parents mean well, but they often make things way worse when they try to set things straight."

"What should I do then?"

"I want you to go to school and shrug it off. You can't ignore the whole GoFundMe-page thing, but you can turn it on its head. And above all else, do not let them interrogate you."

We talked for hours. Lucía told me about all kinds of stuff she went through when she was a middle-schooler. The more we spoke, the better I felt. By the end of the night I was determined to go back to school and deal with everything and everybody. I didn't want to shrink away from the challenge. I wanted to stand my ground and make her proud.

Because I'd stayed home on Wednesday and Thursday, all I had to do was get through one day—Friday—and I'd be back at home for the weekend, far away from my tormentors. Lucía promised to come over on Saturday so we could go over everything that happened and she could help prepare me for the following week.

## THINK WHAT YOU WANT, SAY WHAT YOU WANT

When I got to school, I got a bunch of stares. And kids I barely knew giggled and whispered stuff as I walked by. But other than that, things were pretty chill. Until recess. I walked out into the glaring sun and crossed the playground to my favorite spot, underneath twin jacaranda trees.

Halfway there, Carmen, Shana, and Brittany were skipping rope. Megan and Kayla stood by like the hangers-on they'd clearly become.

"How's the fund going, Elena?" Megan called out, her words soaked in sarcasm.

"Not that great," I said.

"Why?" she said.

The jump rope went slack. Everyone was listening. I looked at her and smiled.

"A new roof is going to cost way more than $15,000, Megan. And the guest bathroom is a total dump. We gotta renovate that too."

She looked stunned.

"And if I'm going to get new clothes, I want top-of-the-line stuff." I was on a roll now. "I wanna spend the day on Rodeo Drive, not at Walmart."

I didn't wait for a response. I just walked over to my spot and settled in with a book of poems Lucía had loaned me, acting like nothing they had done could faze me.

They left me alone for the rest the day.

On Monday, before school, a dozen kids—Shana and Megan included—were hanging around the main entrance, waiting for the doors to open, when I got there. Without Brittany and Carmen around—which they weren't now—Shana was the supreme leader. Everyone deferred to her.

"Look who's here, guys!" she said.

"Hi, guys," I said.

"Hey, Elena, are you really that poor?" It was Tommy, the boy whose party was the scene of the Jason-kissing rumor that kicked off my monthlong middle-school nightmare.

"I mean . . . a GoFundMe page?" he continued. "That's pretty down and out."

"Yo, that's cold!" someone added.

"What do you think, Tommy?" I asked. "Do you believe everything you see on the internet?"

"Yeah, I do. Mostly." Everyone cracked up.

"It's up to you, Tommy," I said, shrugging my shoulders. "Think what you want."

The doors opened and everyone piled in.

Later, at recess, Megan and Kayla came up to me. Brittany, Shana, and Carmen were close behind.

"We heard your uncle is going to jail."

"Really? What for?"

"Stealing. We heard some kids saying he's part of a gang that broke into a bunch of homes in Beverly Hills because you guys are so desperate for money."

"Doesn't sound like something my uncle would do. He's pretty busy. He works in construction."

"But what if it's true?"

"It's not. I don't know why anybody would need to say that, but I can't stop them. If you want to go along with stuff like that, you can."

"I can do whatever I want."

"You can. I don't mind. I mean, it doesn't make you look that good. It makes you guys seem kinda mean-spirited, you know. Ganging up on the 'poor little Latina girl.' First you spread rumors about me kissing boys. Then a web page goes up that makes it look like my family is a dirt-poor charity case. And now my uncle is a criminal? It's not a good look, guys."

"Is that all you've got to say for yourself, Elena?"

"Yeah. There's nothing else worth saying. You can go along with whatever you want."

I smiled and said, "Guys, I gotta go get my lunch. See you later," and I walked away.

I stopped caring when kids laughed at me or talked about me when I walked into a classroom or down the hall. And it seemed like the less I cared, the less often they did it. After about a week, Kayla stopped being mean and Megan stayed away altogether.

About a week later, at recess, Brittany asked me if I wanted to skip rope with her, Shana, and Carmen. Things were way better now. I was able to focus on my schoolwork again. Just in time too, because I had a huge math test coming up in a few days.

On Saturday night, Lucía came over for dinner and we talked things over. She was so proud of me. And my appetite was back at

100 percent. I ate four of Tío Leo's pork taquitos and three of Tía Carmen's chicken quesadillas. I was happy. And Mami was too.

A few days later, in English—which was the last class of the day—I was asked to read a poem I'd submitted. I stood up in the front of the class. Just as I was about to start, Megan pretended to cough really loudly as she called out two words: "Fund Me." Everyone was silent. Brittany, who sat in the front row, turned around and shot her a death stare. Megan slunk back in her chair, silenced.

## MI MAMI

Mi Mami is a selfless woman
Fierce is her glare.
Watching over us,
Our Mami bear.

Long hours she works
In long-term care
To ensure the elderly
do not despair.

A smile from her
Is worth a thousand kisses
Her tender warmth
our fear dismisses.

At home I help her.
It's only fair.
Because on double shifts,
she works her fingers bare.

At school I focus
To make her proud,

And honor the opportunity
Her love's labor has allowed.

As I finished, the bell rang, signaling the end of the school day. I sat down and started packing my book bag.

"Hey."

I looked up. It was Jason.

"Hey," I shot back.

"That was a great poem."

"Thanks."

"Can you help me write mine? I have to read it on Thursday."

I smiled. "Sure, Jason. That would be fun."

He walked me out of class and all the way to my bus.

---

This story was about . . .

- How subtle and hurtful rumors can be
- How belittling and embarrassing cyberbullying can get
- That you can't control what's being said about you online
- That it's important to realize that how you respond changes everything

Elena discovered that fire can't burn without fuel, that you can't control what is being said about you in person or online, but you can be fully in charge of how you respond to it.

# 13

---

# TRUTH TELLING
# AND TATTLING

## *Emma's Story*

It's always good when kids sort things out among themselves. But there are also times when a dispute crosses the line and adult help is needed.

What makes this issue complicated is that children often have differing ideas about how their play should be organized and what is fair.

Some kids are easygoing and happy to construct a game as it evolves. However, this can mean the activity is so open to change that it can become formless or chaotic. Kids who have clear, fixed ideas about how a game should be played can become rigid and controlling. Either way, the fun often gets lost in disputes and arguments. In this story, Emma works her way through just such a confusing tangle.

## POINTS OF UNDERSTANDING

- Being bossy can leave you with no one to play with.
- Others need space to have their say.
- Brothers and sisters don't like playing with a sibling who always wants to have it their way.
- Needing things to be clear, with proper rules, can seem controlling to others, even if all you want is for games to be fair.

## POINTS OF HOPE AND LEARNING

- Being with others goes better when you understand that everyone has their own way of seeing things.
- When you seek help from an adult to genuinely find a way to work things out, you are not being a tattletale.
- Friendly and relaxed ways to connect with other kids can be learned.

Imagine a world in which we raise our children to be inquisitive rather than accusative. Helping them learn to honor their own sense of fairness while also becoming more open to the viewpoints of other kids is vital. That way, rather than fighting against opposing opinions, they can begin to see them as differing perspectives that need to be acknowledged and understood.

---

*My name is Emma. I'm eighteen. I've always been a neat, organized person, and now that I'm in my first year of college, that is a big advantage. I know how to keep my social life and schoolwork balanced. Many of my dormmates stay up all night goofing around or watching YouTube videos or Netflix and then get overwhelmed by classes, tests, and social commitments. I don't get too stressed out because I organize my time well.*

*I've already made some really good friends in college. We hang out together and laugh a lot. But as I think about it now, I realize my life could have taken quite a different turn if it hadn't been for my second-grade teacher, Mrs. Johnson.*

*But let me backtrack a bit more, to when I was in kindergarten. Back then, things didn't go so well between me and my younger brother and little sister.*

## MY WAY OR THE HIGHWAY

Ryan, Susie, and I were close in age but we seldom played well together. I'm a rule keeper. And even as a little girl I was really clear in my mind about what was right and what was wrong. But Ryan and Susie seldom saw things my way. They often accused me of being bossy—and our games almost always ended up as big arguments.

Ryan, who is currently finishing high school, has become an amazing musician and songwriter. He's always been really creative. He's so different from me that sometimes it's hard to believe we are from the same family.

But when we were little, he made me so angry. When we played together, he liked inventing scenarios and changing things all the time, whereas I always wanted to be clear about things and stick to what we decided to do.

I liked to be in charge and to plan things out like you do when you create a script for a movie. I was really good at mapping out every detail. We'd spend ten minutes working out how we were supposed to play: who would be the doggie, who played the master and the fireman, what clothes everyone should wear, and how we should act.

When I'd set everything up and we started playing, Ryan would suddenly come up with a new scheme and try to change everything. That bothered me so much because I wanted to stick to what we'd agreed to do. Ryan and Susie had their own ideas—and it seems pretty clear to me now that I didn't allow them any space to speak up or try different things.

But Ryan did things that didn't make any sense at all. When he was the policeman, he'd wear weird stuff like a feathered scarf or shiny red shoes. He'd assure me it was okay, no matter how much I insisted it was wrong. I figured he just didn't care. He was certainly as stubborn about being weird as I was about our play being true to life.

Susie was easily distracted, and she would drift in and out of our games. But whenever she joined in, Ryan made sure to act extra goofy to make her laugh and win her over to his way of doing things. She always sided with him because he was "way more fun." If we didn't do things their way, he'd convince her to quit and sabotage everything. There I'd be—left standing alone with no one to play with.

That's when I'd stomp over to our mom. "Everyone is ganging up on me," I'd say, angrily. "They're so unfair." And if Mom didn't pay enough attention to my complaint, I'd add something more incriminating, like "Ryan even used a really bad word, and now they've taken the costumes and toys and won't play with me at all," just to get him in extra trouble.

I behaved the same way at school, trying to set the rules and control how we played at recess. I guess I didn't know any better. Pretty soon I was having the same kind of arguments I had at home with my classmates in kindergarten. That didn't go so well either. Sometimes I was able to get them to do what I wanted. Other times I'd run to our teacher and tell on a classmate who wasn't doing what I said. She would help us find a way to sort things out between us. Sometimes that meant I'd go off and do something with her while things calmed down. But eventually things got bad enough that some of my classmates would stop playing and run away when they saw me coming. Or if they were older or bigger, they would just push me away and call me a teacher's pet. I often ended up with no one to play with and nothing to do. I felt like a lonely general with no army to command.

This went on all throughout kindergarten. I kept getting bossier and bossier at school and at home. The harder I tried to make people play with me, the worse it got.

In first grade I had a chance to start over with a whole bunch of new kids. We had a set recess time then—and there were more kids from different grades out playing at the same time. Our first-grade teacher didn't supervise recess as often as our kindergarten teacher had. So any time something went wrong—by which I mean "didn't go my way," I had to find an on-duty teacher to complain to.

At first the teachers would come over and try to help us sort things out. But as soon as they went away, the other kids would get mad at me or give me mean looks and say, "Why did you have to do that?" or "Everything's fine when you don't play," or "Why do you always have to be the boss, anyway?" After a while, even the teachers started to get frustrated with me. They'd say things like, "We can't come over for every little thing," and "Emma, you're a bigger girl now. I think you can try to sort this out." But I really couldn't. The only way I knew how to act was to control things: to stick to the rules. The teachers got tired of me running to them and telling them everything that was happening. Looking back on it now, I sure don't blame them. But I just didn't feel welcome anymore.

## THE BIG BLOWUP

Things didn't change much when I started second grade. Until one day, about a week into the school year, there was a really big blowup at recess. Five of us girls were playing jump rope. It was a game where you jumped to the rhythm of a specific song, like:

A sailor went to sea, sea, sea
To see what he could see, see, see.

But you weren't supposed to just sing and jump. There were also hand signals that went with the words. Julia and Clara kept messing those up.

"That's all wrong, Julia," I said. "You don't put your hand up to look when it's a 'sailor went to sea.' You do it only when the sailor sees stuff."

"Whatever, Emma. It doesn't really matter."

"It does matter," I replied. "That's what the whole game is about."

And then she started doing it on purpose and smirking at me.

"You're ruining the game, Julia," I said.

Everyone was laughing because Julia was being so goofy.

"Stop it!"

They all laughed even harder.

"Why do you get so angry, Emma?" Donna asked.

"Because you guys are doing it all wrong," I explained.

"But it's just a game," Clara said.

"Yeah, but—" I stammered.

"Whatever," Donna said. "It's just funner when you aren't here, Emma."

That comment hurt. It also made me mad. So I stepped in and grabbed at the rope to stop them. But they yanked at it, and it burned through my hand.

"Ow!" I yelled. "That hurt!"

No one said or did anything. Then Clara and Donna started chuckling.

"What's so funny?" I said.

Everyone else in the playground had stopped what they were doing and were staring at me.

"You did that on purpose," I continued.

"No I didn't," Donna insisted.

"Right. I'm telling," I declared.

I spotted a teacher near the swings. As I marched toward her, I heard Clara behind me call out, "What else is new, tattletale. You always do that."

After I told on Donna, Clara, and the others, everyone stayed away from me. No one in my class was willing to risk playing with me anymore. I sat on a bench most days pretending not to notice that everyone was having fun all around me. And I spent my recess time reading or making up songs I could ask Ryan to put to music on his piano at home.

Then one day I wandered over to where a bunch of first graders were playing. They had their recess period at the same time as us second graders. Since they were really new to the school, they saw me as a big kid and welcomed me into their games.

Things went really well at first. I showed them how to play two of my favorite jump-rope games and a really fun tag game. We had a great time playing them for two straight weeks.

Then things went sour. I guess I started getting bossy again and tried to "make" people play with me the way I wanted them to. After all, I reasoned, I'd taught them these games and I knew all the rules inside out. But they got tired of me trying to arrange everything. When I walked over to them, some of them began to melt away, and pretty soon they started intentionally avoiding me just like my second-grade classmates did.

## A FRESH START

One day I walked over to a group of first graders. When they turned and walked away, I saw that one girl, who I'd hardly noticed before, stayed where she was. She was different from the other kids—a shy, thin, pale girl who looked really lonely. I remembered vaguely that when she'd played with us before, she never seemed to know how to join in and always backed away when things got rowdy.

I walked up to her that day and asked outright: "What's your name?"

"Mai Lin," she whispered.

"I'm Emma. Will you play with me?"

She nodded, and we walked around for a little while, talking quietly, until we ended up next to the school garden. We admired all the different plants and flowers and talked until recess was over.

"You're really good at working things out," Mai Lin said as the bell rang.

"Thank you," I replied.

"I like talking with you," she said sweetly.

"Me too," I replied. "Let's meet here tomorrow."

The next day we met and sat for a while on the edge of one of the garden beds that the first and second grade looked after. I noticed some buckets and gardening tools lying about. The buckets were half full of water because it had rained the night before. I thought up a game in which we carved out rivers and streams next to the garden, where there were several dirt piles.

We had so much fun building walls and designing tunnels that we returned there during recess for the rest of the week. I felt good about playing with Mai Lin. She needed me. I secretly wished it could be that way with everyone else, because that's really what I wanted: to connect with her and help her.

Mai Lin was a different person when she played with me. She wasn't nervous or shy. She laughed and relaxed. I guess my bossiness wasn't such a problem for her. By planning things out and playing with her, I was able to help her out. I think I made her feel safe and happy at school. Having someone to play with certainly made me feel a lot better too. I felt I could let go more, that I didn't need to be in charge all the time. Playing with her became so easy and carefree. I'd never really experienced that before. I didn't feel like I had to be in control of every detail, though I was too young then to know why.

Having a steady playmate at recess made school so much better. Until one day Mai Lin didn't show up. I waited at the garden. Then I looked around and even went to her classroom.

"Hello. You're Emma, aren't you?" It was Mrs. Smith, Mai Lin's first-grade teacher. I nodded.

"You've been playing a lot with Mai Lin, haven't you? It's been so nice to see that she's found a good friend."

I felt my heart swell up hearing that.

"Yes. We have lots of fun," I said. "But I couldn't find her today, anywhere."

"Mai Lin is going to be out for a little while," Mrs. Smith said.

"Okay," I said sadly.

I waited all week by the garden, but Mai Lin did not return. I found out later that she'd gotten very sick. As it turned out, she was out for the rest of the year. For a while I tried playing by myself at our spot next to the garden. But it just wasn't the same, and I felt really alone.

## A DIFFERENT WAY OF SEEING THINGS

The following week I tried to join in with my second-grade class-mates again, and at first, things went okay. They were playing a new chasing game that didn't have that many rules. The bases were trees, bushes, or benches. But they changed every day. It wasn't easy for me but I did alright. Until one day, when I was just about to capture Julia. I tagged her but she called out:

"Base."

"What do you mean?" I asked.

"I'm standing on it," she said.

"That's not a base," I argued.

"Base," she repeated. She was pointing at a thin crack in the ce-ment.

The other girls gathered around us as we argued.

"There is no way that's a base, Julia," I declared.

"This is our game, Emma," Isabel said. "We made it up."

"But that's totally unfair," I said.

"How do you know?" Isabel shot back. "And anyway, all you do is argue when you join in. You always have to be the boss of everything."

"That's not it at all—I just—it's a crack, not a base," I replied, starting to cry. "She just made that up on the spot so she wouldn't get tagged."

"We're allowed to make things up in this game," Julia replied. "That's the fun part."

"That's not fun," I said. "That's cheating."

"Well, we allow it," Isabel added. "So just don't play with us."

"But I want to," I pleaded.

"Well, you just can't anymore," Julia stated.

"But Mrs. Johnson said, 'You can't say you can't play.' It's even up on the wall in our classroom!" I shot back, thinking I had her stumped.

"Well, we're saying it anyway," Isabel said emphatically. "Aren't we?"

Everyone nodded their consent.

"Fine. But I'm gonna tell on you guys."

"Right, Emma. I guess nothing's changed," Julia said. "Go ahead. Run to an adult, you tattletale."

I scanned the playground for Mrs. Johnson, who happened to be one of the recess supervisors that day. When I spotted her close by, I ran toward her. I was so upset. I wanted to explain everything that had happened—how unfair it all was, like I'd done before.

She must have seen our argument because she was already walking toward me.

"Did you see that, Mrs. Johnson," I said, out of breath.

I started to explain but she raised her hand.

"Emma, stop," she said. "I've got something important to tell you. Sit down here with me." She pointed to a large tree stump and sat on a bench beside it.

"But I—"

"You don't have to tell me what happened," she said. "I saw the whole thing, Emma. And I want to ask you an important question: Why do you think that your classmates often don't want to include you in their games?"

"Because I speak out," I said. "When the game doesn't go the way it should, that's cheating. And I don't let them get away with that!"

"I really appreciate how much thought you put into the way games should go. And you try your best to have it work out that way. I really do," she replied. "Do you think it's also possible that Clara, Julia, and the others may have different ways of seeing what is right? And how they imagine the game should be played might be different from the way you picture it? They may have a different perspective."

"What do you mean by perspective?" I asked, puzzled.

"Here is a good example, Emma. You think you are telling the truth and correcting something that's wrong, but some of the other children in the class may feel you are tattling."

"But that's not—"

"Hold on, Emma. I know you like things to be right and that's very honorable of you. So I've come up with four new rules that will help you understand the difference between truth telling and tattling."

"Okay, Mrs. Johnson."

"Rule number one: Only tell if you are not trying to get people into trouble."

"But—"

"I'm going to tell you the four rules, Emma, and you think about them and see how things go, okay? No interruptions."

"Yes, Mrs. Johnson," I replied.

"Number two: Only tell if you are not trying to draw attention to yourself. Rule number three: Be willing to accept that others may see things differently. And finally, number four: Be willing to help set things right if there is an argument. Okay? I can write them down for you when we are back in class so you can memorize them."

She got up, and smiled.

"Okay, Emma?"

"Okay," I said. "I'll do my best."

"I know you will, Emma," she responded. "I can always count on you. I just want you to think about them. Keep them in mind as you go through each day, and whenever you get the urge to tell me or any other teacher about something you've seen or heard, go over the four rules first. Then do what you think is right."

As Mrs. Johnson walked away, I sat there on my tree stump, thinking about everything she'd told me. I could come up with a hundred reasons why she was wrong: all the times my classmates had been unfair or sneaky or just plain wrong or misbehaved. But a little seed of doubt started to grow inside of me. And just in the few hours of school left that Friday afternoon, I counted four times when one of my classmates did something that I believed was totally wrong. Each time, the urge to tell them they were wrong—or raise my hand and point it out to Mrs. Johnson—nearly overwhelmed me. But I kept silent.

And I started to wonder if maybe Mrs. Johnson had a point.

## AN UPHILL CLIMB

On Saturday morning—while Ryan raked the leaves in our backyard and Susie skipped around imagining she was a giant butterfly—I started setting up a project on the living room floor that I'd been planning for a month. I'd been collecting different kinds of cardboard containers: shoeboxes, delivery boxes of all shapes and sizes, toilet paper and paper towel tubes, and the like. I planned to create—with the cardboard, scissors, glue, and tape—a big city that we could all play with on a thick rectangular cardboard base. Ryan could use his cars; and Susie, her miniature dolls. And we could add LEGO figures and buildings and draw on it and paint it all too.

"Emma, could you come into the kitchen for a minute?" I heard Mom call out.

"Sure, Mom," I said. "I'm just setting up my city-building project."

"That's what I wanted to talk to you about, dear."

When I got to the kitchen, Mom was wiping her hands on a dish towel.

"I was wondering if it would be okay with you if we let Ryan and Susie help you build your city." she said.

"I don't know, Mom," I replied, crestfallen. "They kind of mess things up a lot of the time."

"I know, Emma. But you said you were building it for everyone to play with, and it might be nice if they participate in making it too."

"Okay, Mom," I sighed.

That afternoon I let Susie and Ryan help me work on the city project. I'd mapped out all the streets and buildings in pencil on the cardboard base. I gave them each instructions on how to build a section. For twenty minutes we cut, pasted, and taped the structures together.

Everything was going great—until Ryan messed things up by gluing a toilet paper tube on top of a shoebox-sized gas station.

"Why are you doing that?" I asked, perplexed.

"I like the way it looks," he replied.

"Come on, Ryan! What kind of gas station has a tower on top of it?"

"The kind I build!" he replied defiantly.

"It doesn't look right at all!" I cried. "It looks more like a tiny factory now."

"I think it looks great!" he said, digging in.

We argued back and forth until I got so mad that I yelled at him to leave.

"Fine! But I'm gonna go build myself a whole planet," he cried. "I'm not playing with you anymore. Come on, Susie. Let's go do it in my room!"

He grabbed a bunch of my materials and stomped up the stairs. Susie bounced up after him dutifully.

"Stop taking my stuff, Ryan," I yelled after him.

When he failed to reply, I shouted out, "You've ruined everything now! I'm telling Mom."

"Go and tell on me—again. I don't care," he replied, slamming the door to his room behind him and Susie.

I ran to the kitchen and told Mom what had happened, hoping she would be on my side.

"Ryan can be difficult sometimes, I know. He has his own way of looking at things and all kinds of different ideas like this one about a tower, which doesn't make much sense on a gas station, I'll admit!"

"It's totally wrong—right, Mom?" This was going better than I'd thought.

"Do you want a glass of milk?" she asked. She poured me one and we sat down at the table together. I'd calmed down quite a bit.

"I spoke with Mrs. Johnson the other day, Emma," Mom continued. "You know there was something she said that really stuck in my mind. She thinks you are a very sweet, kind girl and you are very imaginative."

I beamed with pride.

"She also said you always seem to have a very clear picture in your mind about how things should be. Is she right? Do you think a lot about how things should go?"

"Yeah, I do, Mom. I get this picture inside me, and it's really real. And every part of the game—I see it. How it should go so that it will be the most fun."

"I see," she said. "And what happens if it doesn't turn out the way you planned it to?"

"If it doesn't work out, I just get really mad," I said.

"I see," she nodded.

"And it's not just games, Mom. It's other stuff too. Like how things should get put away in the kitchen or what roads we should take when we drive to school."

"That happened last week, didn't it?" she asked. "You got upset because we didn't drive by the field with all the horses."

"Yeah. Because when I woke up that morning, I thought about them and I wanted to see that big white one," I replied. "And when the policeman said we had to take a different way, I got really mad. That's not the way I'd planned it. I wanted us to go the way of the farm."

"You know, Emma, it's taken me a while but I've learned that everyone has a different way of getting where they want to go. We all have different ideas about how we want things done."

"I guess so," I said, wondering where she was going with this.

"I'd like to tell you a story about when I was younger."

"When you were little?" I asked, excited. "When you were my age?" I loved Mom's stories about her childhood. We all did.

"Not quite that young, Emma," she replied. "When I was twenty-five, I was a serious hiker and trekker. I even worked as a trail guide for several adventure companies out in Colorado and Alaska."

"That's where you met Dad. At Alaska, right?"

"Yes," she said. "But this is a story about a climb I did the year before I met your dad. I was hired to guide a group of hikers to the top of a mountain in a national park in Alaska. I'd climbed this peak at least a dozen times before and knew all the trails you could take—from the easiest to the most challenging.

"We met up at base camp where we checked all our climbing equipment—stuff like our hiking boots, ropes, water bottles, trail maps—and spoke with other hikers who were getting ready for their hikes. There were five or six other groups checking in with the ranger and preparing for their hikes. As I walked around and looked at everyone, I couldn't help noticing things that I thought were wrong. 'That's a pretty grimy old backpack. I can't believe she's using that,' I thought to myself. 'And look at his hiking boots. They are worn out and won't grip the ground well.' But I didn't just think these things. I stopped and talked to some of the groups. 'Really, you're going to take that route?' I commented to one team. 'That's for much more experienced climbers.' And to another group who told me they were going to go over an ice bridge I said, 'That's crazy. I wouldn't take that trail. It's been warming up lately. That bridge is not safe in this weather.'

"One group had way too little climbing rope and I told them so. Another group had much more than they would need. I made my opinion clear to them too. So I basically walked around base camp making all kinds of judgmental comments to these people I didn't really know, giving them advice they hadn't asked for, like a real Miss Know-It-All. Some folks smiled and thanked me; others didn't look too pleased. But I really couldn't help myself. I just had to tell everyone what I knew and thought. And I acted like I knew better than anyone else.

"The teams all took off up the mountain taking different trails. About midway through our hike, we got to a point where several paths intersected. There we came upon the group I'd criticized at base camp because they were lugging too much unneeded rope with them. They had stopped because two members of a third team who had started their hike earlier that day had fallen down into a crevice, and they were using the extra rope they'd brought to pull those two hikers out of the hole. The long rope I'd scoffed at was their rescue rope. And if they hadn't brought it along, they would not have been able to save the two fallen climbers, who could have died if they were not pulled up quickly enough."

"Wow. That's incredible, Mom," I said. "You got to see them save the hikers who'd fallen into the giant hole."

"Yes, I did. But what I learned that day is that there are many ways to do things, and the way I think they should be done is not always the best way. I found out that there are many ways up a mountain."

"So you were kinda being super bossy at base camp," I said. "And in the end, it turned out you were wrong?"

"That's right, Emma."

"I get it," I said excitedly. "That's a great story, Mom."

"Well, there's one more thing. Do you remember the group I told not to go on the trail that had an ice bridge you had to cross, because the weather had been too warm?"

"Yeah, because the ice might be melted and it would be too slippery, right?"

"Exactly. Well, it turns out I was right. They weren't able to cross there. They had to take another route."

"That's great, Mom. You were right."

"I was right, but the way I told them made them mad. And that's why they didn't listen to me. I was just being rude and bossy. It would have been much better if I'd been polite when I made the suggestion, instead of being bossy and a bit snarky about it."

## A NEW APPROACH

On Sunday morning, Dad took Ryan and Susie out to do some shopping at the hardware store. Mom and I did a few house chores together and went for a walk. On the way back, she suggested we give building the city together another try.

"This time," she said, "let's all sit down together and talk about what we'd like to do before we start working on it. What do you think? Could that work?"

"I guess so," I said.

When Ryan and Susie returned, we had lunch and then sat down on the living floor, where Mom and I had laid everything out.

"Susie, what would you like to make in the city?" Mom asked.

Susie's eyes got big. She described a store she wanted to make where dolls, dresses, and toys were sold. She wanted it to be a two-story building with huge windows on the bottom floor where she could draw displays, like she'd seen at a big department store downtown that morning when she was shopping with Daddy.

"That's a lovely idea, Susie," Mom said. "Isn't it, Emma?"

"Yes, I like it a lot," I confessed, looking at my baby sister with some surprise. I had no idea she could come up with such good stuff. Probably because I'd never bothered to ask her.

"What about you?" Mom said, looking at Ryan. "What would you like to add to the cityscape?"

"Well, what's missing right now is maybe a parking garage like the big open ones Dad sometimes parks at when we go out to dinner. I could park all of my mini cars there."

"Okay," Mom said, smiling and looking over at me. "I guess you two have proven to us, once and for all, that there are many ways up the mountain."

She winked at me and turned back to Ryan, who had stood up and was jumping up and down.

"And, and . . . I want there to be a garage with two large spaces cars can fit in when they are getting an oil change or being fixed. And a car wash, too, on the other side."

"That sounds lovely, dear. What do you think, Emma? Could your brother work on that and add it on as a separate section of the city? And maybe even put in a big factory building behind it so he could add three or four towers on top?"

"Yeah! That would be so cool, Emma," Ryan cried out. "Can I? Can I?"

I thought about it. Giving Ryan a section to do the way he wanted solved two problems. It gave him something to do that he liked and he could build the way he wanted. And it would keep him from doing weird stuff to other buildings, like putting a factory smokestack on a gas station.

"That's a great idea, Ryan," I said. "Why don't we draw in a river and the factory can go on the other side of it. I'll go to the basement and get you some of the thicker cardboard to use as a base for your parking lot and auto shop."

"And for the river and factory too?" he said, jumping up and down. "Yes!"

I was truly surprised that day. Just like Mrs. Johnson had told me at recess on Friday and Mom had told me on Saturday, everyone—not just me, or just my classmates, but my little brother Ryan and baby sister Susie too—has their own really clear pictures of how things should be done. Or as Mom put it, there are many ways up the mountain.

The next week at school there were several times when we were out playing or in the classroom when I got frustrated because things were not going the way I'd imagined them. But I tried my best to remember that other kids have their own ideas and pictures of how things should go, like my brother and sister. It wasn't easy, but I resisted the urge to criticize or threaten to tell on them. I tried to keep in mind what I'd learned from Mrs. Johnson and my mom.

Things slowly started to change. When everything didn't go my way in a game at recess, I didn't just stomp off hurt and angry, as I had before. I stayed put and tried to talk things out with the other kids. Mostly I listened, like I had when Mom sat me down with Ryan and Susie to talk about what they imagined we could do for the cardboard city-building project.

I realized then that other kids had really good imaginations and ideas too, and that my way wasn't always the only way or the best way. This made me a much better classmate, teammate, project partner, and most importantly—friend. As I got older and better at controlling my urge to plan and direct everything, more kids wanted to play with me and become friends. Not only did no one run away when they saw me coming at recess but sometimes kids would seek me out and ask me to help them solve a problem or argument, because they knew how important being fair and correct was to me. "Let's ask Emma what she thinks," they'd say. "She's honest. She tells it like it is."

I'm not saying things were easy or perfect for me from second grade on. I had my share of arguments at school and at home as I got older. And I had difficulties fitting in and making friends in middle school and high school, like anyone else.

But those difficult times I had in kindergarten and first and second grades—and the advice I got from my mom and Mrs. Johnson—helped me see how much the way I acted mattered. If I came across as bossy or tattled on kids a lot, it was my responsibility to understand why that was and to work hard to change the way I saw things. Otherwise I would never be able to connect with my classmates and form lasting friendships.

I also learned that running to a teacher and telling them what's going on isn't always a bad thing. In certain situations, it can be exactly the right thing to do. One day, at recess, when a bunch of us were playing tag together, Joey and Tyler did something no one was ever allowed to do. They climbed up the big oak tree behind the gym building, at the back of the playground. Joey was acting really goofy. He yelled at us as he dangled upside down from a long, leafy branch. Suddenly we heard a loud crack. The entire branch—with Joey still clinging to it—crashed down onto the ground. Everyone stopped playing and just stared at him as he lay on the ground, groaning. Except for me and Clara. She ran to see if Joey was okay. I raced back to find Mrs. Johnson and told her what had happened. An ambulance came and took Joey to the hospital, and two teachers got a ladder and helped Tyler—who was too scared to move—climb down safely. In front of all of us Mrs. Johnson said, "I'm so glad you came and got me so fast, Emma. That was quick thinking. It was exactly the right thing to do."

"Way to go Emma," Clara said. "Yeah, thanks," Tyler, still a bit shaken up, added. I smiled. Now I knew exactly what Mrs. Johnson meant about the difference between truth telling and tattling.

---

This story was about . . .

- Being too bossy and trying to control others
- How when a kid seeks adult help, others see them as tattletales

- Learning the difference between truth telling and tattling
- Realizing that other kids need to have a say too

Emma struggled to coexist with her siblings and classmates until she realized that her need to plan and direct everything or complain to adults is what kept her from becoming friends with everyone around her.

# 14

---

# STANDING UP AND SPEAKING OUT

## *Darpan's Story*

We hear a lot about the need for empathy these days, but how does that translate in a complex school situation? Intervening in conflict is not easy. When you stand up for someone else, you may be told to mind your own business and end up feeling rejected or embarrassed. You also run the risk of drawing unwanted attention to yourself and becoming the next target of the aggression.

But as Darpan demonstrates in this story, you can keep your help low-key and practical and find like-minded kids to help you make a difference. What's more, you don't have to be one of the more popular, confident kids to be effective. In fact, if you have survived your own difficulties and navigated social challenges successfully while finding a way to fit in, you will be an authentic and appreciated mentor to others who struggle socially.

## POINTS OF UNDERSTANDING

- When adults bully a bully into stopping bullying, they are actually inadvertently modeling strange, questionable behavior.
- If we punish children who are teasing, it only drives the problem further underground.
- No matter how upset you get, reacting to taunting will only make things worse.

## POINTS OF HOPE AND LEARNING

- When kids are helped to realize that joking around can cross the line and become hurtful, they are capable of changing their behavior.
- If blame and shame are avoided, true accountability and enduring solutions can become part of the problem-solving process.
- Self-effacing humor is a very effective way to deflect teasing.
- Shy and quiet people notice a lot and can learn to convert their emotional sensitivity into helpful social action.

From little things, big things grow. In this uplifting story, we see how the kind actions of a quieter kid are noticed and motivate others in unexpected ways. A school's entire social climate can change when emotionally resilient, motivated students are taken seriously and given the encouragement and space to become leaders who inspire the whole community.

---

*My name is Darpan. I'm twenty years old. I'm in college now, studying international relations and social sustainability, but I became interested in how people relate to one another years ago, when I was a skinny seventh grader in middle school. You see, I wasn't a big talker or man-about-campus back then. In fact, I was pretty shy. But I didn't stick out like some of the other loner kids who always seemed to have a KICK ME sign pinned to their backs. I got along okay with a lot of different types of kids who I met in our big class.*

*But that was because of what I'd been through when I was even younger—in third and fourth grades. Back then I was teased a lot. Kids called me "Dustpan" instead of Darpan. And "PB," which made no sense to me for the longest time. And I learned the hard way not to take taunting and teasing too seriously, because kids who were too sensitive got picked apart at my grade school.*

My *amma* (my mom) packed me a lunch every day because she didn't like me eating cafeteria food. "They put all kinds of nasty chemicals and preservatives in the food, Darpan," she'd said.

On my very first day as a third grader, I sat down at a table next to a bunch of kids I didn't know and dutifully pulled out the three plastic containers Mom had stacked in my shiny new *Star Wars* lunch box. I peeled off the lids and gazed happily at Amma's chicken curry, soupy mung dal, and freshly made naan, as I inhaled deeply. Then I froze. My tablemates had stopped chewing their burgers and fries and a crowd of kids had formed behind me. Everyone gawked at my meal, a pungent curry smell wafting up into their noses.

"OH MY GOD!" Violet cried.

"What the—," Bryce exclaimed.

Joey, Sam, and Eli watched in mock horror as Jonah "fainted" and fell to the floor. They tried their best to "resuscitate" him.

"That looks like puke, my guy!" Benjamin added thoughtfully, as he took a massive bite out of a greasy slice of pizza.

My face and neck caught fire. I tried my best to disappear into my chair but the entire lunchroom was now silent. Everyone stared, then they cracked up.

For the next month, some version or other of the same scene played out each day. There was nothing I could do about it—no matter how embarrassed I felt, no matter how angry or insulted.

I wasn't the fighting type, and it was useless to get all riled up and yell at everyone to stop. Because that would just make them laugh harder and act deliberately meaner. I tried disappearing, hoping everyone would move on. I skipped lunch for three straight days.

But when I reappeared on the fourth day, they all made such a mega fuss about the return of Curry Man, which everyone now called me everywhere I went, that I decided it'd be best to just eat my meal in the designated area and pray that Violet, Bryce, and the rest of them would eventually get bored and stop tormenting me.

They didn't. They just kept coming.

Finally, two torturous months into the school year, I drummed up the courage to try a different tactic. Violet and Bryce, the most vocal hecklers, started their gasping, stomach-clutching, retching routine, I stood up and said in an exaggerated Hindi accent, "Dearest darling Violet, won't you please do me the distinct honor of sampling Amma's exquisitely conceived mung dal."

She pretended to strenuously object to my offer, but then opened her mouth and gulped down the spoonful I held up.

"Hey!" she cried. "That's really good, Darpan."

When everyone called out, she silenced them with a majestic wave of her hand.

"Hold on, you ingrates. Wait a sec. You try it, Bryce!"

Bryce grabbed my spoon, dunked it into the dal, and dutifully swallowed a heaping spoonful.

"Isn't it delicious?" Violet asked. Bryce nodded, and they both sat down and tried dipping pieces of the naan I offered them into the spicy curry sauce. And that was it. No one teased me about Amma's lunch menu ever again.

I learned a bunch of other things that year and the next that helped me roll with the punches—taunting and teasing and such—that went on all around me in elementary school. In most cases I was able to get along with kids from all kinds of backgrounds and social cliques.

By the time I entered middle school I was even pretty good at standing up and speaking out for other kids who were being pushed aside or excluded, without triggering too much nastiness from the bully types.

Then something really cool happened in ninth grade that set me on the course I am now on.

## AN UNLIKELY FRIEND

One brisk Friday afternoon, as I'd just turned the corner past the school parking lot and headed down a quiet tree-lined block, someone called out.

"Hey you!"

I spun around, troubled by the sharp tone in the voice.

"Hey," I replied hesitantly.

Bearing down on me was a kid I'd never talked to before. Everyone knew him, though. Scott Barlett was the star power forward on our varsity basketball team—and a giant for his age, really. Scott-the-Jock, as we mere mortals called him, was 6'4" and *still* growing. A mere tenth grader, he was mad popular. He hung out with the ruling class at school: the coolest juniors and seniors, who lorded it over everyone and partied together every Friday night.

His incredible athletic talent had catapulted him to instant A-list status at our school. And his celebrity had definitely gone to his head. He'd already developed a reputation for being cocky and rough with kids like me: smart, quirky, ninth graders who circulated in small, protective clusters on the fringes of the school's social scene.

"What were you up to with the seventh graders yesterday at recess?" Scott asked huskily when he'd caught up with—and towered over—me.

"Whadd'ya mean?" I asked as innocently as I could. I was already scanning my surroundings, wondering if I'd just walked into an ambush, if others were lurking behind a tree or bush down the street. Had I absentmindedly wandered into one of those after-school lunch money grabs I'd seen on TV shows?

"The kid you were talking to. Timmy. That's my little brother," he said.

I gulped. Nothing in his facial expression hinted at what he was driving at.

"Great kid, funny little guy" was all I could mumble.

I was ready to smile and engage, or sprint—whichever would guarantee my survival.

"Yeah, he can be annoying," Scott said, his voice softening. "But he's quite the jokester at home. Can I walk with you a bit?"

"Sure," I said, my entire body relaxing as it dawned on me that Scott-the-Jock did not pose an imminent threat.

"I'm Scott, by the way," he said, pausing to shake my hand.

"I know."

"Just wanted to say thank you, uh—"

"Darpan," I offered. "I'm in ninth."

"Right. Darpan," he said, looking a bit puzzled. "What kinda name is that?"

"My parents are Indian. You know, from Asia, not out West."

"Cool. Does that mean you play that weird sport with the wacky-shaped bat and the stakes?"

"Kinda, I guess," I replied. "I've lived here in Pennsylvania my whole life, but my uncles taught me how to play cricket."

"Yeah, cricket. That's it. Weird sport."

"I'm on the lacrosse team here at school," I said.

"Sweet."

I was warming up to Scott-the-Jock. One-on-one, he didn't come off as the thoughtless, brutish, cool kid I'd been warned by classmates to steer clear of—a card-carrying member of the alpha crew.

"I was just wondering what you said to him?" Scott asked. "He's a bit of a smart-ass at home. But he's been having a rough time ever since he started middle school. Then last night he comes home all cheerful, laughing and cracking jokes like his old self."

"Nice!"

"I just don't know what the deal is with him when he's here," Scott added. "He walks around by himself all the time, looking sad. He doesn't seem to have a single friend or anything!"

I wondered about this big, tough kid walking beside me. He didn't fit the profile of top gun or act at all like the Scott-the-Jock I'd seen at school. This guy was kind and thoughtful. He seemed genuinely concerned about his little brother.

"Yeah," I said, deciding to risk opening up to him a little myself. "When I was younger, I didn't have the best of times fitting in either. Too shy to join in, I'd walk around the playground and just watch everyone else. So I get what he's going through. I'm much more comfortable at school nowadays. And I hang out with the seventh and eighth graders sometimes. Join their games, even. I know most of them pretty well."

Scott-the-Jock looked at me quizzically.

"If I see something flaring up—like a potential argument or fight," I continued, "I kinda like to step in when I can, without making it too awkward."

"Really?"

"I noticed your brother was being teased because he's a bit of a loner."

"Three or four kids were targeting him yesterday," Scott said. "I was thinking 'bout knockin' their heads together, but then I figured that might embarrass Timmy, make things worse for him in the long run—his big brother rushing over to save him. Anyway, he'd just be pissed at me for interfering."

"Yeah, good call on holding back, Scott," I said, gently. "Rescue operations like that never end well."

"That's why I was so surprised. You show up, and thirty seconds later, everyone is laughing and getting along. Whaddya do?"

"Nothing really," I said. "They were taunting Timmy a little—calling him 'freak show' and 'weirdo.' 'No one likes you,' they said."

"I could feel it in my bones," Scott replied, his fists clenching. He looked ready to pounce.

"When I was younger and got treated that way, my best defense was to say something strange or funny," I said. "I told them, 'You dudes better watch out. Timmy here is probably plotting your demise. He's a genius tactician.'"

"Ha!" Scott replied.

"Yeah, that kind of stumped them for a second," I said. "Then Timmy, who they probably never heard speak before, says in this scary oddball-robot voice, 'That's what eight hours a day of *Fortnite* and *Call of Duty* does to a man.' Then he puffs up his chest and declares, 'I'm invincible right about now, fellas. Let's do this!' Which was pretty funny all by itself. But coming from a skinny, little waif like him? He had them rolling around on the ground. Best of all, Timmy, all serious and belligerent a second earlier, fell down laughing right there with them."

"I saw that," Scott said excitedly. "Couldn't believe it!"

"They loved it and immediately asked him if he'd join them in a game of manhunt."

"That's awesome," Scott said.

"I stuck around," I added. "Teamed up with Timmy, just to make sure things went smoothly."

"That's really cool, Darpan," Scott said, grinning. "I really appreciate what you did for my little brother." He shook my hand vigorously. "Anything you need, you can count on me. No matter what. Okay?"

"Just hook me up with some courtside tickets to your game against Middletown High next Friday night, Scott, and we're even!"

He looked puzzled for a split second, then broke into a grin.

"Good one, Dar-man! Good one," he said, knowing full well that high-school games in our school district were free. "I'll have four waiting for you at Will Call. I promise!"

Then, just as quickly as he'd appeared, Scott-the-Jock disappeared down the block.

A week later, Scott caught up with me after school. He said he'd been thinking a lot and suggested we do something together—to help kids like Timmy feel less awkward in school. He had an idea that was pretty awesome: to get athletes from all sports—girls' and boys' teams, JV and varsity—to buddy up with kids from the seventh, eighth, and ninth grades. Each athlete-mentor would welcome their "buddy" at school and do stuff with them to help them feel more comfortable socially. "If each kid has an older student—a confident, popular, athlete type—to talk to and look up to, maybe figuring out the social thing wouldn't be so scary," Scott said.

"We could sometimes, like, sit with our little buddy at lunch or hang out with them at recess," I suggested. "That way they wouldn't feel so lonely. They could come to us for advice, even, whenever they got into trouble, or whatever.

"This is such a great idea, Scott," I said. "And it would work both ways, of course."

"What do you mean?" he asked, puzzled.

"Well, since popular jock types tend to, uh, sometimes bully younger, more vulnerable kids. If their job is to help them, to look out for them, then maybe they'll be less likely to be mean to them—and to other kids too."

"I see what you mean," Scott replied, nodding thoughtfully. "I gotta go, Dar-man," he said, turning away abruptly.

I could see that what I'd just said had shaken Scott up, though I didn't know exactly why.

"Let's talk more tomorrow," I said.

"Def," Scott called out over his shoulder as he headed to the boys' locker room to get ready for basketball practice.

I loved Scott's idea, and I decided to introduce him to Tammy, Jin-hai, Samara, and Javier, who were my friends on the student council. Tammy, an eleventh grader, had a big heart and a lot of influence with teachers and Assistant Principal Lestmann. Jinhai was a senior, a top student, and the president of the student council. Javy and Samara were quirky, cool juniors who headed up several after-school clubs. If anyone could help us organize and implement Scott's idea, it was those guys.

Getting teachers and administrators to agree to any kind of student proposal, even something simple such as having extra water fountains installed, was always a steep climb. But over the years, I'd developed into a pretty decent strategic thinker. And I knew that with the right team—Tammy, Jinhai, Samara, Javy, and maybe even Scott too—I could figure out a way to get this done.

## SLOWER BUT STRONGER

I wasn't always all that strategic or confident. I was actually quite insecure when I was little. In first grade I was diagnosed with dyslexia. My case wasn't too extreme, I was later told. But I had all kinds of trouble reading and writing, and I was, well, basically just a really slow learner. I got anxious and frustrated when I couldn't figure things out. And having to skip certain classes or other activities to meet with my special needs teacher (SNT) three times a week made me feel isolated and disconnected from my classmates. "Where do you disappear to all the time?" they'd ask me. I'd stare back at them in silence, biting my lip. I was way too embarrassed to admit I needed all that extra help.

But as I got older, I realized the challenges I faced in my early school years, learning and social, were, in a weird way, a blessing in disguise. The daily struggle had just made me more determined and harder working. And with help from my SNT, I learned creative ways to figure things out.

By middle school my teachers were telling me I was "a good problem solver" and "a strategic thinker." And I kinda was, I guess. Not just with schoolwork. I got good at handling social stuff too. If kids were arguing or teasing one another, I'd devise a way to distract them—to shift their focus away from the kid they were targeting. Drawing from my own experiences in elementary and middle schools, I helped younger kids develop strategies to cope with bully types and fit in better.

People often ask how I came up with the idea of launching a Student Social Action Committee (SSAC) at school. I'm not 100 percent sure. The seed for the idea came to me after I helped Timmy at recess that December day, and met his older brother, Scott-the-Jock, after school. But I used recesses to connect with younger kids long before we formally started our SSAC program.

In fact, it was at one such recess, just after I started ninth grade, that I first met Mrs. Sullivan.

I walked by a group of seventh and eighth graders who were having an intense argument about a rule violation in a game they'd been playing.

"Yo," I said, "can I join you guys?"

Utter silence.

"You're a ninth grader," one kid proclaimed, as if that disqualified me from cohabitating in the same galaxy.

"That doesn't mean I don't like playing tag or manhunt," I shot back sternly. Then I smiled.

The kid shrugged. "Sure, why not."

And just like that, their big argument was ancient history.

I played with them for the rest of recess period.

"Did you do that on purpose?"

I spun around. A kind-eyed teacher stood before me, her arms folded across her chest.

"I'm Mrs. Sullivan," she said with a wink. "Some of those kids you just played with are my seventh graders"

"Oh. Huh, Darpan. At your service."

"We call that redirection. What you just did."

"Just wanted everyone to chill out and play, me included," I replied.

"Well, that was quite clever and effective," she said. "You may have a future in psychology."

"Thank you!"

I watched the friendly teacher disappear through the doors into the school's main hall, clueless as to what a massive influence she would have on my life in high school and beyond.

I got to know Mrs. Sullivan pretty well over the next few weeks. We talked at recess a few times. Three months later, when I told her about the club I was forming with Scott and the others, and about how we wanted to help kids fit in better at school, she got excited.

"Why don't you guys meet with me and go over what you'd like to do," she suggested. "Then you can try it out on my seventh grade. They could definitely benefit from working with high-school student mentors."

The six of us met with Mrs. Sullivan twice, and she presented us to her class a week later at recess. We introduced ourselves briefly and then broke off into three groups. Scott and I spoke with ten seventh graders, Tammy and Jinhai with another ten, and Samara and Javy with the rest. We talked with the kids about our experiences of being left out, teased, and bullied, and then we asked them to speak about theirs. At first the seventh graders listened carefully. They were a bit spellbound by Scott, the alpha-male, superstar athlete, I think. But after a few minutes that wore off. Then things quickly went downhill.

"You guys are way too uptight," one kid said.

"Yeah, Darpan. You've always been cool with us, but this stuff is kinda dumb," another declared.

"It's not like we're beating anybody up," argued a third. "All we do is joke around. What's wrong with calling Oswaldo 'sequoia' anyway. Isn't he the tallest kid in the seventh grade?"

"It's not that, guys," I tried to explain. "It's just important to consider the other person. You may think something is hilarious, but your classmate might find it really hurtful."

"I dunno, man," said the first. "My dad says everyone's become a total baby and we should all just suck it up and deal."

"Yeah," others chimed in. "This being all PC is ridiculous."

When we were done, we gathered around Mrs. Sullivan's desk.

"That didn't go so well," I told her.

"Don't let it get to you, Darpan," she replied, smiling. "They're a tough crowd. I like what you guys are doing. Keep it up."

"Thank you, Mrs. Sullivan," Jinhai said as we left the classroom.

"That sucked," Tammy blurted.

"Yeah. Some of those kids are *not* cool," Javy lamented. "That Davey kid kept mimicking my voice and dissing my look." Javy wore a light-blue denim jacket with every protest pin and button known to humanity attached. For him, each symbol was a point of pride. Most of the kids at our school weren't all that conscientious or caring. Behind his back they called him "Button Boy Freak."

"He really crossed the line," Javy added.

"Yeah. They say they're 'just joking around,'" Jinhai grumbled. "They say, 'Come on. You did it. Everyone does it.'"

Tammy was close to tears. "But the way they talk is so *not* joking around. It's just plain mean. It might be funny to them, but it totally crosses the line."

Scott nodded. "Totally crosses the line!"

"Wait, guys," I said, stopping suddenly in the middle of the corridor outside Mrs. Sullivan's classroom. "Say that again."

"What, Darpan? Don't be weird," Javy chided

"Hold on a sec," I said. "You guys just used the phrase 'crossing the line,' over and over."

"So?"

"Well, that's what they're doing. It's joking around, but they don't realize *when* it crosses the line. We need to show them the exact moment when that happens."

"Okay. But how?" Scott asked

"Why don't we do skits," Tammy suggested. "We do them all the time in drama class to convey emotions."

"Really? Are you serious?" Scott asked.

"Actually, yeah," I said. "Tammy's right."

"What do we have to lose?" Jinhai offered. "Talking to them clearly didn't work like we thought it would."

"They need to be able to see and feel what we are talking about," Tammy said. "Visualize it."

The six of us designed three skits that depicted situations in which kids who thought they were "just joking" got progressively meaner—until they'd crossed the line into teasing, or worse, bullying behavior.

We talked it all out, pulling ideas from our personal experiences.

"Kids often have no idea where that line between joking around and being hurtful is," I told the group. "And they don't realize that for people like me and Jinhai, that line can be really different. Some things that you all say to one another as American kids are perceived as really offensive in other cultures, like ours."

"Darpan is right," Jinhai said. "The line gets crossed in a different place when you're from a different culture."

"Can you give us an example?" Scott asked.

"Well, you guys often joke about your backgrounds," I said. "Where you are from or how you look. And you make comments about us too, but we find them really offensive."

"What's the nastiest thing you've been called, Darpan?" Tammy asked.

"In third and fourth grades, everyone called me 'PB,'" I confessed.

"What does that mean?" Scott wondered.

They all looked perplexed.

"I've never told anyone about this before," I said.

"Whatever you say, Darpan, stays in this circle of trust," Tammy assured me. "No one is going to repeat anything we talk about outside this group. Right, guys?"

"Right."

"I couldn't figure it out myself for the longest time," I said, my voice cracking. "Then one day at lunch at the end of the school year, an older kid who'd always been especially nasty toward me, called out to me at lunch.

"Hey, PB, you want some of my PB&J sandwich?"

"Peanut butter?" Scott asked.

"Yup."

"What did that have to do with *you*?"

"Peanut butter is brown, Scott," Jinhai said. "They were making fun of the color of Darpan's skin."

"Oh my god," Tammy gasped. "That's so racist."

"Yeah," I said. "For two years they called me that. And I acted like it was nothing. I had no clue."

We approached Mrs. Sullivan after school one Friday afternoon about using our new crossing-the-line skits, and we even enacted one of them for her. We'd developed it to make it more clear to kids when joking around becomes hurtful or even nasty and downright mean. She loved it and asked us to show it to her class the following week.

Scott and I were nervous at first. But Tammy was such a good actress, she carried the rest of us. And it really came together. The class cheered when we wrapped up the third skit, and then Mrs. Sullivan led a twenty-minute-long discussion about attitudes and feelings. Javy and Samara opened up about some experiences they'd had in fifth and sixth grades. And several seventh graders spoke earnestly about things they or friends of theirs had gone through. It was a real breakthrough for all of us.

When the bell rang and all the seventh graders filed out, they shook our hands and high-fived us. Mrs. Sullivan beamed. "You guys were fantastic," she said.

"Thank you!" Samara replied.

"We had no idea how it would go," Scott confessed.

"Well, I think you guys should present to the other seventh-grade homerooms. And to the eighth grade as well."

"We've got other ideas," I said. "We want to develop a walk 'n' talk recess buddy system."

"And a sit with a senior athlete lunch program," Scott said.

"All this sounds great. Have you guys thought of a name for this . . . er . . . club?"

"We were thinking of calling it the Student Social Action Committee," Tammy replied.

"Some of us are on the student council, and we're going to make a proposal to Assistant Principal Lestmann next week," I said. "Would you consider being our faculty adviser for the program?"

"I'd be honored, Darpan. You kids are really onto something. This could go a long way to improving the social health of the school."

## WE'RE ALL DIFFERENT AND THAT'S OKAY

We were all pumped up about our successful session with Mrs. Sullivan's seventh grade. But an incident the following week made it crystal clear to me that we were just scratching the surface of the social apathy kids in our school faced day in and day out.

Scott and I were talking excitedly about how we should present our student-athlete mentorship program to the players on his team. As we turned the corner, past the first row of portable classroom trailers, we happened upon three seniors. Two I recognized as Scott's varsity basketball teammates. The third was a brick house we'd all nicknamed Larry-the-Large. At six foot four, 275 pounds, Larry was our football team's mammoth linebacker.

Their backs were turned, but we could tell from their body language that they'd cornered some hapless kid.

"I done told you that already, my guy," Larry said. "Why you gonna go around disrespectin' me like that."

"Come on, guys. What'd I do?" the voice cracked.

"Hey, guys!"

Scott's booming baritone made the hunched trio jump.

Larry spun around, then softened instantly. "What's up, Scotty?"

"Nuthin' much, little man," Scott shot back, smiling. He glanced at their target.

"Sup, Javy! We've been looking all over for you, yo. We gotta plan out next week's SSAC meeting. You still wanna meet with those pesky eighth graders?"

"Oh hey, Scott," Javy replied as calmly as he could, clearly overcome with relief. "What's up, Darpan!"

As Javy slipped past the big three, Scott turned squarely toward them.

"You guys are in, right?"

"Whaddya mean?" Larry mumbled.

"Coach approved the lunchroom buddy program. Said it's mandatory. And I've picked out two seventh graders and one eight grader you guys can team up with. You down?"

"Sure thing, Scott. Count us in," Larry said. The others nodded their ascent.

Javy and I said our goodbyes to Scott and the three alphas and headed back to the main building.

"Catch up with you later, Javy," Scott called out as we walked away.

What Scott did that day impressed me more than anything else he'd ever done, anywhere: on the court—where he was already one of the best power forwards in the state—or off. He was way more than just some popular jock now. He was a decent human being. A real person. Someone who could withstand peer pressure and still be cool and inclusive; who did what he thought was right. Scott treated Javy the way any good friend would. Sure, he knew that differences existed, but he didn't label Javy as gay or straight, Hispanic or Irish, male or female, popular or nerdy. He just saw Javy as, well, Javy—student, fellow SSAC member, and friend.

When his athlete buddies saw him do that, they were suddenly drained of all their animosity and aggression. Was Javy different from them? Of course he was. Had that made them fearful and aggressive? Definitely. But when Scott acknowledged Javy the way he did, their anxiety and ire faded.

Now they saw Javy differently; they saw him the way Scott and I did, the way he should be seen—as a human being, as our friend, as someone who could count on our unwavering support, come what may. With that one act of quiet heroism—simple acceptance—Scott ensured that no one would ever bother Javy again about, well, being Javy.

With Mrs. Sullivan's help we convinced the school to let us set up our six-person Student Social Action Committee. And after she'd spread the word about our when-joking-around-crosses-the-line skits, other seventh- and eighth-grade teachers invited us into their classrooms to perform them in front of their kids and talk about our experiences.

Scott's idea of convincing his basketball coach to help us set up an athlete lunch-buddy program also took root. And within two months it had become so popular that our athletic director and Assistant Principal Lestmann asked to attend one of our SSAC meetings.

"We love what you've done with the junior high–schoolers at lunch," Assistant Principal Lestmann said.

"We want to formalize it around all of our teams," athletic director Harmen added. "Can you help us organize that and pair up kids with our athletes? With guidance from their homeroom teachers, of course."

"We'd love to," Tammy exclaimed.

"That's awesome, sir," Scott added.

After they'd left, we high-fived one another.

"This thing is really taking off, guys," Jinhai said.

"Sure is," I declared.

"What's wrong, Scott?" Tammy asked suddenly.

We all turned. He'd propped his elbows up on his knees and buried his face in his hands.

"I'm sorry, guys," he moaned.

Tammy kneeled down in front of him. "That's okay, Scott." She put her arms around him.

"You don't have to talk about anything if you don't want to," I said cautiously. "But if you do, we're here for you, bro."

"I can't believe I never once spoke to him or even just said hi."

"Who? Scott?" Javy whispered.

"My little brother. I could have helped make things so much easier for him by just being there for him."

"That's okay, Scott," Tammy said. "That's water under the bridge. All that matters now is that you came through. You care a great deal for him. That's clear to everyone."

"You show him that every day," Jinhai insisted. "You always touch base with him. I've seen you."

"I owe that all to Darpan," Scott said, clearing his throat. "If he hadn't done what he did—"

"You're the one who came up with the athlete-buddy system, Scott," I said. "And it's working. Not just for your brother but for everyone. Now even Coach Harmen and Assistant Principal Lestmann are into it—really into it!"

"Thank you, guys—for everything," Scott said, standing up and looking a little embarrassed.

"That's what we're here for," Tammy said. "Go SSAC!"

## MAKING CONNECTIONS

Later that spring, the newly formed SSAC faced its biggest challenge—in another seventh-grade classroom, which Mrs. Sullivan had arranged for us to work with. It was a class she supervised once a week, which she'd noticed was struggling socially.

She spoke with Assistant Principal Lestmann, who recommended us to their homeroom teacher, Mrs. Hammerstein. With her blessing, we set up a meeting during recess period with the entire class, supervised by Mrs. Sullivan.

The first thing I did at the meeting was ask everyone to push all the desks to one end and form one large circle of chairs, so that we could all face one another. The idea was to position ourselves so we could speak openly and directly to one another. There were twenty-seven of us; Mrs. Sullivan, six SSACers, and twenty seventh graders, including Scott's brother Timmy.

Mrs. Sullivan spoke to the class about us first and then asked everyone to introduce themselves and say a few words. I talked for a few minutes about why we formed the SSAC and what its goals were. Then we asked the class a few basic questions about how the year was going for them. Silence. As I looked around the room, all I saw were sullen or fearful faces. What a contrast to Mrs. Sullivan's seventh graders! At our meetings with them, three or four kids always put up their hands or blurted things out. Pretty much the entire class had been bursting with enthusiasm to participate.

Mrs. Hammerstein's seventh graders, on the other hand, looked nervous and hesitant. Mrs. Sullivan and I tried for a few more minutes to spark a conversation among the students, but nothing worked. So we ended the meeting early, and Mrs. Sullivan told them they could all head out to recess. "Why don't you guys go out there with them?" she suggested. "That way you can connect with them when they are more relaxed and hopefully figure out what the class dynamic is."

Tammy, Samara, Javy, Jinhai, Scott, and I fanned out in twos, joining different cliques that had formed throughout the playground.

We met afterward and compared notes.

"My group was four girls, popular types," Tammy reported. "One of them was clearly in charge. A bit stuck up. Very much the bossy type."

"Is her name Lisa?" Scott asked.

"How'd you know?" Tammy replied, surprised.

"Darpan and I spoke with my brother Timmy," Scott said. "He told us that Lisa kinda runs things behind the scenes in that class."

"The other kids don't dare cross her," I added. "But he told us they're even more cautious around Mrs. Hammerstein."

"Exactly," Scott interjected. "Timmy said, 'In our class, we get in big trouble if we do or say anything wrong. So we don't tell Mrs. Hammerstein anything. Because you run the risk of getting punished by her, and if you get anyone else into trouble, Lisa and her squad will come after you too.'"

What it boiled down to was that Mrs. Hammerstein was strict, and the severity of her punishments escalated quickly. One strike meant you stayed in for recess. With two, you had to stay after school. After three strikes you were sent directly to the principal's office and your parents were called in for a meeting.

This was so different from how Mrs. Sullivan handled things. She didn't make a big deal out of anything. She just talked quietly with whomever was involved. No one got blamed. No one got "punished" the way they did in Mrs. Hammerstein's class. It made total sense that Mrs. Sullivan's seventh graders spoke freely, that they talked things through. Because Mrs. Sullivan didn't use what kids said about one another against them. What you disclosed didn't lead to punishments; without severe consequences, kids never got angry with one another. They kind of turned tattling into truth telling—and things got worked out.

"Mrs. Hammerstein's strictness has totally backfired," I said. "Instead of helping create a more disciplined classroom, it's become a snake pit. Like Timmy said, kids just got sneakier about their meanness."

"You know what else Timmy said?" Scott pronounced proudly.

"What?" Javy asked.

"He said, 'It's really weird, but our teacher is like, trying to bully the bullies into stopping bullying.'"

"That's just plain stupid!" Samara exclaimed.

"Yeah. Timmy's totally right!" Jinhai declared. "What Mrs. Hammerstein does makes no sense."

"Why?" Javy asked, not quite following.

"Think about it," Jinhai replied. "If you punish a kid who's bullying, they end up feeling like they are the ones being victimized, like they're the ones being picked on, targeted by the authorities: the teacher or the school."

"That makes them even more likely to keep bullying the other kids," I said, shocked at how this all played out.

"But it gets worse," Jinhai declared. "Because once the bullies have been punished—and are on notice—everything goes underground. The bullying doesn't stop. It just gets craftier or 'sneakier,' as Timmy put it."

We thought about everything we'd discovered.

It was clear now why kids in Mrs. Hammerstein's seventh-grade class didn't communicate well with one another or their teacher. When we told Mrs. Sullivan what we'd learned, she recommended that we divide the class into groups and spend more time with the kids. If we hung out with them, like we had at recess, and they began to trust us, we might learn a lot more about what was actually going on in the class. Then we could figure out the best way to step in and help.

Over the next few weeks, we spent time with our new charges at recess, in the library, and during lunch. Details emerged about bossy Lisa and her three closest friends. We found that they had been targeting a girl named Joni, pretty much since the beginning of the school year. They'd started by teasing her in class about the way she talked and dressed. Then their taunts migrated to social media—with texts and posts, and even unflattering photoshopped photos.

We gathered that Joni was a sweet girl who didn't hang out with older kids much and hadn't been exposed to a lot of TV or movies. Lisa and her crew made fun of her for being old-fashioned and naïve, or childish. They'd also scared the rest of the class into steering clear of her.

As a result, Joni had become nervous and withdrawn, according to her mother, who dug around and discovered some of the cyber taunts. When she brought the cyberbullying to Mrs. Hammerstein's attention, heads rolled. Lisa received a two-day suspension, three other girls were given Friday-afternoon detention for a month, and all of the parents of the kids involved were called in for meetings with Mrs. Hammerstein and the school leadership. Everyone apologized and swore this would never happen again. And things appeared to have been resolved.

But what the uproar actually did was make things ten times worse for Joni. Now she was not only the weirdest, most isolated kid in her class but also the most hated. Everyone blamed her—and her pesky mom—for the fallout.

Lisa and her clique pretended to be kind to Joni when Mrs. Hammerstein was present, but they did everything in their power to intimidate and torture her when she wasn't. And as Timmy put it, no one else said a word, because "those girls will totally squash you if you do."

A couple of other kids told us Lisa and her crew "don't do anything outright mean to Joni anymore. They just, like, roll their eyes when she talks, turn their backs on her when she enters a room, or make strange squeaky noises because they say she's meek and mousy. No one can pin anything on them because they are so subtle. They make her feel bad—without ever being punished."

By the time we were asked by Mrs. Sullivan to work with the class, it was May. The school year was coming to a close, and Mrs. Hammerstein and the school principal thought things were back to normal. It wasn't until our Spanish teacher, Señora Sanchez, caught Lisa's clique passing notes and a drawing in her class that the adults realized that the bullying had not stopped. It had simply gone underground.

Señora Sanchez caught Sara passing Laura a drawing of a chubby brown-haired mouse in a sweater with the letter *J* emblazoned across its chest—Joni—prying open a cookie jar and getting electrocuted in the process. When she asked the class what was going on, no one confessed. No one said a single word.

Having heard about the work Mrs. Sullivan was doing with the SSAC, Mrs. Sanchez decided to show her the drawing and notes she had confiscated. Mrs. Sullivan spoke to Assistant Principal Lestmann, who agreed to allow us to work with the class. "This is a very sensitive situation," Mrs. Sullivan told us. "No one is to speak about the notes and drawing outside of our group. I want you all to think about everything that we've learned about what is going on in this seventh-grade classroom. We will meet next week and come up with a plan. Let's see if we can handle this situation ourselves."

I thought about what we'd learned all week. I thought about what had happened in Mrs. Hammerstein's seventh-grade homeroom class and how different it was from what went on in Mrs. Sullivan's; why adhering to a strict set of rules and school code about bullying had made things worse, not better, for everyone involved; and how the SSAC could best handle the new stuff Joni was dealing with.

"I think I've got it, guys," I told Mrs. Sullivan and the others at our next SSAC meeting. "In your class, problems come up and get worked out. No one gets into deep trouble. The person who causes a problem is held accountable, but they don't get 'blamed' or 'punished.' There's got to be a way we can hold kids like Lisa, Sara, Tara, and Laura accountable without blaming and punishing them either. They've gotten that enough already, and all its done is trigger resentment and spur revenge.

"You remember how, when we did those skits, kids realized how hurtful certain things they say and do can be—even though they'd had no clue at first? With bullying it's totally the same. Kids who bully often don't truly understand how hurtful what they say and do can be. They need to be confronted about the pain they are causing, without being blamed for it. And we can help do this because we are older than these kids and have been through more stuff than they have. But we are also their peers and can connect with them more directly than adults can."

I suggested that since talking to Mrs. Hammerstein's class as a whole had not worked—it was clear that no one was willing to share anything in a group setting—we should divide up the kids who were at the core of this problem into much smaller groups and see if hanging out with them would help them open up to us more. Tammy, Jinhai, and I got together with Joni, the primary bullying target, and Scott, Samara, and Javy met with Lisa, Tara, Laura, and Sara, the power-girl clique that was making her life miserable and intimidating the other kids. We were able to assure all the kids involved that they would not get into trouble because Assistant Principal Lestmann had put Mrs. Sullivan in charge of this situation. And we explained to them, much to their relief, that that was not how she operated.

Over the next two weeks, our two SSAC groups met with the kids assigned to us. Then we shared our findings. The biggest surprise for all of us was that the "mean girls" were not as bad as we'd thought, and Joni was not Miss Total Innocence either.

"The girls find Joni really annoying," Samara revealed. "Because she follows them around a lot. And they don't like her mom because they say she's way too protective of Joni and is always complaining about things at school."

"Yeah," Scott agreed. "They actually feel unjustly targeted by Joni's mom."

"Like she blew everything out of proportion," Javy added. "It's kind of like our joking-around/crossing-the-line exercise. They said they always tease one another and joke around all the time, and no one makes a big deal out of it. But when they did it to Joni, her mother went nuts. She came after them and got them into huge trouble with the school and their parents and everyone."

Once we'd heard everyone's accounts of what their seventh graders had told them, Mrs. Sullivan suggested we bring everyone involved together for a meeting.

"Can we call it a no-blame meeting?" Jinhai asked.

"Yeah. That would be perfect," I added. "It makes it clear no one is in the hot seat. We're all just trying to work together to make things better."

"Great idea, Jinhai," Mrs. Sullivan replied. "And along those lines, we should invite two neutrals—kids from the class who aren't close to Lisa, Sara, Tara, and Laura or friends with Joni. That way we can get another hopefully unbiased point of view of what's been going on."

## A NO-BLAME MEETING

When the day finally came, Lisa, Laura, Tara, and Sara sat with Javy, Samara, and Scott on one side of a long, rectangular table. Tammy, Jinhai, and I sat with Joni on the other, and Mrs. Sullivan and two neutrals, Carla and Sam, sat at each end. We started the meeting by explaining everyone's roles. Then we SSAC members shared our assigned seventh graders' accounts of what had gone on in the class.

Scott's team spoke first about what Lisa, Laura, Tara, and Sara had experienced. I snuck a glance or two at Joni to see how she was handling things. She looked frightened and sad when Javy and Samara repeated what the girls had said about her trailing them, and she bit her lip hard when Scott told everyone what they thought about her meddlesome mom.

Then Tammy spoke to all of us about Joni's experience, how she'd begun to feel sick, even stopped wanting to come to school at all. She felt nervous all the time, and she had so much trouble focusing on her schoolwork because of the teasing and exclusion that her grades had plummeted.

I looked closely at Lisa, Laura, Sara, and Tara. Their faces were ashen. Laura, Sara, and Tara were close to tears. Lisa hid it better, but she was clearly stunned. It was clear that they hadn't the foggiest clue how much pain they'd caused Joni.

The neutrals proved to be a big help. At one point, when we were talking about the teasing, Sam piped up: "The girls do that stuff all the time *to each other*. To them it's no big deal because they've been friends forever."

"That's true," Carla interrupted. "And, sorry, Joni—I don't want to sound mean saying this—but you sort of follow them around a lot, and I think they might sometimes say mean stuff to you because they just get annoyed."

"That's true, Carla," Laura said. Lisa, Sara, and Tara nodded vigorously.

"Yeah, but that's no excuse," Sam countered. "You can say stuff to friends because you know they can take it. You guys trash-talk each other all the time and it's totally cool. But you can't talk like that to everyone. It just doesn't work. And it can be really hurtful."

Everyone was silent for a moment.

"I can see you girls didn't really understand how hurtful this all was," Mrs. Sullivan offered gently. "I don't think any of you meant for things to go this far."

"Yeah," Laura confessed, looking straight at Mrs. Sullivan. "I feel kinda bad about what we did to Joni now."

"This might be hard to do, Laura," Mrs. Sullivan replied. "And I understand if you can't. But could you say that directly to Joni? Because she's right here."

As Laura turned to Joni, I felt a lump forming in my throat.

"I really didn't mean to be this mean," Laura said, her voice cracking. "It just kinda got outta hand. I wish we hadn't taken it so far."

"Yeah, me too," Joni whispered back.

"Me too," Lisa said, hugging her shoulders.

Sara and Tara just stared at the floor.

"Thank you, guys, for being so honest with one another," I said, hoping to lighten the mood and shift us all to problem-solving mode. "What we'd like to do now is brainstorm a bit about how we can make things better for everyone."

Samara suggested that Lisa, Laura, Tara, and Sara sit with Joni at lunch a few times, and that the neutrals—Sam and Carla—join them. "Jess should join us too," Carla exclaimed. "She's really chatty." Everyone nodded.

"One of us from the SSAC will try to find you guys once a day," I added, "to check in and talk about stuff."

"Good idea, Darpan," Mrs. Sullivan said.

"What about if we all do a group project together?" Sam asked. "That really works because you don't have to talk about feelings and stuff. You just get on and do things together. You five girls could be in it, and I could too."

Everyone liked Sam's idea. Mrs. Sullivan volunteered to speak with Mrs. Hammerstein about grouping them all together on the next class project assignment.

"Okay, everyone," I said. "We've got lunches, daily check-ins with your SSAC buddy, and a group project planned. A great start. We'll check in with you guys at pickup each day to see how everything is going."

"But I want you all to keep in mind," Mrs. Sullivan added, "that some of these ideas may work and some might not, and that's okay. It's really important that we try them, that we give it our best."

The kids really did try.

They ate lunch together four times over the next two weeks. It didn't feel weird at all that Lisa, Sara, Tara, and Laura ate together with Joni because they were joined by Sam, Carla, and chatty Jess. In fact, Mrs. Hammerstein liked the idea so much that she arranged for the entire class to be divided into what she called "rotating lunch bunches" twice a week. Kids in the class who barely ever talked to one another now ate together twice a week and got to know one another a lot better.

Mrs. Hammerstein also arranged for Joni, Lisa, Laura, Sara, Tara, Sam, and Carla to work on a recycling project under their science teacher's supervision. The girls all got really into it and convinced some of the boys, including Timmy, to join in.

Mrs. Sullivan invited Mrs. Hammerstein to our follow-up meeting with seventh graders. We caught up and discussed what was working well and what wasn't. Lisa talked about how much she liked the recycling project, and Joni spoke about how lunchtime was so different for her now. Mrs. Hammerstein didn't say a word. She just took it all in.

Over the next few weeks, I noticed that she and Mrs. Sullivan had become much friendlier. They hung out together at recess, and Mrs. Hammerstein seemed much more relaxed. Timmy told Scott and me that the mood in the class had shifted. Mrs. Hammerstein hadn't turned into a softy, but she didn't seem as uptight. I realized that the whole cyberbullying ordeal in her class must have been really stressful for her too. It was the first time I'd ever thought about what teachers go through when big problems arise in their classes. It must have been a huge relief for her that our no-blame meeting had gone well and things were improving between Joni and the others.

Over the next few years, the SSAC expanded. By my senior year we'd come up with a host of ideas to improve the social scene throughout the school. The athlete-buddy lunch program grew and was in full swing. Mrs. Sullivan and the SSAC conducted regular no-blame meetings when things got out of control in specific classes. And seventh- and eighth-grade homeroom teachers regularly deployed our rotating lunch bunch strategy in the first few months of each school year to keep their classes from getting too cliquey. We came up with other cool ideas, such as our welcoming group or circle of friendship, for new students; and our recess walk 'n' talk sessions with younger students. In fact, I felt kinda sad a week before graduation day when I attended my last-ever SSAC meeting. I looked around at the other students—a whole new cast since Scott, Javy, Samara, Tammy, and Jinhai had all graduated in the last few years—and realized how much I was going to miss them and Mrs. Sullivan.

I guess she felt the same way because at graduation, Mrs. Sullivan looked over toward me from the rostrum and smiled. Then she approached the mic.

"There has never been a student that I have taught in my thirty years here who has had more of a positive impact on his or her fellow students from all grades—seventh to twelfth. We are proud of you and the fine young man you have become. The Outstanding Leadership Award goes to . . . Darpan Raju!"

The entire seventh and eighth grades stood up and whooped and cheered. And my classmates pounded me on the back and stomped and clapped with the same unhinged intensity they had minutes before when Mr. Ferrera, our varsity basketball coach, had announced the names of our championship squad.

I looked over at my family as I accepted the award. Amma seemed bewildered.

"What is going on?" she stammered, my sister reported to me later.

"Why is everyone cheering Darpan like he's Tom Cruise?" Papa asked.

"Everyone loves Darpan, Mr. Raju," said a booming voice behind them. They swiveled to find Scott-the-Jock, back from his first year of college to see us all graduate. He was grinning from ear to ear. "Your son is a true gentleman, sir," he said, shaking my startled dad's hand vigorously.

The SSAC has become a permanent school program. Every year, dozens of students work with the kids from the younger grades. And our entire school culture has changed as a result. I'm amazed when I think that this all started from something so small, from me talking to Scott-the-Jock's younger brother Timmy one day at recess when I was in ninth grade.

---

This story was about . . .

- How your own struggles can help you understand what other people are going through
- Finding friends who can help you change your school culture
- How little steps inspire big change